F SIGHT, OUT OF MIND

JOHN PODMORE

OUT OF SIGHT, OUT OF MIND

WHY BRITAIN'S PRISONS ARE FAILING

\Bᵇ\

Biteback Publishing

First published in Great Britain in 2012 by
Biteback Publishing Ltd
Westminster Tower
3 Albert Embankment
London
SE1 7SP

ISBN 978-1-84954-138-1

10 9 8 7 6 5 4 3 2 1

A CIP catalogue record for this book is available from the British Library.

Set in Garamond and Modular by Namkwan Cho
Cover design by Namkwan Cho

Printed and bound in Great Britain by TJ International, Padstow, Cornwall

*This book is dedicated to the long memory of my late mother
Alice and to the all too brief memory of my granddaughter
Eva Alice, so beautiful the angels wouldn't let her go.*

CONTENTS

ACKNOWLEDGEMENTS

My thanks to Robin Horsley, who introduced me to Biteback, and to Bruce Jones, who is a proper author and helped me with the original outline and gave invaluable advice on various chapters. Without Sam Carter, my editor, I would have the right words but not necessarily in the right order.

To Jim Semple for teaching me about humanity in prison; the Brat Pack (the late Eddie Kiloran, Shereen Sadiq, Paolo Pertica, Andy Stonnard and Aidan Gray) for teaching me about addictions; John Hewitson, Kate Quigley, Kay Featherstone and Jacqui Ceglowski for my survival in south London. To Georgina Nayler, Mark Woodruff and Alison Liebling for invaluable help with research. To the many former residents of Her Majesty's prisons, without whom this book would never have come about. I have not named them but they know who they are and we haven't finished yet. Despite wrestling with their past demons and struggling with the prejudices and barriers to life outside, their openness and honesty and overwhelming desire for improvement was inspirational. To Fay Deadman for teaching me about children in prison.

To my daughters Gemma and Rachel for their love and forbearance towards a dad trying to be a prison governor and single parent at the same time, and regularly failing on both counts. To Amy, Daisy and Matilda for their love and support throughout this project, and of course for Matilda's keyboard and mouse, without which nothing would have happened.

INTRODUCTION

'While we have prisons it matters little which of us occupy the cells.'
George Bernard Shaw

Prisons are like schools: everyone has an opinion about them. All of us have been to school; far fewer have been to prison. But that is changing. As the prison population increases inexorably, more and more people are being caught in the net of incarceration – not only offenders themselves, but husbands, wives, siblings, parents and friends. Prisons change the lives of all who come into contact with them and only rarely for the better. Something that costs billions and affects millions should interest a nation more than it does. From *Porridge* to *Bad Girls* and from Louis Theroux's exploration of America's scariest jails to fly-on-the-wall documentaries about Her Majesty's Prisons (HMP) Holloway and Manchester, prisons provide entertainment, but this creates more heat than light.

Dostoevsky said: 'The degree of civilisation in a society can be judged by entering its prisons.' His words are often conflated with those of Churchill: 'The mood and temper of the public in regard to the treatment of crime and criminals is one of the most unfailing tests of the civilisation of any country.'

If they are right, then why do we as a nation have one of the highest incarceration rates, have more people serving life sentences and lock up more children, from an earlier age, than most of the rest of the world? And if we do all this only to see three-quarters reoffend and end up back in prison, and if we regularly read about prison inspectors criticising the treatment of and conditions for those locked up for ever longer periods, isn't it time to do something about it?

Do we really understand what goes on, do we care, or do we simply disagree with Churchill and Dostoevsky? Is there a properly informed debate or simply a series of knee-jerk reactions? A high-profile child murder will have people clamouring for harsher punishment – even the death penalty debate will be resurrected from time to time. The riots of August 2011 precipitated a more constructive debate about the appropriateness of prison in certain circumstances, as well as considerable criticism of incarceration's effectiveness, not least from the man in charge of them, Secretary of State for Justice Ken Clarke. But even that debate went barely beyond the belief that all will be well with greater competition and payment by results. If we were truly operating on payment by results then we would be in the process of closing down most of the prisons in this country.

The whispers of those who believe that there are too many in prison and that the system is broken have been shouted down by others hoping to retain power or gain it by out-toughing each other on crime.

The public are not being represented. Extreme events get extreme headlines and extreme opinions, but when properly consulted most favour community punishments where they see reparation taking place. They get satisfaction out of making an offender confront his or her victim. When asked about sentencing they defer downwards. Most victims know perpetrators. Many perpetrators become victims themselves or always were. All too often they come from the same impoverished communities that governments seek to empower, inevitably ending up doing the opposite.

The aim of this book is to offer an insider's view, from somone who was both a prison governor and inspector, of how we got here and how we might get out of the mess we are in. It is not designed to condemn but to help us reconstruct. Much has been asked of the prison system in the past; much more needs to be asked of it in the future. What it should do and what it must do need to be decided through a wider and more informed debate. This book aims to offer insight in order to promote that debate.

We will always have prisons. They are there to protect society, to provide an opportunity for it to intervene and to demonstrate its humanity. Pope John Paul II said: 'Prisons should not be a corrupting experience, a place of idleness or vice, but instead a place of redemption.' To be so, they cannot remain out of sight and out of mind.

ONE

SECURITY

HMP BELMARSH: THE END OF THE LINE

The police Range Rover sped through the already raised barrier, turned sharp left parallel with the concrete prison wall and slewed to a halt at forty-five degrees to the side of the main gate. Three cops in flak jackets leapt out and, in a carefully choreographed sequence, took up their respective positions, sub-machine guns pointing outwards in an arc, one resting his weapon, sniper-like on the bonnet. Seconds later the rest of the convoy hurtled through the same barrier, two prison vans leading the way. The main vehicle gate had opened in readiness and the mobile prison cells disappeared into the 'air lock'. There was no need to knock. The support vehicles and motorcycle outriders screamed to a halt, parked up and went to the officers' mess for a cuppa. The helicopter banked sharply and disappeared over the Thames. Their job was done and mine as prison governor was just beginning.

Belmarsh now held the six men who had escaped from the country's most secure unit, located within its most secure prison. They were soon to be joined by the three men who had escaped from the notorious and hitherto 'impregnable' Parkhurst prison on the Isle of Wight. Alongside them, already on trial or facing long sentences, were the best catches of the Serious Organised Crime Agency, drug and murder squads from across the country and the finest offering from the officers of Customs and Excise. Belmarsh had become the end of the line in terms of incarceration in the British Isles. But the country's most dangerous and most

OUT OF SIGHT, OUT OF MIND

infamous joined 800 of the capital's more ordinary: men over the age of twenty-one on trial, on remand and under sentence for everything from murder to drink driving. They typified the vast majority of the prisoner population. These were the difficult, damaged, chaotic and disordered from the estates of south London, including the nearby 1960s social housing development of Thamesmead, the iconic backdrop for Stanley Kubrick's 1971 film, *A Clockwork Orange*.

Belmarsh looks after an incongruous mix of the dangerous and the disaffected, the politically high-profile and the socially excluded. Whilst there are differences internally as to how these two extremes are treated – the type of work they could do, how they moved around the prison and where in the prison they could be held – they are all under the same expensive roof.

Belmarsh is a local prison, built in 1990 on the site of the old Royal Arsenal in Woolwich. Holding some 900 souls, it was pitched on Thames gravel and every structure required 5-metre piles to hold it up, making it very costly. Built on modern structural principles and rumoured to be able to withstand everything short of a direct nuclear strike, its design also incorporated the very sensible Victorian standard of having its own courts, Woolwich Crown and Belmarsh Magistrates' Courts. These are accessible by a purpose-built tunnel, which was a unique feature in a modern prison then and now. In terms of security and the costs of prisoner transport, it should have proved very cost-effective.

At this time, however, for reasons that were never really clear to me, some trials still took place at the Old Bailey in central London, including high-profile terrorist trials requiring armed escorts. Such escorts were costly, stopped for nothing and no one, and were reputed to cost thousands in wing mirror replacements for those too slow to get out of the way. It was said that judges didn't like to traipse out to the wilds of Woolwich, where a good lunch and a gentleman's club were hard to find. Other more reasonable explanations cited included the problem for jurors of travel – more particularly of being identified, potentially threatened and nobbled whilst en route. Protecting juries outside is one of the more intractable problems of the criminal justice system, which vexes police forces but rarely hits the headlines.

Belmarsh also had the 'Unit'. Variously christened as the HSU (High Security Unit) or SSU (Special Secure Unit), its existence and security dominated every aspect of life at Belmarsh. It was quite literally a prison within a prison. It had its own 5-metre-high wall and parallel mesh fence with a sterile area between them mimicking the vast outer perimeter of the main jail. It had its own gate and entry system with the usual 'air lock' principle of entry. Housing up to forty-eight individuals, it was by far the largest and most secure of such facilities in the country. It was, in fact, only one of three operating at the time. It had its own gym, visits facility and communal areas. The forty-eight single cells were arranged in four 'spurs', or mini wings, of twelve: two on the ground floor and two on the first floor. Each spur had its own 'bubble', or observation post, housing one officer, with up to three officers patrolling inside each short, claustrophobic corridor. The pressures on staff who worked there on a day-to-day basis were intense. Relationships with prisoners in such an environment, with men on trial for the most serious of offences or already facing long terms of imprisonment, were often strained. My admiration for the staff was immense. Whether I gave them the support they needed, to this day I still doubt.

It was into this unit that I watched the Whitemoor six escorted by a phalanx of staff. Despite the formidable firepower of the escort through central London, it was jail-craft from here on in. The fact that we have never debated the arming of prison officers, even on external prison perimeters, is something of which we as a nation should be proud and must maintain. With their wrists handcuffed together and with another handcuff attaching them to an individual officer, the six escapees made a strange sight in their 'escape list' uniform. If a prisoner had recently escaped, or there was intelligence he might try, he would be placed on the e-list (escape list). This required individuals to wear a dark blue set of overalls with a thick, bright yellow band of material sewn down one side from head to toe. The six were not only on the e-list but also classified

Exceptional Risk Category A – the very limit of the system. These were the most notorious prisoners the service had had since the 1960s and I could not help thinking how small and insignificant they seemed. It was as if there were an inverse relationship between infamy and physical stature. Although you would not find anyone willing to admit it, we would often choose our burliest staff to escort notorious prisoners on public occasions: a look at black and white photos of the diminutive Ronnie and Reggie Kray handcuffed to the biggest and broadest officers the service could find at their mother's funeral betrays what could happen. But this was not the case here. There was no public view of this particular group and so no point to try and make.

BANG-UP OVER THE CENTURIES

Imprisonment has been with us for a long time, as has been punishment for offending against the norms of society. Some reasons for imprisonment have changed considerably; others have not. There has also been a shifting relationship between offending, punishment and imprisonment that continues even today.

Archaeological excavations reveal Roman and pre-Roman structures that appear to have been for various forms of incarceration. Most seem to relate to military issues. POWs (prisoners of war) were probably the first detainees. Others offending against their communities were dealt with summarily – killed or disfigured.

Written evidence of prisons in Britain does not appear in any significant detail until the ninth century and was more about politics than crime, kings isolating opposition to their power, for example. Branding, whipping and execution were the fates of others, and it was not until the eleventh century that such actions were taken on the back of any type of legal process.

Medieval Britain saw an incremental rise in the number of prisons. Sheriff's prisons began to appear. The word sheriff is a combination of 'shire' and 'reeve', a reeve being a 'keeper of the peace'. The term has been exported to Ireland, Australia and Canada. Sheriffs are judges in

Scotland. In the USA they have been immortalised in literature and drama ever since their inception.

In Britain, the sheriff was the principal legal officer and based in the counties. He also had political and ceremonial duties. The ceremonial aspect of the role remains in the title of High Sheriff today. The position is unpaid and expenses are borne by the post-holder. A significant number of High Sheriffs today use their year in office to promote aspects of criminal justice and regularly act as a focus for fundraising. Succession is planned four years in advance, a unique concept in any walk of life. Nominations are routinely made by existing High Sheriffs, with oversight by Lord Lieutenants (the sovereign's personal representatives) and the Privy Council. The High Sheriff of Greater London recently set up a shrievalty panel, on which I sit as a lay member, to inject greater transparency into the system. This is unique across the shrievalty. London sheriffs also work collaboratively across the succession to promote positive developments across the criminal justice system.

But prisons were not purely the preserve of local sheriffs; some were run by local corporations and the Church also operated prisons, not just as a way of supporting communities but as a means of exerting its political power. A number were operated on a franchise basis, probably the first example of a sub-contracted prison – prison for profit is not new. The jailer ruled the roost and was the chief profit-taker, charging for whatever he could get away with. He would either buy his post or work in conjunction with the franchise holder. Deprivation of liberty was the easy bit for those incarcerated. Eating, drinking, avoiding beatings and disease – simply staying alive – these were day-to-day challenges that many failed.

Torture was seen as a legitimate criminal justice process at this time. It was used to obtain confessions and testimonies as well as to intimidate, deter and exact revenge as well as punish. Methods were extraordinarily barbaric and encompassed a range of horrors from tongue removal, castration, blinding and genital mutilation to the more readily remembered whipping, branding and burning.

Jails became used more expediently in the sixteenth and seventeenth centuries as religious and political upheaval flourished. The Tower of London was effectively Britain's federal prison, housing those who were seen to have offended the State. As the population became more mobile, conventional crime increased. The term 'correction' began to appear, now commonly used in countries such as Australia and the USA but strangely still eschewed in the UK today. Houses of Correction were established after the passing of the Elizabethan Poor Law of 1601 and able-bodied people were sent there, not necessarily because they had committed a crime, to endure strict regimes of hard labour. Technically they were not prisons and there were legal differences between them, but these distinctions were abolished under the Prison Act of 1865 when Houses of Correction and jails were amalgamated.

It was during the seventeenth century that prisoners began to exceed capacity and new methods to deal with felons were needed. Transportation to the colonies began as an alternative not just to imprisonment but also to corporal punishment. An extract from the Breconshire Quarter Sessions makes reference to a woman convicted of theft in 1759 opting for transportation to the American Colonies for seven years to avoid being whipped: 'Elizabeth Thomas, single woman, being indicted and convicted this present session for felony. It is ordered that she be transported to some of His Majesty's plantations in America for the term of seven years. It being at her own request to avoid corporal punishment.'

Transportation could be for life, not just for a finite period. Some felons were required to work on specific projects such as mining and construction, whilst others would be given as unpaid labour to the colonies' free inhabitants. Women became labourers or domestic servants. After a prescribed period felons could apply for a 'ticket of leave', which permitted certain freedoms, most notably to marry and raise a family. Many never returned to Britain and instead formed the basis of a developing society, often in the harshest of environments. There were certainly parallels with today: exile was generally seen as a deterrent, but many felons were living such impoverished lives in Britain that their perception was that it couldn't be much worse. And for these seventeenth-century men and women, time and distance were alien concepts – whilst many may have shrugged their shoulders at having to go to a different country, few would have realised they might not survive the length and harsh conditions of the voyage. Transportation was seen as a humane and productive alternative to execution, which would most likely have been the sentence for many if transportation had not been introduced.

Little is recorded around this time about escapes, but evidence of chaining prisoners in a variety of circumstances is testament to the fact that it was a problem. Sources reveal that payment by results was in existence. Another extract from the Breconshire Quarter Sessions shows that the keeper of the jail in Brecon had his pay substantially cut after losing a female prisoner: 'It is ordered that the sum of five pounds additional salary to the jailer be struck off for his misbehaviour in letting a convict under sentence of transportation make her escape.'

There were further parallels with today in the legal process of the time. Whilst it was now the norm to be sentenced after a trial, there were often unacceptable delays before this took place and people were held in custody, on remand, for long periods.

The Habeas Corpus Act of 1679 helped to alleviate the problems of a few. Habeas corpus (in Latin: 'you may have the body') is a writ that requires a person detained by the authorities to be brought before a court so the legality of the detention can be examined. Sir William Blackstone, an eminent eighteenth-century commentator on English law, recorded the first writs of habeas corpus in 1305, but found equivalent writs going back before Magna Carta. At the time of Magna Carta it was thought to have been common law. Article 39 states: 'No freeman shall be taken or imprisoned or disseised or exiled or in any way destroyed, nor will we go upon him nor will we send upon him except upon the lawful judgement of his peers or the law of the land.' Over the next few hundred years, concern grew that kings would whimsically intervene on matters of detention, so the Act of 1679 enshrined this ancient prerogative in law.

Where it stands today is described by Michael Zander QC, Emeritus Professor of Law at the London School of Economics:

> Habeas corpus has a mythical status in the country's psyche. In reality it is no longer of great practical significance as there are today very few habeas corpus applications, but it still represents the fundamental principle that unlawful detention can be challenged by immediate access to a judge – even by telephone in the middle of the night.

Habeas corpus did not help those caught up in one particularly vicious cycle. Many were imprisoned for debt but had to pay for their own day-to-day existence, thereby getting into more debt and yet further imprisonment. Extortionate demands by jailers achieved the opposite of the original purpose of imprisonment. It did lead to some legislation in the first half of the eighteenth century, but the endless dance of poverty, social exclusion and incarceration was here to stay.

The plight of people in prison began to attract the attention of humanitarians, reformers and philanthropists in the second half of the seventeenth century. In 1773 John Howard was the High Sheriff of Bedfordshire and surveyed prisons not only in Britain but also in Europe. He was the first commentator on and critic of 'prisons for profit'. Disciples of Howard included Sir George Paul in Gloucestershire, who introduced visits to prisoners by the governor, a doctor and a chaplain. This powerful triumvirate remains enshrined in many practices and procedures today. Informal 'rounds' have been superseded by more formal audit and monitoring processes, but prisoners in segregation today are still required to be seen daily by a senior manager and healthcare official, as well as a member of the Independent Monitoring Board (IMB), a watchdog body for prisons once known as the Board of Visitors. Although staff quarters for people working in prisons have almost disappeared, large houses now sold off either to staff or private owners can still be identified as the governor's, doctor's or chaplain's house. Some of these are out in the suburbs; others can be found within existing prison walls, such as the 'Roundhouses' in Brixton and Maidstone prisons.

It was also at this time that Elizabeth Fry came to prominence. Her work to improve conditions for prisoners lasted some thirty years. She now has a modern public building in her name in Marsham Street in central London, which has alternated in ownership between the Home Office and the Ministry of Justice. The National Offender Management Service had its first headquarters there and its acronym, NOMS, was rebranded to stand for the Nightmare on Marsham Street. It is now in Petty France, near St James's Park in London.

Transportation was significantly curtailed by the onset of the American War of Independence in 1776. Sentences of hard labour for up to ten years replaced transportation and brought a need for more places of incarceration in Britain. The justices of Middlesex appointed a man called Duncan Campbell to operate the system of hard labour in that area and he acquired two old ships to hold convicted prisoners. In November 1784 he wrote to the overseer of convicts on the River Thames:

The Censor is calculated for the accommodation and safe custody of 240 convicts and upwards. For that number certain I am willing to engage, and to find ship, officers and crew, four lighters, or more if necessary, sufficient boats and guards, and to find medicines and surgeon, as has been hitherto done for the convicts at hard labour on the Thames. And this I will agree to do for one year to commence 12th October last for the net sum of £6,500 to be paid quarterly. If my Lords have no objection I should wish likewise to enter into a contract for those on board the *Justicia* viz. 250 certain, for one year at the rate allowed me for last installment 12th October. I pray you Sir to lay this before the Board and to take their Lordship's pleasure thereupon.

He was clearly, before his time, writing his own tender and contract; nevertheless, he was given their Lordship's pleasure.

The hulks were even more miserable than the jails. Prisoners would work in chain gangs, lifting gravel from the Thames during the day and returning to the hulks at night. At the peak of the system in 1820 some 500 prisoners were held on hulks; it ended thirty years later. In 1997, however, the system was partially reinvented when HMP *The Weare* was opened as a temporary measure to relieve late twentieth-century prison overcrowding. *The Weare* was a prison ship berthed at Portland Harbour in Dorset. Holding 400 low security adult men, it was designed to last for three years. It was essentially a flat-bottomed barge and its super-structure consisted of steel containers stacked on top of one another to provide five levels of accommodation. There were showers in cells, but only because the accommodation had previously been used as a barracks. This was in line with much other temporary accommodation at the time – frequently Portakabins stacked on top of each other on spare land within prison perimeters, some of which had formerly been used for oil workers in Norway. When *The Weare* arrived in Portland Harbour it did so without planning permission: the application had been rejected by the local council a month beforehand on the grounds that it would be a blight to tourism. It became exactly the opposite and was, in fact, a significant boost to the local tourist trade.

The Weare was sold off in 2006 after conditions on board were criti-cised by the Chief Inspector of Prisons. He complained that the inmates had no exercise and no access to fresh air. He said it was 'unsuitable, expensive and in the wrong place'. Sadly, these were descriptions that applied to too many institutions across the prison estate.

Despite the loss of the American colonies for transportation, Australia provided an alternative and the first ships were dispatched in 1787. So, by the end of the eighteenth century, punishment in the criminal justice system consisted of execution, transportation or imprisonment in local jails, and it was now that the first moves towards the centralisation of the prison system began.

In 1740, as a result of the testimony of John Howard to a House of Commons committee, Parliament passed the 1774 Gaols Act, which abolished jailers' fees and attempted to provide the means to improve conditions in prisons and the health of their inhabitants. Howard had copies of the Act printed and sent to justices and jailers – who on the whole ignored it. Progress was inevitably slow, but advocates like Howard refused to give up. Prison fees were abolished in 1818 and then, after the appointment of Sir Robert Peel, there came the Gaols Act of 1823. This provided for the inspection of prisons by justices and assigned accountability to the Home Secretary. Unfortunately, some 150 jails in the boroughs were excluded.

In 1816 the government constructed Millbank prison on the banks of the Thames, close to where Tate Britain now stands. It was built over a period of five years and at very great expense. This marked a split in the system between state-run Millbank, the hulks and a number of new 'convict prisons' built around the middle of the nineteenth century, and local prisons. The former were administered by a board of directors and the latter by local justices, who were required to make their own rules for the management of their institutions. This was essentially the federal/state system we see today in Australia and the USA, but knowledge of this has not informed the debate around the twenty-first century British system.

Various acts in the first half of the nineteenth century attempted to provide for greater conformity in the system and eventually inspectors were appointed, initially just five. They reported on their findings but had no jurisdiction, a system still in place today. Pentonville opened in 1842 after two years of construction and £85,000 of expenditure. Designed by Joshua Jebb, Pentonville and Millbank both operated the 'separate' system, under which separation, exclusion and silence were seen as methods of 'curing' criminals. The idea came from American experiments in penal reform. So even then, although we had exported incarceration to the United States, we were immediately watching and attempting to replicate their model. Almost 200 years later, we look at the USA, with its prison population of over 2.5 million, and still think we have something to learn.

Pentonville is incorrectly regarded as of Panopticon design. The design was pioneered by Englishman Jeremy Bentham but never actually delivered in the UK. The Panopticon design was an attempt to provide a vision of everything by everyone – true openness. The separate system was, by definition, quite the opposite. Although not delivered by Bentham, the concept of open vision is something that many prison designers have aspired to for years, often as a way of reducing staff costs rather than providing a decent environment. Others went the opposite way and designed accommodation in a series of complex corridors providing little long-range vision, which were variously described as rabbit warrens or no-go areas for staff. The best example of appalling design is HMP Holloway in north London, a veritable maze of levels, corridors and cells defying all logic and delivering bad living conditions.

By the mid-nineteenth century opinion had turned against transportation because it was expensive and no longer a deterrent. Many impoverished men and women sought voluntary migration as a way of escaping the deprivations of Victorian England. Transportation and hulks had all but gone by the 1860s, but the number of new prisons being built accelerated, with the separate system being enshrined in the Prison Act of 1865. This act also empowered the Home Secretary to close inadequate prisons and establish a code of rules that obliged jailers to visit the prison daily, to see every prisoner and to make nocturnal visits once a week. Only the last remains today.

Towards the end of the nineteenth century localism, which had been central to the system, was removed and replaced by centralisation; whether the current government, with its advocacy of localism, will reverse the trend, only time will tell – there is little evidence so far that it will. In 1864 a new Conservative government was appointed on the strength of its promises to reduce costs and taxes – in those days it was rates that exercised people. The Prison Act of 1877 transferred all power to the Home Secretary. A prison commission was given delegated authority for administration. Inspectors remained, but these and the prison commissioners were government appointees. The concept of the local prison evaporated on the back of a government promise.

Sir Edmund Du Cane, immortalised by the road in west London that bears his name and on which Wormwood Scrubs prison stands, was the first chairman of the prison commission. Du Cane ruled the new centralised system for the next twenty years, bringing to it a military ethos and discipline that remained for much longer – role boards of past governors in many older prisons bear the names of many a military general. It was not, however, a time of enlightenment, and already poor conditions in prisons deteriorated, causing abject misery for their inhabitants.

The Gladstone Committee Report of 1895 picked up the baton of penal reform and tried to shift the emphasis for prisons from control to rehabilitation. It declared that the primary and concurrent objects should be 'deterrence and reform'. Primarily, the report attacked the silent and separate systems and its influence continued across the next century. Yet another Prison Act in 1898 introduced Boards of Visitors, which lasted until the latter part of the twentieth century when they were renamed the Independent Monitoring Board (IMB). As 'watchdogs', they had power to preside over prisoner discipline, being able to take away remission and privileges. It took almost 100 years before their de facto right to imprison people was removed and handed to proper legal bodies. The power was also removed from governors.

In the 1920s the name of Alexander Paterson was synonymous with prison reform, not least because of his work on the direction and conduct of borstals. Penal servitude and hard labour was brought to an end in 1948, whilst corporal and capital punishment were abolished in the 1960s. But it was a rash of high-profile and embarrassing escapes in the 1960s that led to the Mountbatten Report and the profound changes in the system that lie at the heart of the current system – and arguably some of its major organisational and financial problems.

TWO

SPIES AND ROBBERS

THE SPY

George Blake pleaded guilty at the Old Bailey on 3 May 1961 to five counts under section one of the Official Secrets Act 1911. He was given the maximum sentence of fourteen years on three counts, to run consecutively, and fourteen years on the other two counts (to run concurrently) – a total of forty-two years. This was the longest non-life sentence handed down by the courts until the conviction of Nezar Hindawi in 1986 for the attempted bombing of an El Al jet: he received forty-five years.

Most of the case was held in camera but the Lord Chief Justice in passing sentence said: 'Your case is one of the worst that can be envisaged in times of peace.' Blake worked for the Special Operations Executive and MI6 during the Second World War. After the war he was posted to the British Embassy in Seoul to set up a network of agents in Korea. When the city was overrun by the North Korean army in 1950 he was captured and imprisoned for three years. It was during this time he was 'unknowingly turned'. Returning to Britain as a hero in 1953, he went to work in Berlin, ironically to recruit double agents. It was here that he began to leak the details of British and American operations to the KGB. He was said to have betrayed as many as 400 agents, many of whom died. He was finally exposed in 1961 by a Polish defector, Michael Goleniewski. Blake was no ordinary spy and no ordinary prisoner.

Blake was held on remand in Brixton prison and transferred to Wormwood Scrubs on conviction. He was immediately placed on the escape list, not because there was any evidence that he might attempt to escape but because his public profile was so high. The procedures then, as now, for someone on the escape list were very prescriptive and required many checks and restrictions on things such as work, cell location and visits from family and friends. HMP Wormwood Scrubs was not seen as an ideal location, given that it was not the country's most secure prison and was situated in the centre of an urban area. Blake was, however, still of great value to the security services, which could continue to interrogate him whilst he was located in London. Yet even after his interrogation ended, he remained at Scrubs for some five years – until his dramatic escape.

The subsequent inquiry, headed by Lord Mountbatten, identified a number of occasions when he could and should have been transferred. The first was in 1961 when the security services had finished their inter-rogation of Blake. The second was in May 1964 when it was reported that he had established an outside link with a discharged prisoner. There was a third occasion in January 1966 when the governor attempted to have him transferred to a more secure block, and there was even a fourth in June 1966 when six prisoners escaped from the part of the prison in which Blake was housed: a warning, if one were needed, of the insecu-rity of Blake's accommodation. Mountbatten concluded that the main weaknesses in Blake's security emanated from the hostel inside the Scrubs wall. Hostels in such locations at the time were commonplace. They were often within the wall but with access to the outside from a separate entrance. Hostels were designed to hold long-term prisoners in their last nine months of sentence as preparation for release. Transfer was usually authorised by the Parole Board and was seen by prisoners as a rite of passage in the sentencing process. Mountbatten concluded that it was messages and plans getting in and out through 'hostellers' and trustee prisoners working with them that had allowed the successful escape plan to be hatched, but he felt that supervision of Blake's correspondence and visits was generally satisfactory and had not contributed to the escape. Blake had appeared to settle down to his sentence and had kept a low profile, offering apparent quiescence and cooperation.

What was and remains unusual in the case of Blake's escape was the active involvement of people outside. Given Blake's crimes and past associations with espionage, it might have been assumed that his escape would have been part of an international plot by government agencies. The reality, however, was much more mundane – Blake's conspirators were three men he had met in Scrubs, two of whom were anti-nuclear activists, who orchestrated the escape partly for money and partly because of the perception that his long sentence was inhumane. The plan was for Blake to take his chance the during free time for prisoners between 5 and 7 p.m. on a Saturday evening, when only two officers would be watching over 100 prisoners. Blake was allowed to move around like anyone else, there were no special measures for him. A film was showing and others played games or simply mingled freely around the wing. At about 5.30 p.m. Blake spoke with one of the officers, creating a false sense of security around him, not that one was needed; he opined that the all-in wrestling being shown on the TV was a fake. At the 7.20 p.m. roll call Blake's cell was discovered to be empty. A local alarm was raised, and at 7.45 p.m. the police were informed that he had escaped. He had probably had about two hours following the wrestling conversation to make his getaway.

Blake had escaped through the main window of the second floor landing by breaking one of the cast iron frames. Whether he had weakened or smashed it earlier was unclear. The 6 to 7-metre drop was broken by a covered porch over the hall entrance and by a large bin with a flat wooden top. He scaled the outer perimeter by means of a rope ladder thrown over from outside by one of his accomplices. Torrential rain and poor visibility aided the whole process. Apart from the fact that Blake broke his wrist scaling the perimeter, it was a smooth operation. Blake spent time moving between houses identified as safe by his accomplices before fleeing to Moscow.

TRAIN ROBBER 1

The escape of Charles Frederick Wilson on 12 August 1964 was the second of the three escapes to be examined by Mountbatten – and this one took the concept of outside assistance a step further.

Charlie Wilson was regarded as one of the key organisers of the Great Train Robbery, which netted over £3.5 million – at that time the largest haul in criminal history. After a three-month trial, on 15 April 1964 the proceedings ended with the judge describing the robbery as 'a crime of sordid violence inspired by vast greed' and passing sentences of thirty years' imprisonment on seven of the robbers. Wilson's was to be served at Winson Green prison in Birmingham, the first of many public sector prisons to be privatised.

Wilson's method of escape remains unique within the modern prison system. The essence of prison security is to provide a series of secure layers through which anyone inside has to pass in order to get out. The more secure the prison, the more layers there will be, and the more secure the individual layers themselves will need to be. Low security prisons will have a fence. Medium security prisons will have a wall and a fence. High security prisons will have prisons within prisons – special units. Cell doors in secure prisons will be steel constructions with five-lever locks; in semi-secure prisons cells will be more like rooms, with only privacy locks, for which prisoners themselves will have a key. The essence of prison security is to prevent, or at least hinder, someone from inside getting out. What they are not geared to, then and now, is to preventing someone from outside getting in and taking a prisoner out. This is precisely what happened with Wilson.

An unknown number of accomplices scaled the wall of the prison with the aid of a rope ladder and entered the prison buildings. Some members of staff were bound and gagged but the gang appear to have been facilitated in finding Wilson by some doors being left open. They also had certain essential keys in their possession, not least a cell key.

Wilson had only been at Winson Green prison for four months. As with Blake, he gave the impression of being a model prisoner settling down to a long sentence, even after his appeal failed. He was an impressive and charismatic figure who fellow prisoners either thought well able to sustain a long period of incarceration or well-resourced enough to get out at a time of his choosing. He was astute enough not to share his plans with anyone and cleverly declined to attend his appeal. Had he done so, he would have run the risk of being transferred, thereby negating any plans he had made based on months of observation of routines and getting to know his captors personally.

Despite his quiet and cooperative demeanour, the prison authorities were shrewd enough to place him on the escape list: his criminal associations and outside resources were legendary. Being on the escape list meant he had to wear the same high visibility clothing as the Whitemoor six some thirty years later. His movement was limited and monitored, his cell location was changed frequently and at night he was checked every fifteen minutes by a night patrol, which would be required to look into a cell permanently dimly lit. His clothing was placed on a chair outside on the landing. It was this restriction that helped the escape gang to locate him. Whilst there were over 500 prisoners on this particular wing, only sixteen were on the escape list.

It was about 3.30 a.m. by the time one of the staff who had been bound and gagged by Wilson's aides had managed to free himself and raise the alarm. Police and prison officers arrived to find the cell empty and a rope ladder in the grounds. It was clear that by then Wilson was long gone.

The chief director of the prison department, who carried out an initial in-house inquiry into the escape, made a very telling comment: he declared that all proper steps had been taken to ensure Wilson's safe custody based on the assumption that staff integrity could be relied upon. Mountbatten agreed with this statement but called into question staff integrity over keys. He concluded that the intruders had keys before they broke in and in particular were in possession of a master key, of which there were few but to which many had access. A forensic examination revealed traces of soap on one key, indicating that an impression had been made and a copy cut. Experts affirmed that the fashioning of such keys would require testing and modification before perfecting them for use. It was clearly an inside job.

There was a thorough investigation into all aspects of the escape, but the Director of Public Prosecutions decided there was insufficient evidence to bring charges against anyone. The gang which broke in was never identified. It left a bitter taste in the mouths of the many honest staff whose integrity had been brought into question. Mountbatten, meanwhile, drew some pertinent conclusions:

> The custody of prisoners with very long sentences like Wilson and the very large sums of money at the disposal of their friends is a new development the prison service has to face. A prison officer who is in financial difficulties is clearly vulnerable. It is unrealistic to expect him always to report his difficulties to a superior officer, but he might well talk to a welfare officer about them. Officers should be encouraged to do this and the staff welfare organisation developed, perhaps regionally, so that regular visits can be made to all establishments.

Today, Mountbatten might reflect on a service that has made little progress in this area. With drug trafficking and organised crime making people 'rich beyond the dreams of avarice', the risks for staff and managers are now immeasurably more acute.

TRAIN ROBBER 2

The third escape covered by the Mountbatten Report was that of Ronald Arthur Biggs on 8 July 1965 from HMP Wandsworth. He was another of the Great Train Robbers serving thirty years. This was an even more audacious escape, again with direct outside assistance.

Biggs had been at Wandsworth for a year following his conviction and on the escape list the whole time. He had complained to a member of parliament about the stringency of his restrictions, but to no avail. The escape of Wilson had focused the attention of the prison authorities on Biggs's security and three officers guarded his cell at night, changing at regular intervals. He was one of fifty men on the escape list at that time and they would take exercise in two groups, either in the morning or the afternoon. Although it varied, morning or afternoon, the times of each session remained the same, and if he had not taken exercise in the morning, an afternoon session at a prescribed time was not difficult to work out. In addition, as with many prisons in urban locations, it was easy to view the exercise yard with binoculars from nearby residential accommodation, in this case a block of flats.

The main exercise yard at the time was roughly circular and about 100 metres in diameter. It was the afternoon of 8 July 1965 when the four officers supervising fourteen prisoners saw a head appear above the perimeter wall. The gang had parked a furniture van alongside the wall and from its roof threw two ladders over into the yard. The alarm was raised but several prisoners impeded the staff as they attempted to prevent Biggs scaling the ladders. Biggs and four others made their escape, with Biggs being given absolute priority by the gang. The specially designed van was left where it was and a series of getaway cars were in place for the onward flight. The whole thing was over in less than two minutes.

Biggs fled initially to Australia and then, as the net around him tightened, to Brazil – his celebrity in that country, which could not extradite him, is legendary. In 2001, Biggs's escape ended after thirty-six years with his voluntary return to England, where his rapidly failing health resulted in compassionate release on 6 August 2009, the day before his eightieth birthday.

The inquiry looked at the fact that there were other yards that did not have a perimeter wall bordering the outside and that the exercise timetable was too predictable. The simplicity and audacity of the escape did not, however, throw into question the integrity of the staff, but it was yet another embarrassing debacle for the prison service. Mountbatten looked at other escapes around this time, including that of the infamous Frank Mitchell in December 1965 from a Dartmoor prison working party. Known as the mad axe man, Mitchell was an East End villain associated with the Kray twins and they were credited with his jailbreak;

although, given that Mitchell was on an outside working party, he had technically only absconded. After the escape, whilst staying in a flat in Barking Road, Mitchell became increasingly violent and unstable. He disappeared and the Kray twins were later charged with but acquitted of his murder. The body was never recovered – some believe Mitchell is helping support a flyover in Barking. It was the escapes of Blake, Biggs and Wilson, however, which were the main influences on Mountbatten's recommendations.

CHANGES

The Mountbatten Report acknowledged that it was right to move away from the nineteenth-century principles of security based on simply isolating prisoners in cells and that the continued development of humane regimes was vital. Mountbatten's conclusion was that escapes should be prevented by secure perimeters and by assigning to prisoners various categories according to their risk and dangerousness. It is this process that forms the cornerstone of the prison system today and it lies at the heart of many of its failures. He recommended that prisoners be divided into four main categories: Category A, for those whose escape would be highly dangerous to the public, the police or the security of the State; Category B, for those prisoners for whom the highest conditions of security are not necessary but for whom escape must be made very difficult; Category C, for prisoners who cannot be trusted in open conditions, but who do not have the ability or resources to make a determined escape attempt; Category D, for prisoners who pose no danger to the public and can be housed in open conditions where perimeter security is absent. Categorisation on these principles, he decided, was the best means of preventing escape and proper machinery should be set up to ensure all prisoners are allocated to the correct category.

One significant recommendation that Mountbatten made was not taken up. He said that all Category A prisoners should be housed in one purpose-built, maximum security prison, which should be made escape-proof. He recommended that it be built on the Isle of Wight and should be called Vectis (the old Roman name for the island). Instead, a further report followed. This recommended the dispersal of Category A prisoners amongst a small number of designated prisons, which would be of very high security but which would hold a combination of Category A and Category B prisoners. The 'dispersal system', as it became known, remained for many years, to be replaced in the 1990s by the High Security Estate. The name was changed but the principles remain.

The concept of one highly secure prison for the most dangerous was seen as potentially inhumane, very difficult to manage and extremely expensive. Many jurisdictions across the world have flirted with the principle and some have embraced it. Alcatraz Island, opened in 1934, was seen as one of the first prototypes. Units within prisons have tended to be more common than standalone institutions. Katingal was built inside the Long Bay Correctional Facility in Australia in 1975, a forty-cell block regarded by prisoners as an electronic zoo, given the level of surveillance inherent in the harsh regime. In the USA the Federal Bureau of Prisons' solitary confinement blocks are known as Special Housing Units (SHU). They have attracted much controversy and litigation. Many have argued that the living conditions in such facilities violate the US constitution, specifically the Eighth Amendment's proscription against 'cruel and unusual' punishments. In 1996 a United Nations team assigned to investigate torture described SHU conditions as 'inhuman and degrading'.

In the UK the 'Supermax' debate occasionally resurfaces, but the prison within a prison concept has prevailed, based on a modification of the Category A process. 'High Risk' became a category above the old Category A, with 'Exceptional Risk' added above that. Exceptional Risk Category A prisoners tend to be few and far between and are housed currently only in units within Belmarsh and Whitemoor prisons.

THREE

WHITEMOOR AND PARKHURST

It was in the allegedly escape-proof Whitemoor jail, Cambridgeshire, at 8 a.m. on the evening of Friday 9 September 1994, that events occurred that were to shake up the prison and political systems violently. It was the biggest security breach since the escapes of Blake, Biggs and Wilson.

HMP Whitemoor had opened in 1991 just outside March in Cambridgeshire. It was modern, 'hi-tech' and the best security the system had to offer. Unlike many older prisons, which were only later in their lives designated as high security, the security systems at Whitemoor had been embedded in the design and build. In addition, in one corner of the perimeter was the SSU. Housing a dozen men of Exceptional Risk Category A status, it was literally a prison within a prison – an impregnable unit within an escape-proof institution. It operated on the same principle that Mountbatten had advocated: that the perimeter was the ultimate safeguard and that if it was secure enough (and in this instance there were effectively two perimeters – that of the unit and that of the main prison), the regime inside could be relaxed and informal. Prisoners could move freely within the unit, there were many educational and recreational facilities, and the number of personal possessions allowed was far in excess of that in the main prison. Staff saw their work there as mundane and unchallenging. In the subsequent escape inquiry, staff spoke of the 'unit running itself'. Despite the nature of those housed there, by definition violent and dangerous, there were perceived to be few problems. As with Blake, Biggs and Wilson, the absence of conflict on a day-to-day basis lured the staff into a false sense of security. In this unit, however, there was a new and hitherto unrecognised factor at play – conditioning.

The IRA had mastered the art of conditioning in the prisons of Northern Ireland, and at the Maze in particular. The Maze was situated in the former Royal Air Force station of Long Kesh, on the outskirts of the town of Lisburn. It was known as Long Kesh for many years during internment in the province. The Maze played a prominent part in the troubles, seeing escapes, hunger strikes, murders and political negotiation. It was closed in 2000 and though many have sought to raze it to the ground the structure remains. The 'H' block configuration of the accommodation made it particularly conducive to the practice of conditioning. Each spur or leg of the 'H' contained a series of cells leading to a dead end. Staff moving out from the administrative centre of the 'H' would routinely be surrounded by prisoners and bombarded with questions, threats or complaints to such an extent that staff would avoid the conflict by not leaving the security of the centre. Such was the control and organisation of the paramilitaries that there were periods when the counting of prisoners was left to the paramilitary commanders in the units. One prisoner who had been murdered by fellow inmates remained undiscovered for days, as did a cell that had been used to house soil from an escape tunnel.

Numerous inquiries in Northern Ireland acknowledged not only the concept of conditioning and its widespread practice, but also its traumatic effect on staff and the lack of training to combat it. It was not only intimidation in the units that acted as a deterrent to prisoner management, there were many other insidious and subliminal tactics. There were few idle threats during this period. A number of prison officers were murdered whilst off duty. One senior Northern Ireland prison governor told me of the day he had a new car delivered to his home. That same morning, whilst on duty, a piece of paper was passed to him by a prisoner with the make, model, colour and registration number of his new car on it.

Northern Ireland learned the lessons of conditioning slowly and painfully. However, in 1994 in Whitemoor, despite the fact that the SSU housed five members of the Provisional IRA, the potential for conditioning was largely unrecognised.

On the night of the escape the normal contingent of seven prison officers was on duty. Two were in a sealed control room monitoring CCTV cameras and phone calls; a further four, one of whom was a senior officer, were playing scrabble or reading. All of the latter four were in the main body of the relatively small association area. The six escapees – five IRA terrorists and a man who had previously been involved in an armed escape attempt – made their way unchallenged by the staff into the exercise yard, where they were routinely unsupervised as CCTV was seen as sufficient. Incredibly, the six men had with them a vast array of equipment with which to facilitate their escape. As well as double layers of clothing ready for a night on the fens, they had a rope ladder, metal poles, a clamping device, bolt croppers, a screwdriver, a Stanley knife and a pair of pliers. Some of the equipment was probably passed to them by other prisoners via the window of an adjacent hobbies room not covered by CCTV. They cut through the metal fence of the SSU perimeter, which was not alarmed, and then scaled the SSU wall. As the remainder were climbing the first wall, the front runners cut through the fence of the main perimeter, this time setting off an alarm and alerting the prison's emergency control room. Events were now being captured on camera and, although staff were able to observe the surreal scene, they were powerless to stop the escape. The SSU officers, jolted into action by the alarm, hurried to the exercise yard, only to see the last of the escapees astride the wall. One officer approached, only to be shot and wounded by one of the fleeing prisoners. The gunman stood guard and fended off staff as the other five negotiated the main perimeter wall with an ingenious array of ropes and badminton and volley ball poles.

Astonishingly for an escape of such sophistication, and unlike Blake, Biggs and Wilson, having descended the outer perimeter wall there was no escape vehicle and no one to assist them. All six simply ran, pursued by a cohort of prison officers, including a number of dog handlers with charges who had been let off the leash. More shots were fired, but then the gun appeared to jam. Some of the dogs attacked the prison officers rather than the escapees and at least one prisoner threw what appeared to be pepper at one of the dogs. Four of the fugitives were enveloped by the pursuing posse; the remaining two were captured using thermal-imaging cameras from a police helicopter after some ninety minutes. There was much speculation about the absence of outside help once the prisoners had breached the perimeter. No evidence was ever found of an escape car and none of the escapees spoke of any plans that had failed. Nevertheless, the after-effects of the escape on the system are to be felt to the present day.

It was left to Sir John Woodcock to do a 'Mountbatten' on the events, with Sir John Learmont following up with a subsequent inquiry into wider organisational issues. On 19 December 1994 the Home Secretary made the following statement to the House of Commons in response to the Woodcock Report: 'Sir John Woodcock's report reveals a dreadful state of affairs at Whitemoor ... I am therefore asking General Sir John Learmont ... to conduct a comprehensive, independent and authoritative review of security throughout the prison service.'

The Learmont team had barely started in January 1995 when more disasters came along, one after the other, like London buses. Frederick West, who with his wife had raped and murdered at least twelve young women between 1967 and 1987, committed suicide in Birmingham prison on New Year's day; Everthorpe, a medium security training prison near Brough in Yorkshire, rioted on the 2 January; and only the next day three prisoners escaped from HMP Parkhurst.

THE ESCAPE FROM PARKHURST

Although Parkhurst was no longer the Alcatraz it had once purported to be, it remained a high security prison holding Category A prisoners. Parkhurst prison started life as a military hospital in 1805 and was later transformed into a prison for boys awaiting deportation, mainly to

Australia. By 1847 a new wing (C Wing) had been built by the prisoners, digging the clay and baking the bricks themselves. From 1863 to 1869 it had a brief interlude as a female prison and then in 1968, despite its age, it became one of the first dispersal prisons following the Mountbatten report. It relied heavily on a CCTV system, which proved to be as much use as an ashtray on a motorbike.

It was early evening on Tuesday 3 January 1995 that the well-prepared escape plan came to fruition. Like the escapes of the 1960s, internal processes were poor and there was over-reliance on a vulnerable perimeter. As in the Whitemoor escape, there was a surprising absence of outside assistance. The three escapees were part of a group of thirty prisoners who were collected in batches from across all the wings. A single officer marshalling an unruly crocodile of men did not spot the three slip away into the dark and, by failing to count them all out and count them back in again, their absence was not spotted for over an hour.

The three had been able to manufacture a range of tools and the constituent parts of a ladder, and apparently arm themselves with a gun and blank ammunition. Most importantly, they had made a key that would open all the doors and gates that stood between the sports hall and the outer defences of the prison. It later appeared that the key had been well tested beforehand. Given the highly secure nature of the prison and the Category A status of the prisoners, simple routine searches should have found such items. The escapees cut through the inner perimeter fence and scaled the outer wall with the ladder, the rungs of which had been hidden in a workshop, and inexperienced and untrained staff monitoring banks of poor quality black and white screens failed to spot them.

Once out, wearing their own clothes and with ample cash, they simply walked the short distance to the centre of the nearby town of Newport and took a short taxi ride to Sandown – where the final part of their plan unravelled. One of the fugitives was a qualified pilot and they had planned to 'hot wire' a light aircraft at the nearby Bembridge airfield. The clumsy attempt failed, as did subsequent attempts to steal a boat and escape by sea. The island nature of Parkhurst and its two sister jails, Albany and Camp Hill, which for years had proved unpopular with prisoners because of the difficult access for visitors, had played its part in providing an effective security barrier. Without help, the three were stuck. They spent another four days and nights hiding on the island before being spotted and captured. The final arrest of the three marked the end of a period of great concern amongst the islanders – concern that was reflected in the considerable manpower deployed to apprehend the three during their time at large. Public anxiety had been further heightened because of threats made during their trial by one of the prisoners involved. The trial judge and a number of police officers and witnesses in his case had been placed under 24-hour guard until the men were all recaptured.

RECOMMENDATIONS

Learmont made a number of recommendations, but most importantly he revisited Mountbatten's security categorisation system. He acknowledged the very different society for which Mountbatten had made his recommendations. He spoke of a prison system now being run against a backdrop of growing violent and drug-related crime. He also raised the issue of the inescapable rise in the number of Category A prisoners (150 at the time of Mountbatten compared with 750 at the time of his report). He drew particular attention to the modification of the categorisation system in Category A since the Mountbatten Report: Exceptional Risk – containing highly resourceful prisoners valuable to criminal organisations outside and highly likely to escape; High Risk – containing prisoners who may be marginally less likely to escape; and Standard Risk – containing those with fewer resources. He was critical of the fact that certain security arrangements were left to local discretion and that staff interviewed for the inquiry found it very difficult to differentiate between High and Standard Risk Category As in particular within the same prison. He felt prisoners were able to manipulate, exploit and undermine the system.

Learmont highlighted an urgent need rapidly to develop an improved categorisation system. His proposed interim solution was little more than a clarification based on the existing system. He advocated clear rules for each type of prisoner. Under his proposals, Exceptional Risk Category A became Category 1, and so on, down to Category D – now Category 6. He was clear, however, that what was needed in the longer term was a fundamental review of the whole categorisation system, followed by the provision of a new one that better protected the public, had the confidence of staff and was seen as fair by prisoners. Learmont was adamant in his view that categorisation was fundamental to security. He felt that work to improve the system should be given priority.

RESPONSES: PHYSICAL AND PROCEDURAL SECURITY

Sixteen years on, not only has that work not been done, but the societal changes between then and now are even greater than those between the Mountbatten and Learmont reports.

'Security, security, security' was once the catch phrase of the prison service. The balance between security and the regime was also once a hot topic. In terms of public perception, it would be safe to assume that security is the main priority of a prison system. But what do we mean by security? Simply locking people up? The conventional wisdom within the service at one time was a combination of physical, procedural and dynamic security. Physical security is the simplest to describe and consists of traditional barriers such as walls, fences, bars and keys. It is the type of security that any report or recommendation tends to hide under – the result of the Woodcock and Learmont reports was massive spending on high-tech physical security.

My own tenure at Belmarsh during this period saw some £18 million being spent in eighteen months in a frenzy of activity across the jail. At the peak, we spent £1.5 million in one month alone. The Special Secure Unit – the prison within a prison – was emptied to allow massive strengthening of the physical infrastructure and improvement of the alarm systems. But how to undertake such a task? All nine of the notorious escapees had been dispatched to the Belmarsh unit as the last bastion of high security. One of the four main house blocks was designated as a temporary SSU, but in order to reach that status it had to be made as impregnable as the unit itself was going to be. The operation began, with the help of the odd fag packet as well as imported technology from the Netherlands and Israel. Work also started across the jail on the gate, visitors' facilities and the emergency control room. In all there were some eight major construction sites with over 150 outside contractors carrying out the work – all of whom had to be security cleared, monitored, supervised and searched entering and leaving the jail. All manner of things tested those of us tasked with supervising the work whilst continuing with the small matter of housing the nine most notorious escapees in the system, as well as over 100 Standard Risk Category As and 35 High Risk Category As, not to mention a further 700 of south London's finest.

Things seemed to conspire against but never quite overwhelm us. A day didn't seem to go by without one set of construction plans or another being found in a south London phone box; applicants for work with the contractors continued to throw up wanted villains; tools went missing, whilst tools we shouldn't have had were found – a scaffold pole was found buried in the gravel by the SSU but it transpired that lazy builders had abandoned it during the original construction.

This was all taking place in the sunny borough of Thamesmead, built at the end of the 1960s in an effort to solve the social problems that had already started to affect earlier estates. These problems were a result of working class families from different areas being uprooted from close-knit communities, then sent to remote estates many miles from where they previously lived and where they knew nobody. The design of the estates meant people would rarely see their neighbours, as they would have done in the back-to-back Victorian housing they had come from. Worst of all were those that were based on tunnels and alleyways, which were ideal for crime and drug dealing.

The prison itself is on the site of the old Royal Arsenal in the heart of the Plumstead marshes. It was at the height of the building work that I was sent a flyer offering detailed aerial photographs of the prison, a series prior to, during and at the final stage of construction. These were the days before Google Earth – today such detail is readily available – and I was alarmed at an apparent breach of security. My alarm was not shared higher up the food chain so I bought a splendid series of aerial shots over time as the old Arsenal site metamorphosed into HMP Belmarsh. I proudly placed the framed aerial shots around the walls of the prison's boardroom. I gather they were not held in such esteem by any of my successors.

All such distractions apart, it was the geology of the site that caused the headaches and the costs. Being marsh gravel, everything from a gate post to a lamp post needed a 5-metre concrete pile to ensure it would stay in place and be secure. Piles require pile-driving, which is not a silent task. A building plan somewhere in the bowels of the Ministry of Justice will hold the precise number of piles driven during this time. Suffice to say, there were a lot.

When the work was done, normal life with 900 prisoners and 1,000 staff continued. The team involved, inside and outside the prison, was exceptional. The hours were long, the pressure intense and the humour black as night. For all of us, the learning was not so much a curve as a vertical line. There was corporate learning too. Techniques of CCTV monitoring, alarms, lines of sight, types of construction had all progressed. The emergency control room became more like the deck of the star ship *Enterprise*. Surprisingly, none of the technology was new. The Dutch had, and still have, fence designs that make 5-metre concrete walls seem prehistoric and ineffective. Cameras that could see a flea on a dog's bum at 500 yards replaced those more in tune with old recordings of *Hancock's Half Hour*. A wide steel mesh net, originally used as tank protection in the desert and designed by the Israeli army, was placed over the entire exercise yard of the SSU. This was despite the fact that the yard was within the fence and wall of the SSU, which itself was within the fence and wall of the main prison perimeter. Everything was watched over by more cameras than at the average Olympics. This was extreme physical security. No one, including me, stopped to evaluate its cost-effectiveness. The work at Belmarsh was also replicated across the High Security Estate, not least at Whitemoor, where the nightmare had begun. The concept of Vectis, Mountbatten's plan to keep all the bad eggs in one basket, raised its head again. It was renamed Supermax, but then sensibly put back in the drawer. Home Secretary at the time Michael Howard, presiding over it all, slept easily in his bed.

Physical security was then and still remains a safe refuge in the discussion of prisons. If it looks like a prison and has imposing walls, cameras and big Victorian locks and keys, then it must be a prison. But alongside physical security you need procedural security – the processes and systems. This was not ignored and manuals began to appear in profusion, always red in colour. Counting and checking and, most importantly, signing for things became the norm, and the external auditing of those processes became the greatest growth industry the prison system had ever seen. A warm blanket of measurable outputs began to descend upon the service. Quantity subsumed quality.

What came a poor third in the race for ever better security was the human element. The prison service acknowledged the relationship between staff and prisoners, but failed to embrace it properly and see the importance of dynamic security to creating safe jails that protect the public. The term dynamic security was first coined by the late Ian Dunbar in a publication he wrote called *A Sense of Direction*. Dunbar was one of a very small group of inspirational and highly intellectual prison governors, the like of whom have not been seen since. He demonstrated unwavering humanity and respect for those in his charge, but combined it with a flair for imaginative management and, above all, leadership. He drew on the unique experience of governing many of England's most difficult jails at some of their most testing times and in a bleak political landscape that has not improved. For him, management was about prisons themselves and not the bureaucracies that have since swamped them. He eschewed futile rhetoric for intellectual pragmatism, unsurprisingly, perhaps, given that he had impeccable educational credentials, with a degree in politics and economics from Keele University and a period spent at Reed College, Oregon. Dunbar even pursued his life-long interest in ideas and social issues in the States, establishing contact with the Civil Rights Movement and meeting Martin Luther King and Paul Robeson. In later years, a friendship with Norval Morris, the distinguished criminologist, revived his American ties. As well as tenures in Wormwood Scrubs, Wakefield and Long Lartin, Ian Dunbar held the posts of regional manager and director on the Prison's board. After retirement he continued working as a sentence review commissioner in Northern Ireland, dealing with releases under the Good Friday Agreement. He passed away in August 2010.

Dynamic security faced the same problem that besets many potential improvements in prisons – measurability. How do you measure relationships and their effect on the prison environment? The prison service did eventually make one attempt at embracing the concept by declaring a 'decency agenda'. It was a tacit acknowledgment of the old adage that you cannot manage what you cannot measure. As the prison service struggled with the concept, it was left to Her Majesty's Chief Inspector of Prisons to carry the baton of addressing relationships and human interactions in prisons and it was at this time its most ardent champion appeared. Sat in the governor's office at Belmarsh trying to keep all the plates spinning on the poles, I received a call from the Deputy Chief Inspector of Prisons, Colin Allen. A new Chief Inspector had been appointed to replace Stephen Tumim and he had yet to visit a prison since his appointment the previous day – could Belmarsh be his first? Sir (now Lord) David Ramsbotham appeared, and there began a long association that continues to this day.

The remit of Her Majesty's Chief Inspectorate had been to look at the treatment and conditions of prisoners. Unlike some other inspectorates across the world, its remit did not encompass the management of prisons. This remains the case today and is worth revisiting. Reviews of the prison service's organisational structures have been almost annual since the creation of the National Offender Management Service, but in the last decade there has been no independent review of the management of prisons themselves.

Over the last decade the inspectorate has developed a methodology for inspecting prisons. In 2000 it initiated a debate about the health of prisoners and published a report entitled 'Prisoner or Patient', which resulted in the transfer of responsibilities for the health of prisoners to the National Health Service. It also developed the concept of a 'Healthy Prison', something that was first set out by the World Health Organization, It defined four key tests of what ought to be provided in any custodial environment:

- Safety: prisoners, even the most vulnerable, are held safely.
- Respect: prisoners are treated with respect for their human dignity.
- Purposeful activity: prisoners are able, and expected, to engage in activity that is likely to benefit them.
- Resettlement: prisoners are prepared for release into the community, and helped to reduce the likelihood of reoffending and produced.

In conjunction with this philosophy, inspectors would routinely survey prisoners about what they thought of the prison, how they were treated and what benefits, if any, they were receiving during their incarceration that would help them successfully back into society. This took place both in the form of individual interviews and through meeting groups of prisoners away from the imposing gaze of prison staff. The selection of such groups always initiated some debate between inspectors and prison staff: the latter seeking to select the compliant; the former, the more disgruntled.

Wielding the cudgel for the prison service in its efforts to come to terms with dynamic security was Professor Alison Liebling of the Institute of Criminology at Cambridge. Thanks to her passion for the issue and consummate intellectual credentials, she and her team devised the MQPL (Measurement of the Quality of Prison Life) to back up the prison service's decency agenda. Whilst it too was based on prisoner surveys, it was far more sophisticated and statistically valid than the inspectorate equivalent. It developed, and continues to develop, as a very sophisticated tool, looking at every aspect of a prison through the eyes of the consumer – the prisoner. It was gradually implemented as part of the prison service's own audit processes, to which prisons were all too regularly subjected. The survey would take place at the end of an audit and the results would then be carefully analysed. In the early days of MQPL the results did not contribute to the jail's audit score. Audits counted the beans and beans meant prizes in the form of a rising position in the prison service's league tables. What those on the receiving end of what those beans represented – the prisoners – felt about it was something of an inconvenience, not least because it was common for the bean score to be high but the MQPL score to be low. In other words, the auditors rated the prison highly but prisoners hated it. I witnessed many a conversation along the lines that prisoners would only moan whatever you ask them. I hold the contrary view, based on experience: whilst we all love a whinge, I have found prisoners invariably constructive – after all, who better than the consumer to help improve the product. It may be unpalatable to some but what is true for a supermarket, holiday company or TV programme is true for prisons. No firm which ignored its consumers has ever been successful. Prisoner representation in the forms of councils and consultative groups, on either a democratic or selective basis, have been around in some establishments for many years. HMP Grendon, with its emphasis on therapeutic communities, has led the way for decades on prisoner consultation and has been justly recognised for it. It is to be ignored at our peril.

MQPL eventually drifted into the impenetrable league table scoring mechanism of the prison service, but it is safe to assume that this was done reluctantly and that the process is not used as widely as it could be. The Institute of Criminology is now examining the MQPL further and how it can define a good and bad prison, particularly as part of the process of comparing public and private prisons. The institute has brushed aside the popular concept of 'public bad, private good' in favour of an appreciation that some public prisons are very good and some very bad. Ditto private prisons. The work is unread and unrecognised by those in power or devising policy as we dash towards mass privatisation.

Physical and procedural security remain tangible and, above all, easily measurable. Dynamic security, as the Institute of Criminology has proved, can be too. But whilst it can be measured it is more difficult to manage. It needs a skill set beyond bean-counting: it requires a knowledge and understanding of relationships and their dynamics in the entirely institutionalised environments that are prisons. It requires intellectual rigour as well as an ability and desire to debate the issues. We cannot run prisons by coercion. We can only run them by cooperation. If at any time the entire population of a prison wants to walk out of the gate, there is little to stop them. A jail of 1,000 prisoners may only have between sixty and seventy staff on duty throughout the prison at any time. At night, with everyone locked up, there will be less than a dozen. The alternatives are concrete coffins with armed guards inside and around the perimeter. They have been created in parts of the US penal system but are both inhumane and expensive.

Historically, major incidents in prison are regularly thwarted through dynamic security, often in the form of intelligence and primarily from informants. Be it escape attempts, corrupt staff, bullying, assault or theft, the prison informant network can often be relied upon to protect the prison and the public. The successes rarely hit the headlines. But when the network fails because the staff lose interest or the relationships break down, then all the expensive hardware and process manuals become redundant.

Sarpoza prison in Afghanistan should be a lesson to us all. Early in 2011, 480 Taliban prisoners escaped in the early hours of the morning after a team of eighteen insurgents on the outside spent five months burrowing hundreds of metres underground through the brown soil west of Kandahar city straight into the prison's political section where hundreds of Taliban were held.

As the great escape was a break-in rather than a break-out, there was no need to surreptitiously get rid of the earth inside the camp –

according to one local media report the Kandahar plotters simply filled lorries in the city's bazaar with excavated earth from a tunnel stretching a reported 320 metres. The tunnel started in a compound directly opposite the prison and the activity was thought to be just another of the major building projects in the city financed by American aid. For prisoners tunnelling out, removing the soil is the biggest problem. Second World War films such as *The Great Escape* pictured POWs distributing the dirt down trouser legs. At Kandahar it was much easier. The tunnel was large enough to stand up in and was even supported by metal and concrete beams. It went directly under Highway One, a vital Afghan route between Kandahar and Herat. Electric lights and ventilation systems finished off the ingenious but far from subtle construction. As the prisoners came out in the compound at the end of the tunnel, Taliban commanders were there to whisk them away in a fleet of vehicles.

Prison managers knew nothing until long after the prisoners had disappeared into the night. It took from about 11 p.m. to 3.30 a.m. for cell after cell of prisoners to negotiate the passageway to freedom. The first guard who came on to the scene that Monday morning found an entirely empty building, with just the remnants of prisoner clothing. Suspicions of it being an inside job were discounted when one of the escapees recounted the approach of the prison staff: 'They were just sleeping. The guards are always drunk. Either they smoke heroin or marijuana, and then they just fall asleep. During the whole process no one checked, there was no patrols, no shooting or anything.' In June 2008, 870 prisoners had escaped from the same prison when insurgents attacked the compound, blowing up a section of wall. Millions were then spent upgrading the prison – its physical security. What Kandahar demonstrated, yet again, was the fallacy of depending on physical security and the problem of people breaking in from the outside.

Helicopter escapes are the most well-recognised of prison getaways with outside assistance. The UK has fortunately only had one. It was December 1987 when a Bell 206L helicopter hijacked from a nearby airfield landed on the exercise yard at what was then the high security

Gartree prison in the midlands. Gangland boss John Kendall, serving eight years, was joined in his escape by convicted murderer Sydney Draper, serving life. Kendall remained at large for ten days and Draper thirteen months.

For reasons no one can explain, France has had the most helicopter escapes – at least eleven. One of the most memorable was in 1986, when the wife of bank robber Michel Vaujour studied for months to learn how to fly a helicopter. She then rented one and flew to her husband's high security prison near Paris and plucked him off the roof. In a subsequent shoot-out Vaujour was shot and wounded and his wife captured.

The IRA also used the technique in a 1973 escape from Dublin's Mountjoy prison, when three men got away. One prison officer allegedly told the governor that he thought the helicopter was the new Defence Minister landing. A prisoner is reported to have quipped in reply: 'It wasn't your Defence Minister arriving, it was our Defence Minister leaving.'

Helicopters aside, escape from within a prison perimeter is difficult. Escaping from custody on the way to and from prison or between prison and court is little more complicated than shoplifting. Since the escapees from Parkhurst and Whitemoor in the mid-1960s, there have been a plethora of policies, procedures, manuals and audits around prison security, and it has been largely successful. But all prisoners at some time in their sentence, and many thousands each day, spend hours in allegedly secure transport moving from court to prison, between prison establishments, as well as to and from hospitals. Twenty years ago it would have been little more than a minibus with something to secure handcuffs to; these days they are cellular vehicles – vans with steel cubicles or cells built into them. Some have only four cells within them. Some larger ones may have as many as twelve. These 'cells' are horrifically claustrophobic and conditions can be inhumane in hot conditions or where prisoners have to travel long distances, often stopping off at many different locations. Many reports have highlighted the conditions of such transport, which is now contracted out to private companies like SERCO, G4S and Reliance. However, little attention has been given to the poor security they offer. In the north-west of England there have recently been three escapes of prisoners whilst being transported in this way. Three years ago there was an escape by a young prisoner travelling from HMYOI (Her Majesty's Young Offender Institution) Feltham.

Early in my tenure at Brixton I experienced an escape that typified the methodology and the ease of such travelling security breaches. A secure vehicle with ten prisoners on board was on its way to the Inner London Crown Court near Southwark in south London. On approaching the court, an armed gang held up the van, and the driver, who tried to resist, was shot in the leg. The custody officer in the rear of the vehicle was forced to open all the cells within the vehicle and two seasoned armed robbers heading for their trial were collected, all speeding off in a waiting getaway car. It was that easy. Of the remaining seven prisoners, one ran home to his mother and was picked up by the police shortly afterwards, the remainder stayed put, too frightened to take advantage of the situation or too confused to know where they might head were they to run off. It was rumoured that the two who escaped spent some time abroad before coming home to carry on their activities, which has led to at least one of them being back in custody.

Some twelve months later I was walking through A Wing in Brixton when a prisoner approached me to remind me that he had been one of those left in the van who did not flee. He complained about stress and sleepless nights and demanded post-traumatic stress disorder counselling be provided for him. My initial sympathy evaporated when I became suspicious and asked if he had been released since the escape. When he replied that he had and that this was a new sentence, I politely declined his request and moved on.

The escape caused me some pressure as governor. I was publicly questioned as to why such dangerous men, as they had become in the eyes of the press, had not been taken to court with an armed police escort. These questions revealed not only a public but an official lack of knowledge of process and practice. It was suggested such men should be Category A. Whilst these were unpleasant men wanted for serious offences and prone to violence, as demonstrated by the escape, they were typical of many in Brixton and in other local prisons across the country. They would never have met the criteria. Even if they had been Category A prisoners they would not have had armed escorts. Some, but by no means all, High Risk Category A prisoners have armed escorts, but I have been personally involved with Exceptional Risk Category A prisoners being transported without armed escort. The decision is taken by the senior police officer in the borough from which the escort emanates. He or she will make that decision on a variety of criteria, including intelligence and budget. At the time of the Brixton escape, comments from the head of the security branch for the prison service demonstrated that even he did not fully understand the process. Such escapes are easy to carry out and make a mockery of the elaborate security provided when prisoners enter the gates of a prison. Serious organised criminals know this and can facilitate such escapes at will. They may need someone in the prison van to alert them as to which van is which, or they may need someone on the inside to alert them. But prisoners by right need to know when and where they are going to court. Such things can never be kept secret. And though an insider may help, it is not essential.

The ease of such escapes has not been lost on the serious organised criminals in the north-west. In July 2011 Kirk Bradley and Tony Downes – both on trial at Liverpool Crown Court over an alleged guns and grenades plot – were sprung from a prison escort van operated by the private contractor G4S. The van was attacked shortly after leaving the high security Strangeways prison in Manchester. Being on trial for over ten weeks, the movements of the two would have been highly predictable, as was the change in security from one of Britain's most secure local prisons to a white van operated by two G4S employees on little more than minimum wage.

The methodology was similar to that employed in the Brixton escape in 2003. A gang of masked men, armed with a sledgehammer and a gun, stopped the van in Trinity Way, which encircles Manchester city centre, just after 8.30 a.m. The doors of the van were pulled open and the pair in the back were taken out and bundled into a waiting Saab, which sped off into rush-hour traffic only to be dumped in nearby Salford a short time later. One G4S guard was pulled from the van and beaten in the road, whilst the other was left unharmed.

Fourteen months earlier, convicted murderer Richard Smith was being escorted to Salford Magistrates' Court when the van carrying him was ambushed at the back of the building. Two men who had been hiding in a white Ford Transit parked outside the court jumped out and threatened the security guards with a crowbar as they tried to park the van. The staff released Smith, who made off in the white Transit, which was later found abandoned.

In January 2009, 20-year-old Wayne Connor, charged with burglary, was also being ferried between prison and court. The van was operated this time by private contractor SERCO and was attacked just outside Feltham Young Offenders Institution in west London. Two men in balaclavas, armed with a shotgun, forced the van to pull over, smashed the driver's window and threatened him. No shots were fired but the driver was treated for cuts and bruises. Again there was a waiting getaway car. Ironically, the van was heading for Woolwich Crown Court, adjacent to Belmarsh prison, for which there is a tunnel directly from the prison to the court. Connor's escape did not last long; he was arrested just after midnight the same day at Clumber Park Hotel in Worksop, Nottinghamshire, by officers from Nottingham and the Metropolitan Police's Specialist Crime Directorate. His escape should have come as no surprise – Connor had been due to appear at Woolwich Crown Court on Monday alongside his 21-year-old brother Jason McInerney, who had escaped from custody a year previously when he bit a detective's nose as he jumped from the dock at Reading Crown Court. His other brother, Kirk McInerney, and cousin, Martin Carty, both eighteen, tried to escape during the same incident, but were stopped by police.

Whilst outside help is useful, in May 2011 three prisoners proved that it was not necessary and that prison escort vans are vulnerable to simple ingenuity and opportunism. John Paul Williams from Longsight in Greater Manchester, a 35-year-old man serving a life sentence, was one of four prisoners being transferred from the secure Category B training prison of Garth in the north-west to different jails in the area. This time the transport was operated by the prison service itself. They were on the A59 in Burscough when three of the prisoners simply clambered out of the skylights in their individual cells. Two were caught almost immediately, with Williams captured a short time later. A prison service spokesman said in a press release: 'It is exceedingly rare for a prisoner to escape during transfers.'

Prison escort vans are also used to take prisoners to outside hospitals and such excursions present exactly the same problems. For an entertaining, and of course purely fictitious, account of a prisoner feigning serious illness, then being sprung en route to hospital, I thoroughly recommend *Fat Blackmail* by Bruce Jones. An escapee's template – not that one is needed.

Ironically, escapes such as these do not impact on the impeccable security record of the prison service. An escape from within a prison perimeter is a failure of the most important of the service's key performance indicators; an escape from a secure prison transport operated by a private contractor counts against the company and will incur a large fine. It is not, however, a failure of the prison service.

FOUR

PRISONERS - NOT ALL THE SAME

Personal and professional life inevitably collide. We can try to separate home from work, we can try to balance the competing demands, but some professions make it more difficult to succeed in this than others. The operational demands of running a prison allow little separation and the effects on individuals are rarely acknowledged let alone accommodated. My biggest collision came when the death of my father coincided with the actions of one of the most notorious prisoners in the country.

Charles Bronson was born Michael Gordon Peterson on 6 December 1952 in Aberystwyth, north Wales. His parents ran the local Conservative club and his aunt and uncle were mayor and mayoress of the town. The family moved to Luton when Michael was four years old. As a teenager he became a bare knuckle boxer and one-time circus strongman, and violence and aggression began to dominate his life. He adopted the name of Bronson on the advice of a boxing promoter.

His life in prison started with a seven-year sentence for armed robbery in 1974. His violence in prison extended his sentence and he was out for only sixty-nine days in 1988 before being convicted yet again for further offences. He was moved extensively between prisons and spent some time in Broadmoor. He became a prolific hostage-taker and in 1994 he took a civilian librarian hostage at HMP Woodhill near Milton Keynes. As a junior governor, I was involved in a headquarters monitoring role. On that particular occasion, Charlie demanded a helicopter, an inflatable doll

49

and a cup of tea as ransom. Two months later he took a deputy governor hostage at Hull prison. Both victims suffered considerable trauma and Charlie's reputation was sealed. With consequent convictions for his crimes he was eventually sentenced to serve life.

Charlie came to Belmarsh in 1998 as part of his frequent movement under what was known variously as the Magic Roundabout, shared misery or ghosting scheme – the last resort for prisons with people who were the most difficult to manage. By the mid-1990s it was a more subtle and better planned scheme than it had been in the previous decade, but it was still very disruptive for prisoners and their families. The move was usually from one prison's segregation (isolation) unit to another and arranged either between respective prison governors or, in the case of someone as notorious and difficult as Charlie, organised from prison HQ. Each prison would take its turn and although you might delay the inevitable – because you hadn't moved on and were still struggling with your last difficult prisoner – eventually you just had to get on with it.

Though there was a geographical plan, there was rarely an individual management scheme for each prisoner involved. Whilst there were many psychologists in the High Security Estate there were none in Belmarsh at the time, which was something I had tried but failed to address. These were individuals who had been through various psychiatric assessment processes and some had even been sectioned under the Mental Health Act (effectively declared mad rather than bad) for a time, only to return to prison after a period declared as cured and again bad rather than mad. Managing the aggression and poor behaviour was left to individual prisons with whatever resources they had, which was often simply the segregation unit staff themselves.

'Seg' units, as they were called, showed some of the best and worst of prison culture. There was considerable evidence of brutal treatment of prisoners by staff in seg units over the years as managers failed to manage. Lord Ramsbotham as Chief Inspector of Prisons famously challenged staff in HMP Wormwood Scrubs, where he found blood literally still on the walls. Change did come about, and this particular prison morphed its seg into a 'Care and Separation Unit' under the auspices of a man called Jimmy Hughes, a redoubtable Scot who later came to be my deputy at Brixton. Many other segs followed suit and some exotic names evolved, as did a monitoring process that tried to ensure better accountability, involving senior managers and the scrutiny of the prisons watchdog body the Independent Monitoring Board (IMB).

The very best of prison culture saw seg staff, who had no training in mental health issues or anger management or counselling, simply using people skills to manage some very difficult and dangerous men. Some took great pride in 'sorting' those that no one else could. Some adopted the approach that whatever happened in previous prisons you started with a clean slate in this one. But most difficult prisoners rarely received such opportunities and downward spirals of behaviour and attitude ensued. Special units and techniques evolved over the years, culminating in the Dangerous and Severe Personality Disorder Programme. Like many things in the prison system, millions were spent on it without any real proof of its effectiveness.

Charlie got the clean slate at Belmarsh and resided in a seg that was the size of a small prison. The size of a seg was almost a prison's virility symbol: the bigger the seg, the 'harder' the jail. I spent many years being part of various building programmes and there were always demands for bigger segs. They were the prisons version of the M25. The more cells you put in them, the more you needed. The Belmarsh seg was a six-lane highway with no speed limit. There was even a seg within the special unit, about which more later.

One manager in particular, Roger Outram, a large no-nonsense northerner, decided to take Charlie on as a personal project. Roger had transferred from his beloved Yorkshire when Belmarsh opened. He was a fearless straight-talker and just what Charlie needed. Roger was aided by some equally formidable prison officers and Charlie was soon throwing medicine balls around the way you and I would tennis balls. He began doing sit-ups with medicine balls. He could do hundreds without stopping. I was sure his heart would give out. I was often asked could Charlie have this or that. I left it to Roger and his team, although we almost fell out when I suggested Charlie might benefit from being introduced to computer technology. They gave him a photocopy of a computer keyboard to practice on. I gave up and left wider education to Roger.

I would call in on my daily rounds and Charlie would make the tea. We would sit and chat about nothing in particular. I wasn't into amateur psychology, just normal human contact. We discussed how long he had been in segs. After the onset of his hostage-taking he had never lived in a normal wing. However big a seg is they are not known for their panoramic vistas, nor for any aesthetics whatsoever. The exercise yards are little more than concrete caves. I asked Charlie when he had last looked more than 25 metres ahead of him – you can't see much out of prison vans either. He was unsure of the question or where I was headed. So I simply said, 'Do you fancy a walk outside the seg?' A long 'oooooh, ahhhhh yeah!!!!! That-ed-be-good' followed, but with no expectation that I would deliver. We bred very low expectations in people like Charlie. I spoke to Roger about the possibility of taking him out through the seg's many doors into the large expanse of path and grassy areas that separated the various wings and buildings. If Roger thought I was mad or danger-ous he didn't say. He certainly wasn't going to miss the opportunity for a challenge. Other staff were less enthusiastic, so to allay fears I planned a route where very large German Shepherd dogs (with handlers) would be casually sat on the grass watching the world go by as we walked past them. There were strict no-barking instructions – to the handlers whose control of their animals was consummate.

So one sunny morning out we went – Charlie, Roger and me. No handcuffs and the dogs remarkably unobtrusive. The fact that they would have been useless if Charlie had decided to do something silly hadn't escaped me and probably not Roger, but I suppose it gave some semblance of caution. It was like taking a child into Santa's grotto – much more ooohing and ahhhing. Belmarsh is a big place. However, Charlie became very indignant about the litter that had been thrown out of cell windows into the open areas. It was a constant and infuriating problem. Important visitors inevitably only came just after someone had discharged an entire *Sunday Times* out of their cell window into the wind that swept the Thames marsh. Charlie was keen to go and sort out the litter louts. I said thanks but we would manage. Half an hour later we returned to the seg and Charlie put the kettle on.

Two days later precise details of the escapade appeared in an article in *The Sun* with the title 'The lunatics have taken over the asylum'. Some member of staff would have received a nice little earner from the paper. I got the inevitable 'please explain' from HQ and life carried on. I had featured before in *The Sun* and whilst locally we could see the funny side of it, HQ and the press office were Queen Victoria-like and definitely not amused.

Charlie continued to progress and we discussed getting him into an environment where he could begin to mix more normally with other prisoners. This was something we did not consider lightly but which was a necessary part of any real progress. Major building work was under way across the prison as part of the Woodcock Report written after the Whitemoor and Parkhurst escapes. Money was being poured into security and it was at this time that the SSU – the prison within a prison – was being further armour-plated, with the level of work that the Exceptional and High Risk Category A contingent of the SSU moved to a temporary SSU being constructed at the end of one of the main wings. It was furnished with yet another seg and we moved Charlie there and began to introduce him to life in the adjacent normal wing. All was proceeding well, or so we thought.

I was in my local garage having a broken electric window fixed when the call came that Charlie had taken three prisoners hostage. They were three Iraqis who had hit the headlines by hijacking a plane from the Middle East to the UK. After a stream of Anglo Saxon expletives and a demand to get the bloody window back in, I drove to Belmarsh. As I approached the massive car park an entire circus of media trucks, police and helicopters came into view. I made my way to the control room and took over from Paul Carroll, the duty governor who had been in charge as the incident began. There was no one better in such a situation – Paul was of immense skill and incomparable in his relationships with staff and prisoners. He was also a very close personal friend of Roger and we were both aware of how this would play with him.

Prison service hostage training was outstanding. This was not true of all training but the success of hostage training has been borne out over the years by the successful resolution of many serious incidents that very rarely hit the press. It was so good that it was difficult sometimes not to think of real incidents as just one of the many exercises many of us endured. As well as command suite exercises, we would endure periods at mock cell doors, behind which were psychopathic physical education instructors acting as perpetrators screaming threats and abuse at us and describing sexual depravity that left me deeply worried about these so-called actors. Occasionally, an artificial bloody finger would be thrown down corridors at us. Psychologists would sit behind the doors acting as hostages, feeding back our total lack of concern for the victims in the saga. The trainers were very good at pitching different scenarios at us to throw us off course, although there was one scenario they never anticipated – the one which I was about to experience.

In short, we were well trained and prepared, but that doesn't mean things always go like clockwork. Charlie had developed a methodology and was again demanding a helicopter, a blow-up doll and ice cream. Though it was beyond imagination what the Iraqis were going through as they were literally trussed up by their hands and feet, this was the first time Charlie had taken prisoners, rather than staff, hostage. But we were doing what we had been trained for. Roger was soon in touch and wanted to talk to Charlie personally. If this had been an episode of the American TV drama 24 and Roger had been the series hero, Jack Bauer, I would have succumbed and it would all have been over. But to do so would have been against all the principles that guided such a situation and this one could not have been more serious or high profile. Paul, Roger and I reverted to our training.

A couple of hours into the hostage drama a call came from my home – my father had died very suddenly. The doctor later told me that the 'plumbing had gone and he was dead before he hit the floor'. Seventy-six and healthy until then – there were worse ways to go. But as I held the phone and tried to talk, complete shock and bewilderment took over. I was highly trained and experienced. I had done all this before. But who on earth had invented this sick scenario? Then real life dawned and I broke down. Paul put his arm round my shoulder and led me out.

Sharon Roots, the local branch chair of the Prison Officers Association (POA), drove me home. She was a woman of great compassion and well practised in handling the casualties that often ensued in such situations, although I suspect this was outside even her experience. She deposited me at home. I went to the north-west, where my family home was, comforted my mother and buried my father.

A week later I returned to the jail. Paul had taken over command of the incident, resolved it with consummate skill and rightly received a commendation for his professionalism and judgement. Charlie was sent to the 'cage' in Wakefield – a cell within a cell – the end of the line. Roger was traumatised and had not been part of the decision process. I absorbed the events that had unfolded in my absence and began to open and read the many cards of condolence I had been sent in this more comforting, pre-email era. There was one over-large card that had arrived internally. I prised open the envelope, unfolded the card and read: 'Sorry I made it worse for you, stay strong, Charlie.'

I still have the card, and until her recent death my mother would often ask, 'How's Charlie? What's the silly bugger been up to now?'

Charlie continues to serve his life sentence. He has since married, written books and tested the prison system at every level. He now even has a film about him. He retains the title of 'Britain's most violet prisoner'. He could be more reasonably described as Britain's most misunderstood prisoner.

Incarcerated in Belmarsh at the same time as Charlie Bronson was Paul 'Dingus' Magee, one of the six escapees from Whitemoor held in the special unit. Of equal profile, he posed entirely different problems.

Magee was born in the Ballymurphy area of Belfast on 30 January 1948 and went on to join the Belfast Brigade of the Provisional IRA. In 1971 he was sentenced to five years for possession of firearms and was held in Long Kesh prison. After his release he became part of the 'M60 Gang', so-called because of their possession and use of an M60 machine gun, and in April 1980 the gang killed one Royal Ulster Constabulary officer and wounded two others. Less than a month later the unit was involved in a shoot-out with the SAS. After a prolonged firefight, during which a senior officer was killed, Magee and the others were captured when further security services came to the aid of the SAS unit.

Whilst on trial for murder and held at Belfast Crumlin Road jail, Magee and seven other IRA members escaped after taking staff hostage. There was yet another firefight as they were spotted by security services as they left the jail, but when Magee was sentenced to life it was in absentia, as he had escaped across the border to southern Ireland. He was eventually arrested in 1982 in the south and just before his release in 1989 he was served with an arrest warrant for extradition to the north. He was given bail pending legal challenge but fled to England.

Driving through Yorkshire with fellow IRA member Michael O'Brien, Magee was stopped by two police officers. Both were shot, one fatally. A police pursuit followed, during which O'Brien and Magee fired on officers. They got away, but after a massive manhunt both were arrested in the town of Pontefract. In March 1993 Magee was sentenced to life for murder and O'Brien was sentenced to eighteen years for attempted murder. It was during this sentence that Magee escaped from Whitemoor and came with the other five escapees to Belmarsh.

In the wake of the escapes and the subsequent reports and recommendations, the rules for Category A prisoners in general and Exceptional Risk Category As such as the Whitemoor six were substantially strengthened.

In particular, all visits, including those of legal representatives, were to be 'closed visits' – in other words, behind a glass screen with no possibility of physical contact and with communication only by way of a telephone hand-set. Whilst not uncommon for any prisoner when security or behaviour warranted it, such restrictions on a permanent basis had never been implemented – and for them to be implemented routinely during visits by legal representatives was an exceptional measure. The decision was challenged strongly in the courts by lawyers acting for the six. The challenge went as far as judicial review at the High Court in London but the policy was upheld.

'Dingus', as Magee became known as across the jail, showed his indignation by refusing to accept any visits at all. He remained also fiercely independent of the other five and at odds with much of Provisional IRA policy at the time. As a measure of his anger he went on 'dirty protest' permanently. Dirty protests are regarded as having their origins in Northern Ireland during the troubles. They were used as part of the protests against decisions by the British government not to grant political status to Republican prisoners but treat them as 'ordinary criminals'. The extent and nature of them in Northern Ireland was never repeated in England. By mid-1978 there were some 300 prisoners on dirty protest in the Maze prison in Northern Ireland. Tomás Ó Fiaich, the Roman Catholic Archbishop of Armagh, visited the prison on 31 July 1978 and described it thus:

Having spent the whole of Sunday in the prison, I was shocked at the inhuman conditions prevailing in H-Blocks three, four and five, where over 300 prisoners were incarcerated. One would hardly allow an animal to remain in such conditions, let alone a human being. The nearest approach to it that I have seen was the spectacle of hundreds of homeless people living in the sewer pipes in the slums of Calcutta. The stench and filth in some of the cells, with the remains of rotten food and human excreta scattered around the walls was almost unbearable. In two of them I was unable to speak for fear of vomiting.

Dingus acted alone, fortunately for us all, and adopted a particular approach. Usually, urine, faeces and, in the case of some women on dirty protest, menstrual blood would be used to smear the body of the protester and the cell in which they were held. Dingus chose merely to 'paint' his cell 'brown' but kept himself clean. It goes without saying that the supervision and care of a prisoner on such a protest makes for a particularly unpleasant experience for anyone involved. Care is vitally important, if not a phrase the general public would expect to be used. Many individuals resort to dirty protests whilst suffering from mental illness. Dingus was perfectly sane and fully understood his actions. In either case, protecting the health and well-being of the individual and those around them is essential, if very difficult. Opportunities for the individual to stop and clean up are vital, even if they just start again. The temptation to leave them to 'wallow in their own filth' is often advocated but it is essential for those in charge to resist. Food and drink still have be provided even if it ends up as part of the protest, having been digested or simply added to the mix in its original state. Medical care is essential as well. I have only ever witnessed staff behaving exceptionally well in such circumstances, regardless of the fact that working during such a protest accrues barely an extra £1 per shift. Masks and paper suits are now routinely provided but even as recently as the 1990s this was not the case. The smell is indescribable, but the old adage that the longer it goes on the less it smells is true. It may simply be that you get used to it.

In most prisons dirty protests tend to take place in the segregation units and, if it can be engineered, in the so-called 'special cells' of segregation units. These have variously been described as padded cells, unfurnished rooms or strip cells. Padded cells have now gone, but cells with stark, bare walls, no plumbing and no furniture remain. They are designed for minimal use for short periods in order to deal with exceptionally refractory prisoners. If you are lucky, such cells have a drainage system that allows for the hosing down of cells after a protest.

At Belmarsh we were particularly fortunate because it was a relatively modern prison with well designed facilities for such an occasion. Dingus was held in the special cells of the segregation unit of the Special Secure Unit within the country's most secure jail. It was the end of the line. He was the only resident for most of the time, which enabled us to move him periodically to a clean cell whilst we cleaned and fumigated the one he had left. The layman might argue for leaving someone until they clear up the mess themselves. This is not an option. A duty of care requires you to give the 'protester' every opportunity to desist and to maintain them in as clean conditions as possible regardless. Dingus's protest was permanent in so far as restrictions placed upon him would not change and neither would he.

I would visit him most days when I was on duty as I was required to do with everyone held in a segregation unit and with everyone undertaking any kind of protest. Dingus was a diminutive figure, which belied what he had done and what he was capable of doing. He would appear at his cell door, I would inspect his handiwork and we would regularly chat about the world in general and Irish politics in particular. Our conversation was always held at the door, declining as I would the offer a chair in his cell, and always with him still guarded, given he was awaiting trial for the escape. Our discussions were amicable and interesting. I was alert to conditioning but we talked about the escape from Whitemoor. He remained adamant that the tools and gun they obtained did not come in through their visitors and that they would not have put family at such risk. He refused to elaborate but his strong implication of alternative methods of smuggling in the illicit items was left hanging. We naturally reflected on the principles and practice of the dirty protest, conversations which at times seemed surreal in the circumstances. He felt their origins lay in the violence he said would regularly be inflicted on Republican prisoners by largely Protestant prison officers. Being smeared in your own excrement would cause you to be shunned rather than punched; it was, he maintained, the only form of self-protection. He lectured me about Irish politics. I was ashamed to say that I could only listen as my knowledge was insufficient for debate, at Dingus's level at any rate. He was never angry, always considered and thorough. He even lent me a book (clean and unstained I might add): *The Fight for Peace: The Secret Story Behind the Irish Peace Process* by Eamonn Mallie and David McKittrick. The inside cover is inscribed: 'This book belongs to Paul 'Dingus' Magee, Belmarsh prison 15.5.96.' Inside was a Waterstone's bookmark with a George Bernard Shaw quote: 'An Irishman's heart is nothing but his imagination.' I'm ashamed to say I never gave it him back. I would be happy still to do so.

At around £1,000 per cell the financial cost of cleaning up after Dingus during the many months of his protest was not cheap. It was around this time that I received a transfer to HMP Swaleside on the Isle of Sheppey in Kent. He offered me his full support if only I could get him a transfer there. I suggested that such a move was some way off under the current circumstances. He smiled wryly.

In January 1997 Dingus and the other five escapees from Whitemoor went on trial on charges relating to the escape. However, during the trial an article with pictures of them all appeared on the front page of the *Evening Standard* and identified them as 'terrorists'. Lawyers for the six defendants successfully argued that the article prejudiced the trial, not least because an order had been made at the start of the trial preventing any reference to the background and previous convictions of the defendants. The judge dismissed the case, stating: 'What I have done is the only thing I can do in the circumstances. The law for these defendants is the same law for everyone else. They are entitled to that, whatever they have done.' Dingus was repatriated to a prison in the Republic of Ireland in 1998 and eventually released under the Good Friday Agreement. In 2000 he was granted a Royal Prerogative of Mercy.

Dingus and Charlie were but two of the more notorious prisoners in the system. They are examples of certain prisoners in specific situations raising different issues; they are typical of nothing. They grab the headlines and frustrate the proper debate. The misunderstanding of the nature of prisoners is one of the many problems that beset the prison system and its relationship with the public. Prisoners are not all the same. They are all unique in their own way, a bit like the rest of the world. It is no less discriminatory to stereotype all prisoners than it is to stereotype all Germans, Indians or Americans. It certainly does not help the debate.

Politicians in their fear of voters' reactions to prison issues regularly revert to stereotypes. Prisoners are not all murderers, rapists and robbers. In March 2011, at a time when the prison population was still rising and when the August riots had yet to add a significant boost to our already high incarceration rates, the breakdown of the prison population was both revealing and typical of recent years. Out of a population of 85,000 more than 3,000 were untried – that is, innocent in the eyes of the law, if not the tabloid editor. A further 28,000 were serving less than four years, nearly 8,000 of those serving less than a year; bearing in mind that the current law pertaining to sentences of less than four years requires automatic release at the halfway point, that is 28,000 actually in jail for at most two years, with many serving only a few months. At the serious end of the spectrum there were 24,000 people serving four years or more, with over 13,500 serving indeterminate sentences, i.e. with no definite release date. Nearly 6,000 prisoners had been out on licence, failed to abide by their licence conditions and been brought back to prison. And we still had 148 fine defaulters costing us over £40,000 a year to punish for their financial indiscretion.

Even more revealing are the figures in the quarter October–December 2010, when official statistics show 22,881 discharges. That is 22,881 prisoners let out, released, freed – call it what you will. Extrapolate and that is around 80,000 per year. The same quarter saw nearly 28,000 prisoners coming into the system. So whilst there may be a core of violent and dangerous people in prison, there are tens of thousands of people coming in and going out, sometimes for very short periods. Who is in prison? Members of the community passing through. I should say members of some communities, given that many communities are over-represented – namely deprived communities, ethnic minorities, the socially excluded and the mentally ill. Whether the parliamentary community is under or overrepresented I will leave for wider debate.

Official statistics on the prison population are awash with numbers. There is a lot of counting going on relating to age, types of offence, trends in violent crime, sexual crime, burglary and so on. In short, we are locking people up for longer and whatever goes down quickly comes back up. Predictions on the future prison population have been fraught with difficulties. 'Through the roof' tends to suffice for now.

We seem to be shy, however, of looking at the people rather than the numbers. The August 2011 riots were quick to reveal, to the horror of ministers, that many of the rioters had been before the courts before, prompting Secretary of State Ken Clarke to declare that the prison system was broken. Little was known about the wider social background of these individuals. Many were from deprived communities; a small but sensationalised minority had privileged backgrounds. But the system is not and has never been able to analyse these particular issues, though they might constitute some part of the debate on the causes of crime.

The House of Commons library holds an array of prison statistics and included in it is an important description of the characteristics of the prison population:

- Compared to 10 per cent of the general population, 47 per cent of male sentenced prisoners and 50 per cent of female sentenced prisoners had run away from home as a child.
- Over 25 per cent of prisoners had been taken into care as a child compared to 2 per cent of the population.
- Of all prisoners, 43 per cent had a family member that had been convicted of a criminal offence. 35 per cent had a family member that had actually been in prison.
- Prior to their imprisonment, 81 per cent of prisoners were unmarried, rising to 85 per cent since imprisonment. Almost 10 per cent had been divorced. These figures are twice as high as those found in the general population.
- A quarter of young male offenders in prison are young fathers.

- One in five women prisoners were living at home with dependent children at the time of imprisonment.
- Half of male and one-third of female sentenced prisoners were excluded from school. One half of male and seven out of ten female prisoners have no qualifications.
- Two-thirds of prisoners have numeracy skills at or below the level expected of an eleven year old. Half have a reading ability and 82 per cent have writing ability at or below this level.
- Two-thirds of prisoners were unemployed in the four weeks before imprisonment.
- Around 70 per cent of prisoners suffer from two or more mental disorders. In the general population the figures are 5 per cent for men and 2 per cent for women.
- Prisoners are more likely to be abusers of illegal drugs and alcohol than other sectors of the community.
- Nearly three-quarters of prisoners were in receipt of benefits immediately before entering prison.
- Five per cent of prisoners were sleeping rough prior and almost one-third were not living in permanent accommodation immediately prior to imprisonment.

The source of this data is the work of the Social Exclusion Unit, now disbanded, and dates back to the early 2000s. To most practitioners this information is not counter-intuitive, but in a reasonable society looking to have a more effective and cost-efficient system to reduce high reoffending rates then a regular update and analysis of trends in the prison population would seem to be essential, especially in a world of payment by results. Some prisoners regard themselves as sentenced to assessment given the plethora of information-gathering they are subjected to, be it on drugs, health, education or housing needs on release. There is rightly an emphasis on whether prisoners pose a risk to the public if released and concern over whether they have received the right treatment for their drug addiction or mental health problems. But if we are to begin to reduce the prison population by incarcerating fewer individuals then the characteristics of those we do lock up ought to be of the greatest importance and at the heart of future action.

But the people who best understand how they came to be in prison and what went wrong with their lives are the prisoners and ex-prisoners themselves, not least if they have received support and treatment towards that very end. If we are investing in reducing reoffending and if there is to be any success whatsoever, then it seems logical to use people who have been through the system successfully to perhaps influence those still in it or in danger of joining it.

The criminal justice system, however, is guilty of the same stereotyping of prisoners as so many of the general public, politicians and the media. With all the talk of the importance of employing ex-offenders, the one organisation unwilling to do so as a matter of explicit policy is the prison service itself. It remains more paranoid than ever of former residents and how they might threaten security.

Darren was typical of many south Londoners in that he had graduated from being a young offender to an adult prisoner, emanating as he did from one of the many deprived estates. Where he was not typical was with his acting talent, which had shone in one of our charitably funded arts events. He had found his calling and his talent would be recognised. His misfortune was to be released at the end of his sentence midway through an arts programme to which he was highly committed, not least to the final dramatic performance. Release from prison is not always as planned and calculated as the system would wish. Complex calculations of different sentences with difficult to confirm periods on remand or held in temporary police custody can frustrate a system based on pen and paper and the sharp intellect of a prison administrator. Occasionally, because of either a miscalculation or new information a prisoner can find him or herself catapulted to release, throwing any planning up in the air. Darren was fortunate in one sense but frustrated in another – namely performing in the play. Leaving prison one day and coming back voluntarily for pleasure the next is not a normal prison occurrence and the first response of the system is to disallow it on security grounds. Darren certainly held out no hope but thanks to the vision of those around me running such events I was, as governor and thankfully in charge of my own baili-wick, able to eschew security tradition and allow back in with other volunteers a beaming Darren. There was after all no need to subject him to a security clearance. We knew everything there was to know about him, not least his positive motivation for returning.

Darren's motivation was personal. For others the desire to contribute having had experience of incarceration is altruistic. It was in this vein I was approached by Kate Quill, a journalist that I had had contact with during my time at Brixton. She had attended a number of our arts presentations. She was a travel editor with *The Times* and in that context had been working with a particularly famous ex-prisoner who had also become a travel journalist, Howard Marks or Mr Nice, as he was later christened and which formed the title of his autobiography. His own website sums him up.

During the mid-1980s, Howard Marks had forty-three aliases, eighty-nine phone lines, and twenty-five companies trading throughout the world.

Bars, recording studios, offshore banks: all were money-laundering vehicles serving the core activity: dope dealing.

Marks began to deal during a postgraduate philosophy course at Oxford and was soon moving large quantities of hashish into Europe and America in the equipment of touring rock bands. The academic life began to lose its allure.

At the height of his career, he was smuggling consignments of up to thirty tons from Pakistan and Thailand to America and Canada and had contact with organisations as diverse as the CIA, MI6, the IRA, and the Mafia.

After many years and a world-wide operation by the Drug Enforcement Agency, he was busted and sentenced to twenty-five years in prison at the United States Federal Penitentiary, Terre Haute, Indiana, the site of America's only Federal Death Row.

He was released on parole in April 1995 after serving seven years of his sentence.

Kate described how Howard was interested in contributing to prisons and in particular promoting the importance of education for prisoners. He had been thwarted in his attempts to get into a prison and could I help? The story did not surprise me. Such was the suspicion by the prison service of ex-prisoners and its risk aversion that, despite the potential benefits, the baby inevitably went out with the bath water. Kate arranged for herself, Howard and I to meet for lunch at Soho's exclusive media-based (private members only) Groucho Club. I wasn't sure what I could do, but this was one social occasion I was not going to miss.

I was ushered into the small lounge and introduced to Mr Nice himself almost buried in a large armchair. Like many larger than life characters he was smaller in real life. He greeted me with a warm but wary smile and broke into a gentle and engaging Welsh lilt. I doubt he had met a prison governor socially before and he seemed uncertain what to expect. Mutual nervousness soon evaporated aided by Kate, our consummate host and referee. Howard recounted how he had arranged to go into a jail to meet with a group of prisoners, only at the last minute for the prison service press office to throw a wobbly at the negative media reaction that would, they firmly believed, follow his visit. He was literally turned away at the door, surprised and disappointed and unable to comprehend such treatment. Although addressing large audiences was part of his current business he was seeking nothing other than to try and share some of his learning for the benefit of others. Wishing I was still in charge of Brixton, my mind raced as to the possibilities of using Howard in an educational context. We concluded a very convivial lunch and I agreed to come up with a cunning plan.

A few weeks later following an equally convivial dinner to plan a prison visit by Mr Nice, which I hosted, with Howard and a prison governor who adopted my policy of seeking forgiveness rather than permission, he did finally get to speak to a group of prisoners. He went down a storm, was controversial but inspiring. Sadly the enterprise went no further.

Alistair Little came to Brixton via the Ulster Volunteer Force (UVF) and a twelve-year sentence for the murder of a Catholic. Alistair's story and his transformation was later documented in a film by Oliver Hirschbiegel and broadcast by the BBC in 2009. Liam Neeson plays Alistair and James Nesbitt plays Joe Griffin, the victim's younger brother who witnessed the murder. The two actors switch their own religions for the film, which begins with a reconstruction of the murder and then explores what might have happened if the two had met in later life – they never actually did. It explores the pain of a perpetrator and a survivor, (a term he uses rather than victim) and wrestles with the concept of reconciliation. Alistair's autobiography, *Give a Boy a Gun*, mirrors his journey, which he gives you the feeling he will never complete.

He came to Brixton with the 'Forgiveness Project', an innovative restorative justice project. Many people have encountered the concept of restorative justice, when victims meet perpetrators with a mediator in attendance to manage the process and the inevitable emotion that comes with it. It has barely a toe-hold in the English criminal justice system despite a number of organisations attempting to place the concept centre stage. The prison service has eschewed it on the basis that there is no evidence it works, palpable nonsense as an international research record exists for all to see. It is often said in criminal justice that the victim is forgotten, yet it is restorative justice that places the 'survivor' at the heart of the process and research over many years has evidenced the very positive responses of victims following the process. The Forgiveness Project is a step before such work. It collects and shares individual stories, explores attitudes and reactions to violence and revenge and promotes forgiveness and reconciliation. But like direct mediation it is tough stuff and with Alistair as a facilitator even tougher. He talked a language of 'conflict resolution', the humanising of offending, and to the prison service it was a foreign language. If the prison service had not invented it and given it accreditation, i.e. official approval by the State, then it was not allowed.

An initial 'exhibition' took place in the prison illustrating some of the stories that the project had collected. Group sessions for prisoners volunteering to explore the issues would take place, with smaller intensive sessions following on for those who wanted to go further. Alistair was a powerful and challenging facilitator but one who held the respect of his audience in a way I had not previously seen. The smaller group sessions were with Alistair alone and I saw some men transformed and others questioning themselves in a way they had never before been asked to do.

In one of the larger group sessions Camilla Carr told her story to a group of about fifty Brixton residents. In April 1997, Camilla and her boyfriend, Jon James, went to Chechnya to set up a rehabilitation centre for traumatised war-children. Three months later they were taken hostage by Chechen rebels. Their ordeal lasted fourteen months, during which Camilla was repeatedly raped by one of her jailers. During her account no one chatted in the margins, all eyes were transfixed. At the end there was silence. No one moved, knew what to say or do. When conversation eventually broke out the astonishment and admiration from the audience was palpable.

Then Marian Partington rose and recounted her story. In 1973 Marian's younger sister, Lucy, disappeared from a Gloucester bus stop after visiting a friend. Twenty years later, in 1994, the gruesome discoveries at 25 Cromwell Street revealed that Lucy had been a victim of serial killers Fred and Rosemary West.

Questions followed about Camilla's feelings about her rapist. Did Marion forgive Rose West? Alistair would prompt, challenge and broaden the debate. It was awe inspiring. The audience had to be forced out at the end, with pockets of conversations continuing as the men left for their respective wings. Unfortunately we only had enough charitable funds for one event.

Around this time Brixton had a visit from HRH The Princess Royal, a passionate supporter of prison issues over many years and consequently well informed. As well as giving her a tour I was keen for her to see the various initiatives which the prison was now enjoying (thanks to charitable funding). In the style that royals are required to meet people, a large room was to be populated with select groups of people who would be introduced by strict invitation. There were to be no random introductions. I was particularly keen that she meet Alistair and the Forgiveness Project. He therefore had to be 'submitted' as a potential 'introducee'. And there started the panic. UVF? Twelve years for murder? I was then bombarded with requests for information about Alistair and his background, all of which was in the public domain. I'm sure if I were a Royal aide I would have demanded the same intensive scrutiny, but whilst I was irritated, for Alistair it was particularly intrusive and distracting. We did discuss the 'sod it' approach and sticking to mainstream introductions. But we agreed to see it through and provide everything the aides required, half-expecting Alistair to be bypassed in the final analysis by HRH. On the day it was the exact opposite. The Princess spent more time talking to Alistair than anyone else. There were no photos and there goes my knighthood.

Not every ex-prisoner has the profile of Alistair or the very different one of Howard Marks. Some want to help with prison issues but wish to do so based on anonymity, especially Narcotics Anonymous (NA). They define themselves thus: 'NA is a nonprofit fellowship or society of men and women for whom drugs had become a major problem. We are recovering addicts who meet regularly to help each other stay clean.' They encourage abstinence. They are not based around any religion and it is essentially a service whereby addicts seek to help other addicts through a frank and open meeting process. They seek no fees just the opportunity to hold meetings. There is a presumption that many of the facilitators are ex-prisoners but they do not say and they operate on the basis of not being asked. The presumption is reasonable given that we regard drug addiction as a criminal rather than a health issue.

At a time when resources are stretched and community involvement is being encouraged then an organisation such as NA should be welcomed into the system. Sadly anonymity and presumptions act as a hurdle which often proves too high to leap. Letting anyone into a prison without a plethora of checks is an anathema to the security culture of the system. But as so often with security it is an attitude of not taking, rather than managing, the risk. Escorting an NA facilitator after a full search to a secure prison wing and placing them in a secure room with willing volunteers to help address their addiction problems hardly equates to an abandonment of all security principles. It could be argued as being a sensible way to augment what an overstretched prison has to offer.

At Brixton, with a major drug problem and little in the way of resources to address it, I warmly welcomed an approach by NA to come and run groups in the prison. The proposal was for one group per week for up to a dozen prisoners. All that was required of me was to allow the group facilitator entry and access to a group of prisoners in a room. Those who volunteered to attend would be vetted by the full-time drug workers operating in the prison. Simple?

Not quite. Even in Brixton at a time when links with the outside world were being actively encouraged, the prejudice around an organisation such as NA was palpable. This was not made any easier by a tendency in almost all prisons not to unlock prisoners if it can be avoided. Ask any volunteer group working in prisons what the main problem is and it will be getting to meet with prisoners. With all the robust management in the world – and I was known for robustness – it is always an uphill struggle. Volunteers will turn up in their own time at their own expense to offer all kinds of support, only to find that the twelve prisoners they expected to meet are now four or five with the remainder locked in their cells frustrated at not being allowed to join in because they were 'not on the list'. The organiser of NA at Brixton I shall call 'Billy'. His real name was only a nickname and I had no surname but I will add another layer of anonymity to prove the point. Billy looked you hard in the eye when he spoke to you. He was direct. Never impolite but never one to beat around the bush. He had all the trappings of a streetwise urban man: the bike, the tattoos, the canvas bag and the piercings. I liked him a lot. I think he liked me or at least had a respect for what I was trying to do. Conversations were quick-fire and challenging. I usually lost the debate because I too often failed to fulfill my end of the bargain, namely getting a group of prisoners together and his group leader to them. He would usually catch me on the way in, an ambush being the most effective way of avoiding the hassle of actual entry into the prison. I gave orders, instructions, threats and bribes to help make it work and was reminded that governing a prison can all too often be an ephemeral concept. In the end I gave Billy my mobile phone number with the request that if he found himself refused entry or with no volunteers or too few he ring me there and then. I would then ring the duty governor and offer him or her career advice and it worked – most of the time.

Prison is part of the past of many people: Keith Richards, Mick Jagger, Stephen Fry, Sean Penn, Sophia Loren, Wesley Snipes. There is a long list and it ranges from drunk driving, tax evasion and drug possession to the freedom fighting of Nelson Mandela and Mahatma Ghandi. There but for the grace of God go many more. A moment of anger, a reckless driving manoeuvre or 'forgetting' to pay for something might have got any of us a criminal conviction. And let's not forget all those who now confess to drug use, inhaling or not, which was and is against the law. If they had been caught and convicted many business and political parties would look very different. It is worth remembering that the people in prison are only the ones who were caught.

FIVE

POLITICIANS

The hot line – the governor's private direct line – rang. This phone was never a social call and usually meant I hadn't done something I should have done or had to do something I would rather not. Sure enough I was informed that Home Secretary Michael Howard and Prison Service Director General Derek Lewis were on their way from central London and wanted to visit HMP Belmarsh, or more particularly the infamous Special Secure Unit.

Michael Howard had succeeded Ken Clarke by October 1993 when in an infamous Blackpool conference speech he introduced a hugely coercive law and order package which included over twenty measures embracing the return of approved schools, electronic tagging, the removal of the right to silence as well as restrictions on bail and the right to trial by jury. It was here he coined his two most famous phrases: 'prison works' and 'decent and austere [regimes]'. It was a significant break from not only his predecessors but also existing academic research. It was also little more than three years on from a White Paper endorsed by Margaret Thatcher which opined that 'prisons were an expensive way of making bad people worse'.

Howard had been rocked by the escapes from Whitemoor and Parkhurst. His Director General (DG) of the Prison Service was Derek Lewis, the first DG from outside the Civil Service. Lewis had been Chairman of UK Gold TV and Chief Executive of Granada TV.

His was an unusual appointment but one seen as an attempt to bring about organisational modernisation in the prison service. He didn't last long.

Howard and Lewis duly arrived and with little pomp and ceremony we made our way through the prison towards the unit. This was Belmarsh at its most unpleasant. Cold, dark and wet with large house blocks rising out of the damp Thames air. The visitors were accompanied by the usual flunkies, who kept up the rear. They were usually people with little experience of prisons and probably found the place quite daunting. Like me they probably could name a thousand places they would rather be on a Friday night. The SSU was in the far corner of the extensive Belmarsh complex – as far from the main entrance as possible. It had its own wall and inner fence through which it was necessary to negotiate a series of electronic gates and searching procedures operated from the unit's own control room. Apart from the fact that food came in allegedly heated trolleys from the main kitchen, it was to all intents and purposes a self-contained unit.

Howard was not in the least phased or if he was it didn't show it. His declaration that prisons should be decent but austere had been placed at the vanguard of Tory policy on criminal justice. These were the days before 'hoodies' could be hugged and we were yet to be tough on the causes of crime, if indeed we ever were. Howard was yet to have, in the words of his then prison minister, Ann Widdecombe, 'something of the night about him', a phrase she later used to describe him when they were both out of office and the Tories out of power. As far as I was concerned he was something in the night and although I could have done without the additional pressure of two such eminent visitors I and my deputy Paul Carroll ambled along with them in the orange glow from the triffid-like security lights that brought perpetual twilight to this mini city. We made our way across to the unit, offering reassurances to our leaders that following the recent security lapses across the prison estate here at Belmarsh at least we had got a grip. A case of whistling in the dark if ever there were one. What all four of us knew for sure was that if any of the Whitemoor or Parkhurst escapers did it again from Belmarsh we would all be getting our P45s.

We approached the first gate through the outer perimeter wall and passed through into a security 'air lock' which bridged the sterile area between the wall and the inner fence. At this point it was possible for prisoners to see out of their cell windows any incoming guests. Normally such movement would be of little interest and in any event only a handful of cells had any vision at all. Whether staff had given some prisoners the tip-off as to who was heading their way I know not, but almost instantly Howard was recognised and window-to-window communication began around the four spurs. There then ensued a cacophony of abuse which even I found a little strong. Walking around prisons, especially as the one in charge, you became used to having your parentage, your looks and all aspects of your personal life questioned as you walked in open areas past cell windows. The odd missile was not uncommon and even after the ending of slopping out the contents of a pot of excrement could seriously ruin one of Marks & Spencer's finest pinstripes. The fury at Howard was fortunately only verbal, but it was sustained and highly imaginative in a very perverted way. Confident that he was in no danger physically and used to the House of Commons banter I could barely hide my grin. Derek Lewis looked a little concerned and the flunkies terrified but I got the impression Howard was in his element. As the torrent of abuse hit our little group of four, Paul Carroll in a moment of inspired genius turned to the Home Secretary and said, 'It's a good job they can't vote, isn't it Home Secretary?' We all roared, no one more than the man himself. We had little idea that votes for prisoners would some fifteen years on not be a source of amusement but of serious political controversy and not a little hypocrisy.

The following weekend whilst grabbing a Saturday morning lie-in I was listening to a review of newspaper articles on Radio 4. My slumber was shattered as I heard the vignette at the SSU being described with total accuracy in a publication that week. There were only four of us in earshot of Paul's comment that Friday evening. Paul and I had neither the time nor the inclination to be leaking such stuff and spent much of our time fending the media off. How it came to public knowledge I will never know.

Howard's image was eventually dented in 1997 when he was being questioned on *Newsnight* by Jeremy Paxman. Derek Lewis had effectively sacked John Marriot, governor of Parkhurst, shortly after the escape of the three prisoners. It was suggested that Howard had threatened to overrule Lewis if he didn't sack John. Paxman asked Howard a total of twelve times: 'Did you threaten to overrule him?' Howard's equally persistent reply was that he 'did not instruct him', ignoring the 'threaten' part of the question.

It was a short time later that his former minister of state at the Home Office Ann Widdecombe made her famous comment. The Tories by then had lost power and Howard made an unsuccessful bid for the party leadership. Many argued that Widdecombe's comments had a profound effect.

What never made the headlines was the tragic death not long after his sacking of John Marriot. John was a governor of huge intellect and great integrity. Many in the service felt profound disquiet about his very public treatment and thought that he had been made scapegoat at a time of huge political upset. His funeral on the Isle of Wight was packed and everyone sported red ties, John's hallmark, in his honour. It was said in the eulogy that the only thing John had of the night about him was the hours of the night into which he worked.

Politicians don't like prisons. Secretaries of State, formerly at the Home Office now at the Ministry of Justice, hate prisons. Appointments to the post of prisons minister are punishment postings. Few come out unscathed and anyone overseeing any aspect of the system knows it is not if, but when.

Prisons were placed under the jurisdiction of the Home Office, or Home Department as it was referred to in Parliament, in 1823. The police followed in 1829. The Home Office itself began life in 1782 when all domestic matters of government were moved into the Home Office and all foreign matters to a new Foreign Office. Its initial responsibilities involved such things as petitions to the king, royal prerogatives and issuing instructions to magistrates. It was tasked with protecting the public and safeguarding the rights and liberties of individuals as well as managing police and prisons. A whole raft of responsibilities have been added and removed over the last 200 years. The control of explosives was added in 1875 as were dangerous drugs in 1914. Firearms were added in 1920, with elections following a year later. Slaughter houses were removed in 1953, reservoirs in 1969 and Northern Ireland in 1972.

It was 9 May 2007, in the panic years of the Labour Government, that the most significant change took place in criminal justice administration in this country. Prisons and probation were moved to the Department for Constitutional Affairs which was renamed the Ministry of Justice. The architect of the change was Dr John Reid. Reid was appointed Home Secretary on 5 May 2006, replacing Charles Clarke after the latter was removed in the wake of a Home Office scandal involving the release of foreign national prisoners.

The foreign prisoners row was one of the many low points of Labour Prime Minister Tony Blair's third term. The revelation that over 1,000 foreign prisoners had been released into the community after serving their sentences rather than being deported and that some had gone on to reoffend caused public outrage, panic in government and hysteria in the media. Clarke carried the can for years of organisational mismanagement across different departments which had neither the technological infrastructure or wherewithal to talk to each other. Clarke had generated some optimism in the penal reform sector. In a speech to the Prison Reform Trust (PRT) in November 2006 he had talked of reducing the prison population, of diverting those with mental illness away from incarceration and of developing alternatives.

It was on this wave of optimism my tenure at Brixton ended. After more than three years of personal turmoil and sleepless nights the prison had turned the corner and, whilst not transformed, the rot had stopped. From Britain's worst performing prison it was now its most improved.

There was in consequence a much improved mood around the place and the local community and many charities were actively involved in making 'The Big House', as we were known in the town, a more respected and constructive institution. Back in 2000 one of my predecessors, Dr Andrew Coyle, had devised a plan for Brixton which involved extending the perimeter wall to make way for workshops. The wall was extended but the money for buildings never came. Left behind was a large tract of land behind a 5-metre brick wall, separate from the main prison but invisible to the outside world. Derelict and full of rubbish, I had turned it into a much needed car park for staff. With an eager group of volunteers, however, I devised a plan to use the space to build what was termed a transitional facility. A place where prisoners could go towards the end of their sentence to integrate better into the community. With the help of some work pro-bono from interested architects we drew up plans for a facility that would house around 150 prisoners but would facilitate treatment and training within and work experience outside. It was not rocket science. Hostels, ten to twenty-bedded units adjacent to urban jails, had performed a similar if less ambitious task for years. This was to be a social enterprise where planning permission was not an issue and where a local community would see it as natural progression to the work in the existing jail. No one in prison service headquarters got it. I might as well have been proposing the building of a brothel for all the enthusiasm I received. However I was blessed with a new breed of High Sheriff in London who were eschewing their ceremonial roles for active engagement in criminal justice during their one-year unpaid tenure.

Economist, journalist and academic Frances Cairncross had enjoyed one such tenure and was a passionate advocate of this embryonic project. She enjoyed personal connections with Charles Clarke and persuaded him to come to Brixton for a visit in order for him to be hijacked on the project. His visit was seen with much suspicion by prison service headquarters. Home Secretaries tended to be sent rather than seek visits. He arrived with the usual pomp and ceremony. He saw the usual things including volunteering to sit in a prison cellular van or 'sweat box'. Clarke, a man of large proportions, sat down in one cubicle only for the van driver to lock the door on him. Seeing my career going even further south I quickly requested his release. To his credit Clarke was unfazed. At the end of the visit I offered to jump in his bomb-proof Rover, have it drive into my 'space' around the corner and persuade him of the merits of my proposal for a new-style transitional facility. We stood together in the vast derelict space surrounded by high prison walls. He got it.

A few weeks later I was told that Clarke had proposed a new unit to develop three prototype transitional facilities across the country and I was offered the opportunity to lead it. This was the only thing that would get me out of Brixton. I had given up hope or expectation of greater promotion or glory and would have stayed at my south London bailiwick quite happily until retirement. This was the challenge of a lifetime. I left Brixton with a heavy heart but fired up imagination. Three weeks later Clarke had gone and Dr Reid was declaring all before him 'not fit for purpose'. If my career was the equivalent of the stock market I had moved into silver just as everyone else was moving into gold.

Storming into the Home Office, like a Celtic supporter heading for the last pie in the shop, Reid was seen by some as one of the government's most effective performers over the previous decade, being described by many commentators as a bruiser, but with a strong academic leaning. He was certainly confrontational, not least when people missed the title 'Dr' when referring to him. His academic standing is based on a doctoral thesis listed on Stirling University's website as: 'Warrior Aristocrats in Crisis: The Political Effects of the Transition from the Slave Trade to Palm Oil Commerce in the Nineteenth-century Kingdom of Dahomey.' Attempts to obtain a copy have never proved successful. The term 'effective performer' is a curious one and symptomatic of problems then and now of how government in the UK operates and how departments within government such as prisons can suffer.

Reid held eight government posts in the space of seven years, running three of the government's largest departments in the space of just two years, Health and Defence before the Home Office. When he became Secretary of State for Health he is reported to have said: 'Oh fuck, not health.' When he joined the Home Office and took on responsibility for prisons I heard one senior colleague say: 'Oh fuck, not John Reid.'

During his brief sojourn in Defence, Reid committed 3,300 troops to Helmand province, Afghanistan in January 2006. He later said troops would leave 'without a single shot being fired'. At the Home Office Reid hit the ground (and anything else in his way) running. He rushed around condemning his predecessors as incompetent and his staff as dysfunctional. His famous description of his new department as 'not fit for purpose' became part of a new bureaucratic lexicon. Reid's comments were rebuffed by Clarke, who criticised his comments in a defence of his own period in office. It was difficult at times to remember they were both part of the same political party. Morale in Reid's depart-ment hit rock bottom as it wrestled with a new leader whose loyalty was to the next election rather than to genuine improvement in his department. He would have been better to have done a PhD on leader-ship and management rather than obscure elements of the Kingdom of Dahomey.

The doctor's first hundred days were memorable. As well as lots of talk of reform and transformation he planned 8,000 more prison places; a 40 per cent reduction in headquarters staff by 2010; and he condemned the probation service for letting people down, and argued for fundamental reform. Reid was a perfect example of a British Cabinet minister drawn from a small pool of underqualified Members of Parliament. We have little to learn from the USA in penal reform but in government it is worth reflecting that in the USA they seek true experts selected by the President and confirmed by the Senate to serve in the Cabinet. The US system is not infallible but the principle of choosing experts to run difficult departments crucial to the well-being of the nation is preferable to leaving it to amateurs who play musical chairs every time one of them has an affair, fiddles his expenses or changes his sexual preferences. Even then forgiveness was in abundance as exemplified by David Blunkett and 'Prince of Darkness' Peter Mandelson, both of whom were 'let go' regularly only to reappear in ever more powerful positions. This was never a trait extended to the real criminal community. The Blair years were probably the worst in recent history and the chair-shifting was at odds with the Blair mantra of efficient and effective government. Cameron and his coalition have to a large extent slowed down the music and increased the number of chairs. Nevertheless skills and qualifications remain largely an irrelevance not least when so many of the new intake of politicians, including those at the highest levels, have experience of nothing other than politics.

If we ever did have Cabinet ministers who knew what they were talking about they might look at other American principles and practices. The US Constitution has not been surpassed by anything in Europe over the 200 years it has been in existence. It does have inbuilt protections for the weak. We remain in this country resistant to a Bill of Rights and antagonistic to every element of the European Union, not least the European Court and the European Convention on Human Rights. Combine prisons and Europe, and politicians not only lose the plot, but throw all sanity out of the window. It has been clear for some time that MPs and ministers don't fully understand the difference between the Committee of Ministers and the Council of Ministers, the Council of Europe and the European Union, or the European Court of Justice and the European Court of Human Rights. Even worse they have demonstrated a desire to ignore aspects of European law to which we are bound when it appears politically and publicly expedient.

From 2006, after the uproar over foreign prisoners and Charles Clarke's subsequent demise, Home Secretaries had a published policy of only detaining potential deportees as a last resort. After the furore around Clarke his successors adopted a diametrically opposite approach. There was a presumption of detention at the end of sentence, with few exceptions allowed on compassionate grounds. The approach was kept secret until in March 2011 the UK Supreme Court struck the policy down, ruling that the hidden blanket ban was contrary to public policy. The secret policy was seen as an abuse of power by many. Lord Dyson in his judgment was scathing: 'For political reasons, it was convenient to take a risk as to the lawfulness of the policy that was being applied and blame the courts if the policy was declared to be unlawful.' He could have added personal survival to the political reasons.

Throw into the mix any issue to do with sex offenders and we see even more principles going out of the window. The sex offender register was introduced in 1997. It requires offenders to inform the police of their home address or any other where they intend to reside for more than a week. They are also required to advise of travel abroad. It has always been regarded as a reasonable method of information-sharing between relevant agencies and an ongoing system of risk management of a potentially dangerous offender group. If sentenced to more than thirty months, offenders stay on the system for life. Those receiving a caution for a sex offence will have their name removed after two years. There are currently around 48,000 people on the register.

In February 2011 the Supreme Court ruled in the case of two individual sex offenders that their indefinite registration with no possibility of review was incompatible with their rights to privacy under the Human Rights Act. Ministers and MPs were apoplectic with rage. How dare they be required to obey the law? The law was there to be obeyed by rapists, murderers and robbers not ministers of the Crown. David Cameron declared that he would do the 'minimum necessary' to comply. The media pitched in with accusations that the court was establishing a 'pervert's charter'. About half of those on the list were affected by the ruling. Removal would not rule out all checks, not least a CRB (Criminal Records Bureau) check. The ruling was simply saying that yet again a blanket ban, this time overt, was unreasonable. The ability to have a right of appeal in the light of changed circumstances was a reasonable safeguard. Nothing was mentioned about the case of one of the appellants whose offence had been committed at the age of eleven, one year above that of the age of criminal responsibility and three years below the age of criminal responsibility for most of the rest of the world. The unpalatable truth that society is at most risk from those who never get near a register was also forgotten. It is of course vital to protect past and future victims of sex offences and there are many ways of doing it. Flouting the law for political capital is not one of them.

VOTES FOR PRISONERS

One of the best and most recent examples was the vote early in 2010 in the Commons defying a European Court of Human Rights (ECHR) ruling. In 2006 the ECHR had found that the blanket ban on votes for prisoners was a breach of their human rights. At a practical level in prisons it was not an issue that particularly vexed anyone. Remand prisoners were allowed to vote on the very reasonable premise that they were not guilty of any crime. Very few actually did and this says much about the nature of remand prisoners. The criteria used to decide are quite specific: the charge may be particularly serious or reflect previous convictions; the defendant may be thought likely to interfere with witnesses, commit further offences, not comply with bail conditions or simply disappear. Class A drug use can also be a factor. Implicit in any decision would be whether or not someone had a place to live. Bail conditions usually require individuals to live at a specified address. Consequently the more socially excluded someone is and the more chaotic their lives the more likely they are to be remanded in custody. Absence of peer or family support or just poor legal representation also plays a big part.

Proof that the decisions were more about social exclusion rather than criminal risk comes from PRT figures from 2007 which show that of the 11,400 people on remand some 21 per cent were subsequently acquitted and 30 per cent went on to receive a non-custodial sentence.

In terms of voting the remand prison population was less likely than any comparable age, gender or socio-economic group to be on the electoral role. Difficult and damaged people leading chaotic and disordered lives are unlikely to fill in electoral roll forms if they ever received any. If any remand prisoners are on the electoral roll and eligible for a postal vote whilst in prison the mechanisms to encourage them to do so do not exist and current procedures for letters and outside contact make the process difficult in the extreme.

The fact that remand prisoners rarely vote and the reasons why did not feature in the debate. The arguments for convicted prisoners voting were put eloquently to the All Party Penal Affairs Group in the House of Commons by the Archbishop of Canterbury:

> If we lose sight of the notion of a prisoner as a citizen, any number of things follow from that and indeed are following from that. The prisoner as a citizen is somebody who can on the one hand can expect their dignity as a citizen to be factored into what happens to them and can reasonably expect that penal custody will bring something that contributes to, rather than takes away, their capacity to act as a citizen in other circumstances. Thus issues around restoration, around responsibility, around developing concepts of empathy and mutuality are all part of what seems to me to be a reasonable working out of what it is to regard the prisoner as a citizen.

Such arguments were lost on hundreds of MPs who competed to denounce the European Court of Human Rights and express their outrage at the prospect of 'rapists and murderers' voting. It was the House of Commons at its populist best and intellectual worst, in a week when two of its former members were imprisoned for expenses fraud. The ECHR, which many members sought to conflate with the European Community in their quest for populist support, had ruled that it was a blanket ban on all prisoners being refused the right to vote that was unlawful. Implicit in the judgment was that not all prisoners were the same. Whilst many countries had adopted the right of universal suffrage across all their society, Britain was simply being required to be more circumspect and arguably more intelligent in its approach.

Debates around the concept of allowing prisoners with short sentences to vote got nowhere. Plans to give judges discretion were derided. There was no mention of the fact that some 80,000 prisoners are released into the community annually and consequently the majority of the prison population is within months of release. Granting the vote to those less than twelve months from release, thereby encouraging them to be on an electoral register, have an address, be a citizen and be less socially excluded gained no currency.

The former Lord Chancellor, Lord MacKay of Clashfern, in a Commons Select Committee Report on the issue underlined the legal point. He told the committee that the key problem for the court was not our denial of votes for prisoners but the blanket and indiscriminate nature of our ban, shared only by Ireland and Liechtenstein. He reminded the committee of the deepest of principles: 'If we believe in the rule of law we are just as much bound to observe the decisions of the European court on matters within their competence as we are to obey the decisions of our own courts in matters within theirs.'

The government response over many years had been to employ a range of delaying tactics to avoid implementing the ruling. Yet again successive Justice Ministers were preoccupied with political considerations and fear of adverse headlines, rather than fairness or the rule of law. Yet again all the court was reinforcing was that blanket bans were unreasonable. MPs and the media invented another 'charter for murderers, robbers and rapists'. It was also a message from the legislature to offenders that the rule of law could easily be broken by those who make it. MPs may be free to change the law but voted overwhelmingly to defy it.

Few nations, with the possible exception of the USA, are so out of step. Looking simply at votes, the government in Hong Kong recently concluded a sensible public consultation exercise prior to enfranchising all, or most, of its prisoners.

In April 1999 South Africa declared: 'The universality of the franchise is important not only for nationhood and democracy. The vote of each and every citizen is a badge of dignity and personhood. Quite literally it says that everybody counts.' According to the Joint Committee on Human Rights, the UK is now also out of step with most European countries. Prisoners may vote without restriction in seventeen countries and may frequently or sometimes vote in a further thirteen. The UK is one of only twelve countries where people in prison are still stripped of their voting rights.

Prisons continue to be held in such opprobrium by our elected representatives because whatever happens they cannot win. The media make sure of that. It is not a party political issue but we have been blessed with politicians over the last fifteen years at least whose loyalty is to the next election rather than to genuine improvement, be that criminal justice or indeed any other aspect of government.

There have been exceptions. Beneath Secretaries of State at the Home Office, and now Ministry of Justice, have been prisons ministers, although their designations are now more complex and varied. Yet it has always been the case that, below the Secretary of State, some unfortunate minister has had prisons as part of his or her portfolio. It would be interesting to see who over the last few years actually saw it as an opportunity to engage with a serious part of government in need of reform and who saw it as a punishment posting. Few were around long enough to make a difference. Some were clearly not around long enough for such an appointment even to make it into their biographies. This is at odds with prison governors, or *alleged* prison governors. Whilst ministers may wish to hide the fact that they held responsibility for incarceration, the number claiming to be prison governors is quite remarkable. It seems to some that having worked in a prison as a junior middle manager entitles the use of the appellation 'former prison governor'. Deputy mayors of London, eminent professors and even a former director general have adopted the term as a rite of passage.

Paul Goggins was prisons minister roughly in parallel with my tenure at Brixton. Ministerial appointments came and went, none more so than under the Blair government. It was in 2003 early in the relegation zone period of league tables at Brixton that my long-suffering but immensely loyal secretary Kay came into my office to announce that there was a minister at the gate to see me. 'Anglican, Catholic, Jewish or Muslim?' I asked. 'Prisons' she replied, in the usual scolding manner she had of dealing with my irreverence. 'Wheel him in,' I said, as if I had a choice. It was Paul Goggins, who had been appointed that morning and probably having never been in a prison and the fact that we were only a few minutes out of central London, had decided to visit Brixton first. Although not immersed in criminal justice, Goggins had the ideal background in the social services sector – ideal, that is, in the eyes of a very few of us. He had worked as a child care worker with Liverpool Catholic Social Services before running Wigan Children's Home in 1976. He was a project director for Action for Children in Salford in 1984 and became the national director for Church Action on Poverty. He was in the people business. He joined me in my office for an introductory coffee before the usual Cooks tour that I gave to a lot of people with varying degrees of enthusiasm. He asked me to tell him about Brixton. I rather cheekily asked him to relate the brief he had been given by HQ and I would fill in the gaps. He was professional and magnanimous, I was weary from lack of sleep and an excess of disasters. I said we should start at the bottom. This was A Wing on what we would call the 'fours', i.e. the fourth floor landing. This was probably the worst accommodation in the prison system. It was best described by freelance journalist Peter Stanford in *The Independent* that year. Peter and I now work together for the Longford Trust. Peter described in an eloquent article how, if you take two public lavatory cubicles, remove the wall between them, take out one lavatory and replace it with a bunk bed, then that was a cell on A Wing. He didn't mention that the door would be a bit thicker but his description has not been bettered. Slopping out was allegedly abolished in 1996 and toilets were put in cells. Some say cells were put in toilets.

I approached one cell at random. It was 'association', a time when prisoners could move freely about the wing. Two, young south Londoners were behind the open door of the cell. I knocked and asked if the prisons minister could have a look inside their abode. There was polite quiescence as they sauntered out leaving the thick Victorian door uninvitingly framing the chaos within. I ushered the minister into the gloom with his flunkey following behind reluctantly and me bringing up the rear. The cell was now full and there was barely room to turn around. Goggins surveyed the scene and I reversed the process as we repaired to the relative wide open space of the narrow landing. My ultimate boss turned to me and said with absolute good grace: 'You've made your point Governor.' Although I was making a point, I lied and said I wasn't making any point, but was simply reminding him of what we were both responsible for.

Goggins later came back to the jail to open formally a new education facility – an old Victorian hospital wing that had been converted as proof of what Victorian architecture could be with paint and imagination. There was consternation at HQ when I relayed to them that the shadow Prisons Minister, Dominic Grieve, had asked to come along to the event. In innocence, an attribute never ascribed to me by my lords and masters, I simply asked what the protocol would be, never having had two such guests. Apoplexy hit the press office who ruled that such a thing was not possible and broke every rule in the book. Flummoxed, I asked if they could therefore tell Mr Grieve that his presence was forbidden. After an hour of radio silence there was a change of mind. I met each man separately as he arrived. Neither was the least bit phased by the other's presence and they chatted away amiably. I felt a little like Mr Speaker and was yet again reprimanded by HQ (not the politicians) for welcoming everyone yet again to Britain's worst prison.

It was a year or so later that I had cause to be grateful for some sort of positive relationship with a prisons minister. Mental health at Brixton had been one of the most intractable problems for years. The prison had not developed a good reputation for dealing with such people. One particular hospital wing, F Wing, had become notorious for conditions and levels of suicide and was for a period before my arrival referred to as

'Fraggle Rock'. Care had improved but the poor mental health of many residents had not. Services were now overseen by forensic mental health consultants as part of contracted out, but effective services. One of the biggest problems was transferring people with severe mental health problems to secure mental health facilities. Courts, faced with people charged with criminal activity but with the real possibility of mental health needs, had neither the time nor the expertise on hand in court to deal with the problem. Remand in custody to 'sort it out' was all too readily the first rather than the last option. We were stretched – at times to breaking point. In one public event encompassing all the London prisons, a fellow London governor described his primary purpose as governor of such an establishment as being to prevent escapes. I described mine as keeping people alive. I regularly failed.

Michael, not his real name, was a typical, if extreme, example. He had been charged with a minor public order offence in south London and after appearing before magistrates was remanded in custody. Immediately on arrival it was clear this man was very unwell. Three days into his custody at Brixton he was in a hospital cell, naked, hiding behind his upturned mattress, banging his head against the wall, defecating and urinating on the floor. Staff did their best to care for him and my consultant psychiatrist battled against the system to have him sectioned under the Mental Health Act and transferred to a secure hospital. This process of transfer and diagnosis has been written about and much discussed by health professionals, prison officials and prison inspectors. 'Waiting times', as the period during which a transfer was arranged was almost flippantly described, could run into months. Agreeing a diagnosis, finding and paying for a bed were all elements in the mix which caused very sick people to remain in an inappropriate and toxic environment however much we all tried to make it a safe and caring one.

But for reasons I was unclear about, perhaps simple expediency in a crowded court calendar, I received a fax from the court that had remanded Michael in custody saying there would be no further action on the charges and the case was dropped. The warrant I had for holding him therefore expired immediately. The system of warrants has not changed for centuries. It is the legal basis on which a court requires the governor of a prison to keep a prisoner in custody. They are not as simple and straightforward as they sound and have not embraced the digital age. One person held on one warrant for a specified period of time is a luxury. Complex, parallel and overlapping warrants for a range of alleged and proven misdemeanours mean that occasionally the arithmetical calculations taking account of a raft of issues across courts and counties result in prisoners being let out too early or too late. Too early is picked up as prisoner on the run due to a cock-up. Too late is compensation at a level better than the minimum wage.

Legally, Michael was straightforward. I no longer had legal authority to hold him. Legally I had to let him go. Governing is a lonely place. The buck stopped here. Fortunately I had an excellent working relationship with my consultant psychiatrist. Simon was adamant: this man was dangerous to himself and others and should not be released. It was unsafe. Without a hospital order, continuing to hold him was without question illegal. There might be a hospital bed for him tomorrow. It might take three months. Seeking advice up the food chain was pointless. The law was clear and I chose to break it. He remained in my custody and our care. A few days later a bed was found for Michael. He had no family and friends to challenge my decision and for once no one leaked anything to the press.

All would have been well if investigative journalist Nick Davies had not come along. Nick is one of the last bastions of true independent journalism. He writes extensively as a freelancer and for *The Guardian* and *The Observer*. Author of one of my favourite books, *Flat Earth News*, an exposer of journalistic malpractice worldwide, Nick has long had a passion for criminal justice issues. Most recently he played a key part in exposing the phone-hacking scandal centred around the *News of the World*.

Nick was also a film-maker and had approached the prison service press office to make a film for *Guardian*/Channel 4 Films on mental health in prisons. Unbeknown to me, agreement had been reached with the press office to film in Wormwood Scrubs. He had asked to come to Brixton but been diverted. Letting me loose with a film-maker was not their idea of sound public relations. At the last minute Scrubs declined for unspecific operational reasons and I was asked to host Nick at very short notice. I was delighted. My passion for addressing mental health issues in prison had been ignited in my time with the prisons inspectorate over the previous three years and as governor of Brixton the need was always in sharp focus.

I was introduced to Nick, who had an easy manner and a leather jacket I coveted for most of the day. From my point of view he had open house. Everyone did. Personal privacy and confidentiality went without saying but I kept nebulous security issues to a minimum. The press office played the central midfield as best they could and Nick did his stuff. There then came the inevitable interview with the governor. It was in my office, with Nick throwing the questions off camera and a press officer taking notes in the background. After a few preliminaries I raised the case of Michael and relayed my law-breaking. As we got going and the story was revealed, Nick paused the filming and asked me if I was sure I wanted to say all this. I doubt he does that very often. The press officer was holding her head in her hands, presumably contemplating her next career move. I was adamant. I had broken the law and was not going to hide the fact. We finished and the film was broadcast on *Channel 4 News* two weeks later. I watched and my mother dutifully programmed her video recorder. At my regular morning meeting in the jail the next day, our review of the previous day's chaos and attempt to forecast the day to come, there were a few gasps and 'oh shit, what has he done now?'; Kay had already obtained some quotes for my leaving party. The silence was deafening from HQ. No calls, no emails, nothing. I was too busy to worry.

The next night there was another prison film on *Channel 4 News*. This time about suicide and self-harm, fronted this time rather more sensibly by a career civil servant. I watched with interest and assumed the previous film had melted into history. At the end of the film Jon Snow, now a fellow trustee on the Longford Trust, announced that in the studio to discuss the film was prisons minister Paul Goggins. Before talking about suicide Jon reminded the viewers and the minister that on the previous night one of his governors had described how he had broken the law. What was he, the minister responsible, going to do about it? I don't know if the minister had prior knowledge of the question but his answer was wholly supportive and I remain grateful for his grace, compliments and understanding of the real issues. The next day the deputy head of the prison service phoned me to ask precisely what I had done. I repeated what I had said in the interview. He said he would have to launch an inquiry into me. I said he had better make it two inquiries. I had done the same thing the day before.

For politicians there may not have been a golden age of prison reform, but there was a time when conviction politicians rather than politicians with conviction were to the fore. Douglas Hurd's tenure as Home Secretary between 1985 and 1989 under Margaret Thatcher was largely uncontroversial, but he was notably of the view that the British prison system did not work effectively and actually argued for more rehabilitation of offenders and alternative sentencing. Ken Clarke, first time around in 1992–3 under John Major, was not around long enough to make that much of a difference but was pragmatic and focused on the problems. At the second time of asking, Clarke in 2010, supported by rational views from the Liberal Democrats in the coalition, began to articulate alternatives, fewer numbers and actually declared the prison service as broken. But the Clarke spring moved into a Tory winter as the public sector prison service was all but declared dead, to be replaced slowly but inexorably by a privatised prison service. Political doctrine outpacing true prison reform, aided and abetted by politicians scared of true debate, will reap a whirlwind.

SIX

CHARITIES

PIONEERS OF PRISON'S 'BIG SOCIETY'

The narrow path that ran through Brixton's austere Victorian buildings and razor wire-topped fences, leading to the steps of the prison chapel, was crammed with vehicles, cables and BBC crew. I wasn't even sure how they had managed to get it all in. Brixton had been designed for the ingress and egress of the horse and cart, not an outside broadcast unit nor the sort of vehicle that transports orchestras. Even I was alarmed at the security implications. Fortunately I had a security department that had risen to the challenge. As I climbed the steps to the chapel that cold December afternoon, the sound from within began to reverberate around the entire prison. The effect was simply angelic. On entering the chapel I immediately realised the genius of Victorian design, even in a place of incarceration. The orchestra and choir filled the huge, crumbling and mould-encrusted roof void with sounds the like of which had never before blessed this place of worship.

The orchestra, wires, amps and speakers were scattered around in what to the uninitiated was a random agglomeration of security breaches. To one side was a choir interspersed in which I recognised the 'Angels'. Some looked slightly incongruous amongst the professionals, others slightly uncomfortable. They all beamed at the experience they were now enjoying. This was David Cameron's 'Big Society', a community working together, at its best.

The Big Society has been alive and well in prisons since the very inception of the principle of incarceration. 'Angel of prisons' Elizabeth Fry spent all her time and energy early in the nineteenth century trying to engage those outside with those inside prisons. She tackled basic conditions such as health, hygiene and overcrowding. Supported by her family's bank, she founded a prison school for the children, who in those days were imprisoned with their parents. In 1820 she created the British Ladies' Society for Promoting the Reformation of Female Prisoners, widely regarded as the first national women's organisation in Britain.

In the late eighteenth century John Howard highlighted the treatment of and conditions for prisoners. In those days if you were unfortunate enough to be behind bars your jailer would have to be paid for everything: food, bedding, clothes and any kind of outside visits. In an age when just being poor was liable to land you in trouble, pauper prisoners could starve to death. It certainly helped to reduce the reconviction rates. In 1777 Howard inherited £15,000 and used it to fund further work in prisons. The Howard League exists today as a tribute to his memory and one of all too few completely independent organisations addressing penal reform.

Whilst there is ample record of the issues they tackled and their interactions with governments of the day, there is little record of how they were received by the prisons themselves. In the days before administrative bureaucracies, press officers and ministerial paranoia, it would be safe to assume they simply knocked on the door and were let in, because they dressed well and spoke with authority. At a time when prisons were barely funded at all, in the conventional sense, and when a prisoner only ate what he or she could afford, one also assumes that if people like Howard and Fry came bearing gifts they were warmly welcomed. Politicians did not run scared despite this challenge to the very basis of the system. In 1774 John Howard gave evidence to a House of Commons select committee and was praised for his 'humanity and zeal'. It is impossible to imagine the barriers facing Elizabeth Fry, as a woman in the early nineteenth century, challenging the most deprived and excluded in society. Nevertheless she made herself heard and made a difference.

This was an age of individuals using their own money to further causes about which they were passionate. It was later in the nineteenth and early twentieth centuries as trade and industrialisation reached its zenith that family trusts and foundations were set up by enlightened individuals attempting to use their wealth for philanthropic purposes.

Whilst the articles of many of these trusts and foundations are not specifically about prisons, prisoners or even penal reform, many of them were set up to tackle the issues that lay at the heart of offending or the issues consequent upon imprisonment, such as housing, lack of employment, mental health issues and general social deprivation. Today they embrace more specific criminal justice issues such as drug and alcohol treatment, restorative justice, and work with prisoners and their families. Some trusts and foundations have developed their own specific programmes. The Barrow Cadbury Trust has a Transition to Adulthood programme; the Esmee Fairbairn Foundation has a Rethinking Crime and Punishment programme; the Monument Trust has focused on diverting young people from prison and resettlement afterwards for decades. Trusts and foundations may not have been tough on crime but they have been, and continue to be, tough on the causes of crime and were certainly cognisant of the causes of reoffending long before the National Offender Management Service (NOMS) coined the phrase 'end to end offender management'.

Two hundred years on from Fry and Howard we have a plethora of trusts and foundations awarding grants to charities and community organisations working in prisons and related fields to the tune of £40 million a year. All the grants support services and interventions in prison, communities and, most importantly, between the two. It is evidence, if evidence was needed, that the Big Society is not a new idea.

PHILANTHROPY AND THE MINISTRY OF JUSTICE
Early in 2011 the Ministry of Justice published a Green Paper entitled 'Breaking the Cycle: Effective Punishment, Rehabilitation and Sentencing

of Offenders' and invited submissions from all across the criminal justice system, public, private, voluntary and community. It was trying to bring to the table new ideas, new ways of working. It was seeking to improve a system which had eschewed real change for years. This was however against a backdrop of a national financial crisis and the need to save public money. Sadly it reflected an organisation routinely cleansed of corporate memory. It had no idea that work with prisoners was routinely receiving around £40 million of charitable funds every year. The trusts and foundations had asked each other what they were doing in the justice system and related fields and simply added it up. Deaf, dumb and blind, the Ministry of Justice was Tommy in a tragic opera.

The Ministry of Justice and NOMS also failed to understand the difference between the two components in the charitable sector: the trusts and foundations which provide funds and the charities which rely on them to provide programmes and interventions across the criminal justice system. The latter are themselves, slowly but inexorably, being divided into two by force of the competitive market which successive governments are imposing on the sector. There are larger traditional organisations like the Rehabilitation for Addicted Prisoners Trust (RAPt) and the National Association for the Care and Resettlement of Offenders, Nacro, formerly NACRO, and much smaller organisations delivering small localised programmes such as Music in Prisons and the Comedy School.

RAPt is a charity which helps people with drug and alcohol problems. It provides services to over 13,000 people per year across the criminal justice system. It is best known for its abstinence-based programme centered around what is known as the 12-step approach. This originated from Alcoholics Anonymous but is now used to address a wide range of substance misuse and dependency problems. It is for many a very effective set of guiding principles for recovery from addiction, compulsion or other behavioural problems. RAPt is now a major provider of services in Britain's prisons, delivering both drug programmes and individual assessments. It has recently begun to provide alcohol services, as it has slowly dawned on the ministry that treating the many alcohol-dependent offenders might be beneficial.

Nacro originated back in the 1920s when it began as the Central Discharged Prisoners' Aid Society. In 1999 it dropped its full name of the National Association for the Care and Resettlement of Offenders to become Nacro. Today it is one of the largest charities in the sector, with an annual turnover of around £60 million. It provides accommodation support, education and training, resettlement advice and an extensive range of services specifically for young people.

Although both these organisations receive money from benefactors, they are essentially businesses competing for work across the criminal justice sector. They are increasingly, if not now entirely, subsumed in competitive market processes. They will survive only if they can win contracts and deliver according to tight performance criteria. Their survival will be dependent upon their competitiveness. Their main competitors over the years to come will be private sector companies such as G4S and SERCO. With that in mind and with perfectly reasonable business acumen both Nacro and RAPt have sought to work in collabo-ration with such organisations and have been part of consortia set up by private providers to bid for large government contracts for new prisons. This has proved controversial and both Nacro and RAPt have attracted severe criticism for their involvement in 'prison for profit' ventures. For the private sector companies it makes eminent commercial sense to incorporate the work of highly respected organisations with a long history of ethical involvement in the sector. For Nacro and RAPt it may well be the only way to compete because the government now sees large contracts with their economies of scale as the best way forward in a world of payment by results. Time will tell as to whether such partnerships are collaborations or takeovers and whether profit will subsume ethics.

At the other end of the spectrum is the Irene Taylor Trust and the work of Music in Prisons. The trust was set up in 1995 in memory of the wife of the late Lord Chief Justice Peter Taylor who had a personal interest in both penal reform and music. The Taylor family wanted an appropriate legacy and invited the passionate and indefatigable Sara Lee, who had been the music coordinator at Wormwood Scrubs, to set up the Irene Taylor Trust 'Music in Prisons'. Sara was the perfect choice. Admired by all in the arts world, she was adept at overcoming the many hurdles placed in her way.

The trust began its working life in 1996, with Sara organising and delivering three projects in the first year at HMP Kingston, HMP Bristol and HMP Ashwell, with the help of Nick Hayes, with whom she had previously studied at the Guildhall School of Music & Drama.

Since that time the trust has gradually grown and it can now claim to have put on performances in over half the country's jails. Prisoners have been motivated, audiences captivated and the mood of jails improved. Sadly for Sara and her team, such changes are not measurable, a source of frustration for those for whom counting is more important than recognising people's sense of their own growth towards new life and prospects. Projects in prisons rely on donations, fundraising and the support and cooperation of individual prisons. The trust's work in prisons is highly professional and it understands the needs of prisoners yet its critics are many and continue to provide obstacles for its development. Its work has been evaluated by academics and its website signposts the evidence. Enjoyment in prison however is not acceptable to a media hungry for salacious stories or for politicians paranoid about public perception.

BACH BEHIND BARS

My own personal experiences at Brixton with Music in Prisons (MIP) were extensive and the memories remain fond. I would often be asked what the point of such work was. For me it was about security. Governing prisons is too often seen as counting (although I would admit counting prisoners is quite important, and should be done at least once a day), measuring and ticking boxes. Prisons have to be primarily about relationships, mood and tone. Isolation, literal and metaphoric walls compounded by introspection, is self-defeating. MIP like so many similar organisations broke down those barriers in small and subtle ways.

The Brixton chapel music that cold December afternoon epitomised all that was best in such work. Sara Lee had approached me with, even for her, a most unusual request. Radio 3 was recording a series of programmes for its 'Bach Christmas'. There were to be a number of recordings about the work of Bach in the run-up to Christmas and they were to do one which highlighted the fact that Bach had been to prison.

Bach had worked in Weimar in Germany in 1717 for two dukes who fell out with each other. Bach was caught in the middle and decided to go elsewhere without telling his employers – a crime in those days, for which he was imprisoned for a month:

> On November 6 [1717], the quondam concertmaster and organist Bach was confined to the County Judge's place of detention for too stub-bornly forcing the issue of his dismissal and finally on December 2 was freed from arrest with notice of his unfavourable discharge.

He was thirty-two at the time, married with four children. It was the run-up to Christmas and he didn't know how long he was going to be there. So like the prisoners nearly 200 years later he wrote some music: a prelude and fugue. One of the soloists that day performed it in the Brixton chapel on a harpsichord. The principal piece was to be *Ein' feste Burg*, a choral cantata in D major, performed by the Royal Academy of Music Baroque Orchestra directed by Lawrence Cummings.

There was a 'normal' MIP project ongoing at the time but Sara modified it to train the participants, Barry, Charles, 'Chosen', Cyrus, Levi, Lloyd, Michael, Quince and Richard (who christened themselves the Brixton Angels) to perform one of the movements of the cantata in German alongside four professional vocal soloists: Pippa Goss,

Alexandra Gibson, Matthew Beale and Alex Ashworth. How difficult could that be?

By now Brixton was well used to outside groups coming in. I had taken over the prison at the time when league tables were introduced across the prison service, and lo and behold Brixton was at the bottom of all of them. My philosophy in trying to turn things round was to open the doors (metaphorically, not literally of course) to the community. The response was overwhelming and invariably supportive. The only exception was prison service headquarters, who kept telling me to stop warmly welcoming people to Britain's worst jail. I added, 'run by Britain's worst governor', but humour in 'Crumbly Towers', as we called HQ was, like opinions, forbidden.

I saw delegation as my forte. My deputy, John Hewitson (whose frame was as large as his heart and his intellect) saw this as idleness and a lack of attention to detail. He could be a cruel man. I therefore left the complex task to Sara and the tenacious Kate Quigley, my loyal prison officer lieutenant who made such things happen. Naively I had somewhat underestimated the size and complexity of not only the musical venture, but the needs of the BBC for an outside broadcast. But Kate, Sara and my security team, who by then had come to the reasonable assumption that I was as mad as a box of frogs but took a secret pride in achieving the impossible, made it happen.

They had 'previous' in the common prison parlance for having done something before. A way of making additional income for the prison was to rent out locations for film companies anxious to save money on making fake sets. Risk aversion meant that few prisons would take the risk and there was active discouragement from HQ. But it was potentially lucrative and could be fun. I had agreed that one wing could be used to film a very short sequence around the pool table. As ever, a few seconds on the final film was an afternoon on location. I was aware that the crew was on site and was interested to see how it was all going and if there were any famous stars to rub shoulders with. I entered G wing, to encounter the usual panoply of trolleys, wires, cameras and gadgets. And there by the pool table were what appeared to be actors and directors talking through the sequence. To my sheer astonishment so too was an entire wing of 160 prisoners out on association. In other words, moving freely around the wing chatting, making tea, telephone calls and other 'domestic' tasks. I had omitted to instruct that the wing be locked up during the process and was thereby hoisted by my own petard as I was always taking to task wing managers for not keeping to the normal routine and reducing the time prisoners had to associate. The scene unfolded around the pool table with three landings of prisoners looking down over the railings through the heavy mesh anti-suicide netting that provided an artificial layer between each floor. With all in place the director shouted 'silence, running, action'. An entire wing of prisoners fell silent as the action unfolded. At the shout of cut everyone broke back into shouts and conversations. If only you could bottle it.

In the Chapel of Angels, I sat down and watched, mesmerised, as music stopped and started, takes were taken and cuts were cut. Encouragement was dished out in buckets as the conductor exercised his control and the recording team wrestled for theirs. In one tea break I observed one large, south London armed robber approach the harp player to enquire what it was she was playing. On the reply 'a harp' he remarked on the wonder of an instrument he had never seen before and asked could he, ''ave a go?' Unfamiliar though he was with this particular instrument he knew strings when he saw them and immediately produced pure notes, much to the amazement of the instrument's professional owner.

The programme was finally broadcast on 22 December 2005 and the music was interspersed with a narrative about Bach's criminal history and comments from the prisoners themselves, some of whom had no musical background, none of whom had heard of Bach or Radio 3. One man vowed to listen to such music more in the future but felt he would need to buy a smoking-jacket and to do so with a brandy and cigar. The response from the Radio 3 audience during the broadcast was startling not only for me but for the Radio 3 team which in my view had been brave in their venture and uncertain of their audience's response.

Perhaps it was Christmas, or perhaps an educated audience, but there were no vitriolic responses, just expressions of pleasure, sympathy and understanding. Many emailed during the programme. One in particular wrote: 'The thing that moved me to tears this afternoon was hearing the Brixton Angels singing *Ein' feste Burg* and listening to their deeply felt and receptive response to Bach's music.'

Everyone was moved by the venture and the way the progamme interpreted the issues. Much was learnt in the prison by the men involved and the staff who made it happen. Other prisoners glued to Radio 3 were inspired by tales of their fellow prisoners and now musicians returning to the wings. Much too was learnt by a radio audience not used to, nor expecting, reflections on imprisonment past and present through the compositions of a musical genius. I don't think I improved my key performance indicators, I didn't move up the league table and I doubt the event fitted with the manual on 'what works', but all those involved had a good time and quietly I knew that in the run-up to Christmas, which is one of the most depressing times in prison, the mood of the establishment was lifted. It was just a pity I couldn't put a percentage point on the lift.

WE ARE NOT AMUSED

In a similar vein was the Comedy School, which I worked with extensively during my time at Brixton. Like MIP it struggled to obtain the funding and permission to work in prisons. Like MIP it did not fit the normal criteria and was adjudged by many of the misinformed and misguided as 'treats for cheats'. The arts in prison have suffered more than most activities from their portrayal by politicians and the media. MIP and Comedy School are part of a valiant cadre of arts organisations active in prisons, which also include the Geese Theatre, Clean Break and Rideout, to name but a few. After pressure from a number of arts bodies the Ministry of Justice finally cooperated in the setting up of an Arts Alliance and Arts Forum designed to promote the arts in prison. One of the most vociferous and powerful advocates was Lord Ramsbotham, my former boss as Chief

Inspector of Prisons. Writing in *The Guardian* in 2008 he praised the initiative, saying:

> At last, the government appears to have recognised the important role that the arts, collectively, has to play in the rehabilitation process by encouraging self-esteem. As triggers, the arts are means to the essential end of reducing re-conviction rather than being ends in themselves, but their contribution is invaluable… All the evidence proves that such an approach works.

It was only a matter of weeks later that Jack Straw, then the Secretary of State for Justice, closed down the Comedy School's course at HMP Whitemoor in a knee-jerk reaction to a headline in *The Sun*. Those on the course had included a prisoner sentenced for terrorist-related offences, and as is often the case a prison officer had sold the story to *The Sun* which created characteristic but unfounded public hysteria. Straw unfortunately had no one around him to say 'Calm down, dear', and he ordered the prison service to desist from such outrageous activity. At this time the Comedy School had built up a reputation over more than a decade of work in prisons. The prison service was too timid to remind Straw of this or that there had been previous positive media stories about the school including one in the prison service's own paper, *Prison Service News*. Keith Palmer, a compassionate and committed man, who ran the Comedy School and who had become a dear friend over the years, rang me in sheer desperation about what this meant for the future of his work in particular and the arts in general. In a Radio 4 interview he commented plaintively: 'I wasn't aware that comedy was a crime, I'm trying to understand what other areas of criminal justice *The Sun* gets to decide?'

Terrified prison officials rapidly issued a Prison Service Instruction, warning governors that all activities had to 'meet the public acceptability test'. In the *Independent on Sunday* (25 January) Lord Ramsbotham called the new diktat 'lunacy' and quite reasonably asked, 'Who's going to be the judge? It was a gross overreaction. What the voluntary sector does in prisons is work to help people rehabilitate. If you say you really are trying to protect the public, you'll damage that, if you don't allow rehabilitation.'

For me the Comedy School had been a complete joy, albeit with considerable pressures. My staff were assiduous in choosing participants who would benefit or help others. I vividly remember one group where we had tipped the balance too far into the 'needy' group. Keith approached me two days into the programme head in hands saying that barely any of them would now speak to each other. Two participants had recently attempted suicide, one having been cut down only a week before. Another had spent most of this and previous sentences on the borderline of being sectioned under the Mental Health Act. I did seriously worry that we had given Keith a challenge too far. As it turned out we hadn't and by the end of the course the thoughts of the participants were not about suicide and self-harm but the terror of delivering stand-up to an audience of family and friends who could make the most experienced of stand-up comedians quiver.

As with anything in prison the programme was about a journey not a cure, a transition where relapse was the norm and the curse. This was amply illustrated in one vignette I will remember for a long time. Minutes before a performance I went backstage to wish the performers well and issue the 'break a leg' cliché. One pallid-looking young man turned to me with wide eyes and sweat on his brow and said in no uncertain terms, 'If I don't get my fucking methadone now I ain't going on that bleedin' stage.'

The Arts Alliance has survived Straw's attack and continues to battle against the odds and argue for the value of the arts in prisons. A report commissioned by the alliance in October 2011 gave empirical evidence that the arts can cut reoffending rates. The report was produced by the consultancy New Philanthropy Capital (NPC),and looked at a project called 'Only Connect'. It showed that of seventy-two offenders involved with the project, producing and performing in arts projects including theatre, film and music, and now released from prison, only fifteen had gone on to commit more offences, a reoffending rate of 25.9 per cent. Estimates using Ministry of Justice reoffending data, considering age, gender and time since release from prison, showed the reoffending rate would have been 57.5 per cent without the arts scheme, saving almost £150,000 for each offender who stopped committing crimes. Former Scotland Yard commissioner Lord Blair said the arts can 'have a transformative effect on a person's life, particularly for young people'. Such schemes 'have the potential to tackle deep-rooted problems' and 'this can help them turn away from crime and start to lead purposeful and positive lives'. Tim Robertson, the enthusiastic and charismatic chairman of the Arts Alliance, said: 'With a spiralling prison population, shocking rates of reoffending and steeply declining budgets, we urgently need to find new ways of working. The criminal justice sector needs to open its doors to arts organisations and find new ways of working in partnership with them.' Tim, who also works with the Koestler Trust, one of the best known prison arts charities, which has been awarding, exhibiting and selling artworks by offenders, detainees and secure patients for almost fifty years, is spot on. But will his views and those of Lords Blair and Ramsbotham and a host of practitioners be listened to in the prevailing climate?

It is a real possibility that the larger charities will be swallowed up by the large multinationals in what will outwardly be described as partnerships but which in reality will be annexation. The smaller organisations, especially those in the arts, may simply go to the wall as prison regimes contract and hard-nosed payment by results interventions dominate the sector. It may well be that trusts and foundations will continue to support them, but whether the prison system will continue to find space for them remains doubtful.

SEVEN

TRUSTS AND FOUNDATIONS

For the charitable trusts and foundations funding projects in criminal justice it has never been simply about giving money away. The Ministry of Justice has never had either the wherewithal or the strategic involvement fully to comprehend the benefit it has been receiving. There has also been a fundamental failure on the part of government to appreciate the body of knowledge held within these organisations, founded on hard data, evidence and evaluation. It was clear not just from the Green Paper but also from the general attitude to the trusts and foundations from both ministers and Ministry of Justice officials that they were seen as amateurs simply giving money away on a 'feel good' basis.

Nothing could have been further from the truth. They have a track record of funding based on informed judgement. They have also been risk takers, trialling new approaches across the criminal justice sector. Where organisations succeeded, the foundations would reward them with continued funding. Where they failed there would be constructive dialogue around alternatives. So, arguably, not only was the Big Society alive and well in prisons but so too was payment by results. The 2011 Green Paper tragically ignored the experience and expertise that the trusts and foundations possessed both individually and collectively. Here, uniquely, was an indispensable contribution to the positive development of offender rehabilitation from outside the prison service itself, implemented in both the prisons themselves and in the community, yet it was apparently invisible to those in power.

MONUMENT FOR BANK: MIND THE GAP

The Monument Trust, one of the Sainsbury Family Charitable Trusts founded by the late Simon Sainsbury, is one notable such organisation that has developed a long-term relationship with prisons and prison issues. The trust's donations to charitable causes over several decades represent one of the leading examples of sustained philanthropy in Britain. At the forefront of strategy and policy of funding in criminal justice has been Mark Woodruff, an executive with the trust. Self-effacing but with a quiet and inspiring passion, Mark has been proactive for many years in developing and supporting a range of initiatives not only in London prisons but across the criminal justice spectrum. He has challenged and nurtured many organisations and individuals. He has what is so lacking in Ministry of Justice officials: knowledge, understanding and corporate memory. He has demonstrated the true long-term, strategic value of charitable trusts and foundations and how well philanthropy can operate in such a challenging environment.

Although known for its focus on work within prisons and criminal justice, the trust's true aims are to divert young people away from prison in the first place and, if they do err, to seek to prevent their ever going back. One of its earliest associations was with HMYOI Feltham. As with everyone working with this difficult and complex institution, Monument was acutely aware of the problem of what was, and is still, described as 'churn', the rapid turnover of young men. They would be arrested and charged, remanded in custody, sent to trial and moved on once convicted. Many would repeat the cycle at the end of relatively short sentences. Many would linger at Feltham only if their trial was protracted. The opportunities therefore for meaningful intervention then, as today, were limited. Around 2000 when Monument became involved, charities such as Nacro were key players delivering interventions, funded by grants from central government. These were not the days of the competitive market place. Pressure groups such as the Howard League and the Prison Reform Trust were there, metaphorically, in the wings highlighting the problems but rightly, as befitted their status, not providing services. It was obvious to all how damaging the churn was and how such a difficult custodial environment prevented anyone doing anything meaningful. Valiant attempts were being made by various groups, including the Linbury Trust, another Sainsbury Family Charitable Trust, to build up a body of work and expertise to address the intractable problems of an institution that was struggling to be anything other than a remand factory.

At the time Feltham, like many establishments, had little idea of what work was being undertaken by the charitable sector within its walls. Few knew even just how many organisations were working with their inhabitants. Feltham eventually calculated that there were some sixty voluntary organisations operating there, which came as a shock to many officials. Voluntary sector coordinators were eventually appointed in jails and there were always senior managers responsible for regimes, but the work of the voluntary sector was neither strategic nor coordinated. Consequently there was considerable duplication, cherry-picking of candidates and self-selection by the prisoners themselves. Confident and articulate prisoners, and there were some, as well as those with internal and external advocacy could monopolise many activities. There were no calculations but a fair guess would see as few as 20 per cent of prisoners accessing 75 per cent of activities. There was a real danger at Feltham, as well as elsewhere, that there was an inverse relationship between need and access. If fault lay anywhere at such a difficult time it was with the establishments whose job it was to manage individuals through sentence plans and not those from outside desperate to meet gaps in prison regimes.

The disarray was not deliberate and the voluntary sector did not think ill of an establishment like Feltham which faced huge difficulties simply managing the work of the courts, the POA (which had a reputation at Feltham of not being entirely constructive) and the basic safety of young people. Resettlement was aspirational and a de facto contract was established between the establishment and the voluntary sector, which was regarded as a free resource doing what the public sector could only aspire to. Although there was a cost, which was never calculated, in facilitating the voluntary sector through staff time and prisoner access, there was no direct funding to support these organisations. At this time there was little pressure on targets and monitoring and the rules and regulations of what was allowed were still to follow. Nevertheless it was a time not to look a gift horse in the mouth.

Monument's first big strategic relationship and associated grant programme with an individual institution was with HMYOI Portland, a towering edifice of an institution built to hold soldiers captured in the Napoleonic Wars, on a peninsula of magnificent limestone to the south of Weymouth in Dorset. The original institution was opened in 1848 and held convicted adults. In the 1850s it supplied prisoners for transportation to Australia. In 1921 it was converted into a borstal and in 1998 re-roled as a Young Offender Institution. It was, and remains, a forbidding place where tall grey Victorian wings rise up from quarried limestone. One disused quarry provided a surreal sunken amphitheatre, at the base of which is a playing field. Being outside the main perimeter it was rarely used. It was accidental architecture of which Norman Foster would have been proud. For the young men from London, Bristol and south Wales housed there, it was as incongruous as it was possible to be with their experiences of urban life.

As with many initiatives, the relationship with Monument arose out of a highly critical inspectorate report in 2000 which highlighted a range of deficiencies, not least the absence of opportunities to prepare young people for release. Nacro had established a relationship with Portland and had resident full-time employees on site. It approached Monument with a view to addressing particular resettlement shortfalls identified by the inspectorate. It saw Monument as a significant funder with knowledge and expertise in the sector. This was the beginning of a substantial long-term relationship between a prison establishment, a voluntary sector service provider and a trust. Monument saw it as an opportunity to establish a template for positive future relationships and good practice in dealing with young offenders.

Initial work was with juveniles, those between fifteen and seventeen years of age. Those regarded as the most hard to reach were targeted first. There was no cherry-picking. This was work aimed at those with whom no one had succeeded in reducing their offending or the damage they were inflicting on their communities. At the time Portland benefitted from something relatively rare and unheard of now, an in-house psychology department, which worked out what the young men needed. Rigorous evaluation by Nacro's own research analysts began to show evidence that the initiative was reducing high reoffending rates and was having a positive effect on the economic and social well-being of communities. However, such was the fractured and competitive nature of research, and this is still the case with evidence now, findings and the value of the delivery itself were initially questioned rather than embraced and developed further. Nevertheless, the prison was emboldened in setting up its own resettlement service and a good working relationship with the Nacro project was agreed, still concentrating on ways to reach young men that others found hard to reach. Yet national measures about the benefit of such an imaginative approach and partnership at the time were prescriptive and unsubtle. Technical breaches of licence conditions became new offences and therefore failures. Nuances around the severity of offending and harm to individuals and communities were seen as too difficult to handle. Difficult and damaged young men leading chaotic and disordered lives were trying with support to improve themselves but found it impossible to get credit for incremental change. The fact that offending, like drug and alcohol abuse, is a chronic relapsing condition did not resonate across the criminal justice system.

The three-way partnership continued despite the internal and external frictions. A continuing catalyst were inspections every three or four years and subsequent reports by the Chief Inspector of Prisons which kept up the pressure to continue the work and which highlighted the partnership as a beacon for best practice. Then along came what is commonly described in the prison system as a 're-role', the change in an establishment's function in terms of, in this case, age, or as can also happen, gender. Portland was no longer to hold young men under eighteen.

The prison estate holding those under twenty-one has for many years been the source of vigorous debate. Although the English and Welsh prison system locks up more young people proportionately than anywhere else in Europe, the numbers remain a minority of those in the entire estate. The numbers themselves fluctuate according to a range of influences and the aim of keeping young people near to home has only ever been aspirational. The debate over whether under-eighteens should be kept in uniquely managed institutions or on split sites has been a Gordian knot for the Youth Justice Board since its inception. All sorts of factors come into play, not least cost. More funds have been available traditionally for under-eighteens and there have always been tensions on split sites over funding creep to the 18–21 year group. Governors of split sites have faced huge pressures managing well-resourced, juvenile populations alongside impoverished young offender regimes behind the same fence.

Whilst trusts and foundations have always understood the complexities of population management across the prison estate, they have found the processes involved in meeting prison procedures and the compromised results of their philanthropy at times frustrating and at other times plain galling. What happened at Portland was typical.

Monument had been funding the Nacro Portland programme to the tune of £120,000 a year. The programme employed case workers, outreach workers and secretarial support. It was a complete package. Evidence of the invisibility of the project to policy-makers however came when the re-role took place without informing, let alone consulting, Portland's most committed and long-standing benefactor. A substantial grant had been made to provide a lasting legacy with a resettlement project aimed at sixty of the most damaged and potentially violent child offenders. The re-role was not seen by Monument as the problem per se. It would have been perfectly possible to take the expertise and the learning to another establishment. The project had risen to the challenge of providing evidence-based interventions to a highly problematic group of young people. Monument argued strongly that it was the role of the Home Office policy-makers to look at the work in a wider context and place it elsewhere or incorporate it strategically into other work. The protestations were seen as the (so-called) third sector being reluctant to fit into the work of prisons. Ironically it was one of many examples of the reverse, the public sector failing to appreciate, support and inculcate its work into the mainstream. That the mainstream was more of a small trickle rather than a raging flood was perhaps part of the problem.

For the Monument Trust this was not the first and only time its funding fell victim to the change of function of an establishment. After seven years of long-term strategic funding to set up the Mainwaring Centre for intensive nurturing support to very vulnerable juveniles at HMYOI Huntercombe, in 2010 the prison was re-roled to become a Category C prison for adult males.

Similarly, until 2006, Bulwood Hall in Essex had been a female establishment with both adult and juvenile females. Monument funded yet another project, a replication of its successful collaboration with the Aldeburgh Foundation on creative arts at the Carlford Unit for serious male juvenile offenders, but this time for young women. In 2006, without consultation and mid-project, Bulwood Hall closed down as an establishment housing women and girls and reopened as another Category C adult male establishment.

On both occasions the strategic population management decisions were sound and based on impossible predictions of the future size and nature of the prison population. What was missing was consultation with philanthropic investors. The gift horse was being repeatedly looked in the mouth.

Back at Portland the decision was taken with Nacro to adjust the programme for young offenders to these eighteen- to twenty-year-olds. This three-year phase demonstrated similar strong results. Despite being older, the problems of this particular group were even more entrenched. At first glance the programme was having little or no effect on reoffending rates, but Nacro were able to demonstrate that the seriousness of reof-fending was being significantly reduced. In particular, it highlighted the problem of young men coming back to prison for trivial and even unin-tended breaches of licence – not for mugging but for being late for an appointment. Some of the prison service's measurements were too crude and did not give young people credit for progress in their lives. Without that credit, they saw their own efforts as futile.

It was clear that there was much to do and much to learn with projects such as this. But one problem dogged the process of continuing improvement and development: short-term corporate memory. During this collaboration at Portland one Nacro case worker and a project support officer remained in post for almost twelve years. Little else was a constant. The in-house psychology department was slowly disbanded as funding became centralised. Whilst governors grew increasingly supportive of the Nacro project, then, as now, they rarely stayed in post for more than an average of twenty months, and the acceleration towards the burgeoning leviathan of bureaucracy known as NOMS was only just beginning.

The result was that, as with a number of other voluntary-funded programmes, there was never anyone around long enough to sustain the narrative of the programme's genesis and benefits, to hold the knowl-edge about its development, what mistakes were made and what lessons should be learned. Apart from rare individuals who stayed the course, as at Portland, corporate memory was only being embedded in the trusts and foundations, a fact that was not recognised by the prison service. Knowledge and expertise grew in the sector, emanating from clear guidelines and years of experience in ensuring endowments of charitable trusts were spent wisely, strategically and to demonstrable effect. Yet, with rare exceptions, the philanthropy of trusts and foundations was all too readily seen as random, well meaning, gift giving, based on whim. Nothing could have been further from the truth.

At Portland something was developed that was demonstrably effec-tive and inexpensive. From this one institution alone, the scheme spread regionally and (with the Depaul Trust) in London a high-quality bank of volunteers for the intensive befriending and mentoring of young men with high hopes but still facing great personal and systemic challenges following release was formed. These were networks that were impossible to buy, involving communities, charities and prisons: the Big Society at work. The Portland project was praised by successive governors over their relatively short tenure and by inspectors on regular visits. Despite its low relative cost and high economic benefit, it was not widely replicated. And despite the strong commitment of the prison's own management and resettlement services and the dedication of the local Nacro team, the charity as a whole decided to proceed no further with what it once described as its 'flagship resettlement programme'. Organisations like Nacro now look elsewhere for programmes that resound to the new mantra of payment by results and social impact bonds, losing sight of the fact that it has presided for some twelve years over something that was achieving solid results and social impact. The current round of Monument's funding for Nacro's programme finished in summer 2011 and it is now left wondering what value Nacro placed upon sustained investment of some £1.25 million. Nacro, as a vital third party in demonstrating what an enlightened consortium uniting public services and the voluntary sector could achieve for young ex-prisoners, did not consult its partners, despite strong representations from the prison, by now long convinced of how crucial the programme was to its success. Thankfully, with new investment from the governor and Monument, it has been taken under the wing of a charity pioneering successful new approaches in the UK from South Africa, Khulisa.

GUARDING THE GUARDS

It was not only prisoner projects that were being supported. It has frequently been observed that behind many successful local prison initiatives has been a committed and passionate prison officer. This is despite the fact that prison officers are recruited without a requirement for basic educational qualifications and placed in post after minimal training. In England and Wales the length of training is barely six weeks. In Norway it is two years and to degree level.

It was against this backdrop in 2007 that the then governor of HMP Leeds, supported by an imaginative personnel and training manager with a distinguished academic career outside the prison service, had approached the Monument Trust with a proposal to add on to the basic and continuing training and development for prison officers a programme for a foundation and even higher degrees. The proposal was based around Leeds Metropolitan University and was an attempt to motivate and professionalise a group of prison officers from across the Yorkshire region. A deal with the Home Office was reached whereby the prison service would select and facilitate a group of officers to undertake a foundation degree course with the Monument Trust paying the university tuition fees. The trust calculated that the effective value of the officer's time equated to the cost of the fees. In other words it was an arrangement by which there was joint funding by both organisations – a relatively rare occurrence given that trusts and foundations generally provided almost everything up front. It was also an ideal opportunity for Monument to demonstrate its commitment to improvements across the criminal justice system by funding an initiative for staff, in the knowledge and expectation that it would improve the lot of prisoners. On the same basis, there was also to be a degree for prison managers responsible for the leadership of officers in work for the resettlement and rehabilitation of offenders.

The first cohort of around a dozen staff was typical. Becoming a prison officer had not been a lifetime career choice. Many had done other work but had drifted into the profession by the force of local economic circumstances. They had been frustrated by entering a profession where many of their co-workers were less than enthusiastic about, and in some cases actively hostile to, the role. Here was an ideal opportunity to develop their skills, gain real qualifications and professional development.

A wide-ranging, holistic, course based around offender management was developed. The aim was for it to be delivered anywhere across the country through the regional university network, which was sustained by Leeds Metropolitan University. In other words it would be a pilot programme that, if successful, could be rolled out across the service as a way of truly professionalising some of its key staff. Whilst the time commitment of prison officers is never a free resource, Monument was optimistic that the government would recognise the benefit of the initiative, continue to allow for contribution of time in kind, and that available national higher education funding could be utilised as well, as a way of minimising the direct cost to the prison service. It was a bold local initiative in all the best traditions of partnership working. Staff from six prisons provided an initial cohort of forty who passed the basic foundation degree course. It was not all plain sailing. Not all governors were as forward thinking as the governor of Leeds and they did not always allow their staff the time for study and work preparation in work time, oblivious to the potential greater benefit to themselves and the wider service, or the outside investment they were receiving.

Nevertheless, a substantial trained and motivated staff resource was built up. Some went on to study for full Bachelor's degrees and even Master's degrees. Each reported the positive effects on other officers and the improvement of team-working in their prisons. But instead of this being the start of a major national initiative, like so many things it hit the buffers; and £200,000 later Monument again found itself questioning the apparent futility of yet another otherwise successful initiative. Senior staff moved on and the bureaucracy at the centre was incapable of grasping the opportunity, even when further investment was offered. Nor, as was proved in an audience granted by a senior NOMS director to a senior executive at Monument, was there even an awareness of the existence of the earlier initiative which had actually brought credit to the prison service for its imagination in delivering such a scheme.

The trusts and foundations face a dilemma as local initiatives become subsumed in a competitive tendering process dominated by complex consortia controlled by private sector international companies. Whilst some trusts and foundations would not see involvement of commercial companies in criminal justice initiatives as a problem per se, many are bound morally and legally by the original principles of their endowments to support only charitable, not for profit ventures. Where there are consortia arrangements between not for profit charitable service providers and commercial companies, it is likely that trusts and foundations will be compelled to keep away from such deals. None would be willing to become arms of government, nor to be mere piggy-banks for government as public expenditure contracts. There is, in this complex mix, a danger that trusts and foundations will be accused of not engaging with the payment by results agenda. Payment by results, effectiveness of funding, success, and return on investment have been the watchword of trusts and foundations since their inception. A vast knowledge and expertise on strategic and meaningful funding has been built up over decades.

TRUSTS AND FOUNDATIONS WORKING TOGETHER: THE CORSTON REPORT

I have had the privilege over the last few years of being a trustee of one of the many trusts involved in the sector, the Pilgrim Trust. It was founded in 1930 by American philanthropist Edward Harkness with a £2 million grant. Around 60 per cent of its annual allocation of funds is given to preservation projects – buildings, churches and their contents, artefacts or documents. The remaining funds are allocated to social welfare causes, particularly alcohol and drugs projects in prison and outside. I have seen at first hand, and been part of, an exhaustive analysis of funding requests and allocation of resources based on all the principles that appear to have been reinvented as part of the payment by results mantra. Trusts and foundations work together and share information with each other and with funding applicants. The object of the exercise is to make best use, in various arenas ranging from church preservation to prisoner resettlement, of available funds. Whilst there may be de facto competition between bodies seeking to do the same thing, many are often brought together in the bidding process as a way of pooling effort and expertise to bring better results.

One of the best examples of trusts and foundations not only working together but galvanising government and service providers was the work of the Corston Independent Funders Consortium (CIFC).

The Corston Report was published in March 2007. Jean Corston is a Labour politician and was the first ever female chair of the Parliamentary Labour Party. She became Baroness Corston in 2005. She was commissioned to produce a report into vulnerable women in the criminal justice system. The report outlined 'the need for a distinct radically different, visibly led, strategic, proportionate, holistic, woman-centred, integrated approach'. There was great expectation that the report would be a catalyst for change. Its recommendations were sensible, cost effective and above all contained a blueprint for dealing with women in the criminal justice system in a more humane and constructive way. There was a deafening silence from within NOMS. The leviathan took stock, had meetings and produced discussion papers. *Yes Minister* prevailed.

Teresa Elwes of the Bromley Trust was one of the most passionate in the sector about women's issues and took the initiative in pulling together some fifteen trusts to call for the full implementation of all the Corston recommendations. A formal letter to government was met with the usual platitudes but little action. The lack of response galvanised the trusts into forming a coalition.

The Corston report provided the perfect vehicle for joint action. It was not because the trusts were solely interested in women's issues but that the report provided a concrete action plan for a particularly marginalised group within the criminal justice system. Here was a 'bite-sized chunk' that gave the trusts the opportunity to challenge the government's lethargy and inaction. The trusts also saw a real opportunity for investment in work and projects that could make a tangible difference.

The Corston report provided an opportunity for a different approach from the trusts and foundations. In the light of the report some twenty-two trusts eventually collaborated to form the CIFC. It was decided to fund and appoint a coordinator for the work and Antonia Bance, with a background in third sector delivery, was appointed. She operated under the auspices of the Prison Reform Trust. It was Antonia's job to engage with policy-makers, civil servants and ministers. She opened a dialogue with the Ministry of Justice's Women's Policy Group. At that time, responsibility for prisons lay with Maria Eagle. She also had responsibility for women's issues and equality generally and this role fortunately resonated with everything in the Corston Report. Ms Eagle became proactive on the issue, eager to leave her mark on an administration which was clearly in its dying days.

Somewhere in the complexities of Whitehall funding she acquired £15.6 million to set up a series of 'one-stop shops', places where women could access a range of support services ranging from housing and employment to help with drug, alcohol and mental health issues, as recommended by Corston. It was apparent that the money was a special Treasury allocation and not part of the strategic thinking or funding of the Ministry of Justice. It was the initiative of a single minister which coincided with the agenda of the twenty-two trusts and foundations. So almost by accident the CIFC was raised high on the ministerial agenda.

It was decided to spend the money in two separate tranches, with anything up to £500,000 to be given to small charitable organisations already delivering these women's services. The process was not to be commissioning or contracting or competitive tendering but rapid grant giving within tight time scales in order to spend government money. There was concern within the Ministry of Justice that the equivalent Women's Policy Group in NOMS did not have the knowledge or experience to orchestrate grant giving on such a large scale.

The ministry therefore approached the CIFC and asked it to nominate individuals from the trusts and foundations to assist with the process. Eryl Foulkes of the Tudor Trust and Georgina Nayler of the Pilgrim Trust were nominated and sat in on the decision-making processes. Their knowledge was invaluable and their experience in understanding the nature and structure of many of the organisations delivering services was quickly recognised. Understanding the commercial limitations around accounts and financial planning of some of these organisations was as important as evaluating their ability to deliver services as one could not happen without the other.

With the second tranche of funding CIFC was asked to participate again. Cathy Stancer from Lankelly Chase was added to the secondees from the trusts and foundations and the level of work was such that the task was split into two groups. It was during this second round that the ministry came to realise that within the time-honoured rule of annualisation (spending of all the allocated money within the financial year) there was likely to be an underspend. Some of the money had been allocated to a capital subhead as it was thought there would be a need to construct extra facilities to deliver the services. This was an inaccurate assumption and, as such, capital monies would go unspent. Unless it was spent by the end of the financial year it would go back to the Treasury and would not be carried over to the following year.

Some £1 million was at stake and a deal was struck with the trusts and foundations whereby the money would be given to CIFC if it was matched by it. The trusts, not being bound by Treasury rules, would then have some £2 million to spend on much-needed services over the subsequent twelve months. The government saw it as a way of levering in third sector funding. It was a win-win situation despite the imaginative interpretation of Treasury rules.

Thus was borne the Women's Diversionary Fund (WDF). This time the independent funders were in the majority in the spending decisions. Two Ministry of Justice members were seconded to the team, one of whom was from the NOMS women's strategy unit. The funds from the CIFC and the government were held by Lankelly Chase, which acted as banker and monitor of the process.

It was not all plain sailing. On the face of it there was considerable cash available to organisations which needed it to deliver vital services to a marginalised group for whom there were huge potential benefits, not only in reducing the size of the women's prison population but from diverting others from custody, as well as greatly improving the lives of vulnerable individuals and as such creating safer communities. The money was, however, short term, effectively to cover an eighteen-month period. Increasing the level of service delivery meant recruiting more people with the right skills, a process which itself could take four months, even if the skills were available in the right place. Many of the organisations lacked the basic HR infrastructure to deliver a larger organisation so quickly. Lack of proper accounting, financial planning, training or HR policies proved problematic. The sorts of cash injections that were made would have been difficult to absorb properly over five years let alone over a few short months. There was a need for Treasury money to be seen to be spent first, with the trust money to follow. In effect it was a pooled budget, but politics ruled over pragmatism. Spending took priority over delivery.

The nature of this process was such that it became very difficult to show what affect these services were having on reoffending. They were short-term, with largely chaotic individuals who required long-term engagement. The work was not being orchestrated through a long-term NOMS strategy. The target group was not only those in the prison system but those at risk of offending, thus making evaluation even more difficult. NOMS did instigate a monitoring system using the seven resettlement pathways that had been identified as key to success. The projects themselves were left to choose their own objectives within the pathway criteria. The statistical validity and accuracy of the data was questionable. One group claimed 100 per cent improvement in drug and alcohol treatment, an unlikely result to put it mildly. Measurement generally was inconsistent and not against any validated scales. NOMS number crunching continued in the usual vein – counting for counting's sake.

It is planned that this fund will operate until April 2012, thereafter commercial processes will kick in and organisations wishing to deliver the services will have to tender for the privilege. It is likely that some of the more successful ones will partner private companies like SERCO and G4S. Some may become sub-contractors to the big players. There is a real danger that the private sector providers will cherry-pick the services and existing providers according to where the best profit can be made. Many of the providers delivering excellent services to women but with poor commercial infrastructures will go to the wall. It would be possible for the government to put in place safeguards to ensure the right balance of commercialism and altruism and that risk is properly shared, but it is more likely that the payment by results mantra will dominate, whether or not anyone will ever fully understand quite how it all works. Payment by results may soon become the criminal justice equivalent of the banking sector's credit default swaps and mutualised debt obligations – bringing discredit and ruin in its wake.

To further complicate matters what the centres have needed to achieve has changed from a largely holistic approach to improving the general well-being of women, reducing the risk of offending and diverting women from custody, to a very simple and pragmatic reduction in the female prison population. This will require cooperation from sentencers and from probation trusts, whose relationship with the WDF has been inconsistent. Some trusts have embraced the work and cooperated to huge benefit. Others have seen the small organisations delivering the services as direct competition and a threat to their survival. It is for the Ministry of Justice to ensure a collaborative approach across the board despite the onset of competitive tendering and the very real dangers it presents.

WRESTLING WITH THE LEVIATHAN

Trusts were frustrated that were there too many people being locked up and that little was being done to address the problem. They regarded NOMS as an ineffective bureaucracy and felt that the scatter gun approach to funding prison projects was too ineffective and often poorly supported by individual prisons and governors. It was felt that NOMS in general and prisons in particular were not making the best use of the considerable sums that were being provided.

Much was being made within NOMS of the principles of end to end offender management based on the assessed needs of prisoners. There was much talk of partnership with the voluntary and community sector and the bureaucracy expanded as new departments were set up to ensure proper liaison. There were as ever units in NOMS duplicated by units in the Ministry of Justice. There was, however, no evidence that the trusts could see of any strategy. Above all, the trusts felt that they were being regarded simply as a cash cow operated by well-meaning but naive individuals and boards. Nothing could have been further from the truth and the professionalism of the trusts and the inexperience of NOMS shone through as matters progressed.

Outside the Corston initiative voluntary and community organizations were tripping over each other in their enthusiasm to initiate programmes and projects and engage with prisoners. There was clear evidence that many prisoners fell through the gaps as the low-hanging fruit was picked repeatedly. Many governors were still unaware of the numbers of organisations that were active in their prisons and nor were they aware of how, on what basis and by whom they were funded. NOMS quite reasonably wanted to exercise some control. A free-for-all was inappropriate at many levels. It was important that interventions or programmes did no harm. It was important too that the individuals delivering them were appropriately trained and supervised. Funding needed to be understood and propriety in expenditure ensured. Access to a wide range of prisoners was vital. As was access according to need. Above all, whatever was delivered had to fit logically and strategically with everything else.

Unfortunately, NOMS was failing to deliver these principles with its own interventions, let alone those provided by the voluntary and community sector. At the heart of it all was the process of needs assessment. Identifying and meeting need had been at the heart of its objectives at the birth of NOMS. Ostensibly there were a variety of systems in place which provided the basis for such a process. There were education assessments, medical assessments, drug treatment assessments. The list was endless and many prisoners felt themselves sentenced to assessments. They were also frustrated at the repetition of the process as they moved prisons or returned to prison, as many did after only a short time back in their communities.

Any attempt to deliver an overarching strategy was hampered by the absence of an IT structure. Until well into the twenty-first century the prison service and NOMS was operating with probably the oldest free-standing IT system on the planet. The Local Inmate Database (LIDS) had been set up in the late 1980s and little progress was made for decades in improving it. The National Offender Management Information System (known as C-Nomis) was eventually designed to drag the service kicking and screaming into the twentieth, not the twenty-first, century, but was initially a financial and strategic debacle as described in a report from the Public Accounts Committee (PAC). The committee described it as a singular example of poor project management. Scheduled for delivery in January 2008 at a cost of £234 million, it was stopped in August 2007 because the costs had trebled.

C-Nomis was originally designed as a single database for end-to-end offender management across the prison service and the national probation service. According to the report this was ambitious but technically feasible, but NOMS was accused of losing control and completely underestimating the technical complexity and the need to standardise ways of working.

The programme was also described as suffering from poor planning and financial management, inadequate supplier management and too little control over changes. Over the first three years there was no monitoring of costs or progress, in part because the senior responsible owner had no relevant training or experience. The project board, the NOMS board and the Home Office senior management only became aware of the true cost and progress in May 2007, and NOMS was unable to provide full details on where the £161 million spent up to October 2007 went.

Edward Leigh MP, chair of the PAC, said: 'This committee has become inured to the dismal procession of government IT failures which have passed before us; but even we were surprised by the extent of the failure of C-Nomis, the ambitious project to institute a single database to manage individual offenders through the prison and probation systems.' He added that 'there was not even a minimum level of competence in the planning and execution of this project', and described it as a 'shambles'.

But it was not simply a matter of adequate IT. There was silo thinking and an inability to put the prisoner at the heart of the process. Those serving less than twelve months were ignored, despite being responsible for most crime and returning to prison most rapidly. Interventions were wrongly targeted and money was wasted.

A prime example of the inefficiency was in drug treatment. There had been considerable improvements in the delivery of clinical services in drug treatment. It was now accepted that getting people off drugs or at least treating their addiction properly saved lives and reduced crime. Detoxification, methadone maintenance and a range of clinical interventions available outside prison were now being delivered in prisons. There was also better interaction between clinical treatment inside and outside prison. Some of it had been made necessary by a legal challenge. A large number of prisoners had received compensation after a claim that treatment in the community should continue in prison after sentence. The budget for such treatment in prisons lay with Primary Care Trusts. The budget for the range of drug treatment programmes and the assessment process known as CARAT was at the behest of the prison service. CARAT (the Counselling, Assessment, Referral, Advice and Throughcare service) was the key to drug treatment service in prisons for prisoners aged over eighteen. The budget and management however lay with the operational side of the prison service, overseen by a department which seemed to change its name annually. The type, nature and location of drug treatment programmes defied logic. Prisons delivered programmes based on historical accident and who shouted loudest, rather than on prisoner need and a cohesive strategy. Prisoners were as baffled as governors and often sought transfer to other prisons merely to repeat courses they had received earlier in their sentence. There was little available for the many thousands with combined drug and mental health problems and even less for those with learning disabilities or speech and language problems. There was virtually nothing for those with alcohol problems despite increasing public concern over alcohol-related street and domestic violence.

A report was commissioned by the Offender Health Division in 2008 from accountants Price Waterhouse Coopers into the whole question of expenditure on and delivery of drug treatment. It concluded that the split between clinical treatment and drug programmes was illogical, inefficient and not based on recognised treatment models outside prisons. It was the CARAT process which best illustrated the problem. It had been developed internally by the prison service in the mid-1990s and whilst at the time it was a laudable approach to assessing and delivering against need, the fact that it continued at odds with the rest of the drug treatment world is testament to the isolationist policy in the delivery of non-clinical drug treatment. Over fifteen years some £150 million was spent on the process. To date the process has never been evaluated.

All of this rang hollow with trusts eager to use their endowments to best effect in a field of social welfare where there was huge need. As well as the absence of IT and an effective strategy, prisoner churn, the rapid turnover between courts, prisons and the community, further complicated the matter and further undermined the ability of the service to deliver effective interventions. Yet again it was the voluntary sector which stepped in, in the guise of the Prison Reform Trust, which constructed and attempted to have delivered a 'Prisoner passport'. This highly logical move to produce a simple document which would record everything that a prisoner had or had not done during his sentence. It was yet another testament to the fact that end to end offender management was but a myth.

The trusts felt that policy-makers were unwilling or unable to engage constructively. Community Links in Prisons (CLINKS) had been set up as an umbrella body but there was a feeling that it was mere window dressing.

Yet another indication of the way in which the service did not engage was the Pilgrim Trust's support of a Shelter housing project at HMP Leeds. Over £2 million was put into the project by the Pilgrim Trust. Not only was the establishment unappreciative, it was at times obstructive and particularly so when the trust attempted to evaluate the project. Evaluation was important to the trust in properly delivering against the aims of the endowment. It should also have been in accord with the aims of NOMS to deliver the 'what works' agenda. Approaches to the establishment and the regional manager to support the principles and the costs of such evaluation were effectively ignored. The trust tendered for, paid for and delivered its own evaluation. Faced with equivocal results and a general lack of cooperation in all that was trying to be delivered the project was abandoned by the trust in 2009.

A fundamental question remains for 2012. What will be the relationship between the trusts and foundations when the market kicks in, not only for these women's services but for all interventions? Many believe that the collaboration between WDF and the CIFC has been a real victory for partnership working despite the lack of long-term strategic thinking.

Yet another example of the commitment of trusts and foundations and the voluntary sector to research and evaluation was the publication in April 2010 by New Philanthropy Capital of *Measuring Together: Improving prisoner's family ties: Piloting a shared measurement approach*.

Funded by yet another of the Sainsbury Family Charitable Trusts, the Indigo Trust, it looked to evaluate the work around prisoners and their contact with families. Identified by the NOMS as one of the key components of successful reintegration into communities, such work has traditionally received little government funding or centrally funded evaluation. Many prisoners receive no visits at all or visits tail off over sentences as relationships break down. Prisoners who are visited by a relative are significantly less likely to reoffend within a year of release than those who receive no visits. This emanates from significantly improved chances of finding employment and housing.

Many charities, often funded by trusts and foundations, work with prisoners and their families to build and maintain these relationships. They provide a whole range of services especially visitors' centres. However, measuring the difference these activities make is difficult. Outcomes can be very intangible and have complex links with other factors such as health and drug treatment. They are an anathema to the target culture.

NPC worked with six charities to understand how different activities could improve family relationships, and how this could be measured. This report recommends how government, funders and charities could strengthen measurement in the sector and help to improve family relationships. It did not mention any business opportunities.

So is the government really serious about the Big Society or is it simply about Big Business? Is the gift horse about to be scared off into the hills, and in all of this will there be room for Branstaff?

Branstaff Jacobs is a thoughtful and engaging 55-year-old south Londoner who came out of prison in 2008 after serving a six-and-a-half year sentence. After a lifetime of offending and many years in prison (we had crossed paths in both Belmarsh and Brixton) he decided it was time to stop his own offending and do what he could to prevent others spiralling out of control. Living off housing benefit and jobseeker's allowance, he moved from being a client to become a voluntary worker. Subsequently he opted to do voluntary work with a range of local charities working with ex-offenders. Despite his successful rapport with clients based on shared life experiences and results in finding them accommodation, he was unable to secure employment with the very groups designed and funded for this. His was an effective unpaid internship, but not perhaps the one Nick Clegg was focusing upon in early 2011 as he promulgated his social mobility agenda. Eventually Branstaff decided to set up his own business finding accommodation for ex-offenders. Conscious of a critical world, he achieved funding for and successfully achieved an NVQ level 3 in Information, Advice and Guidance Services. He is a man as thirsty for personal development as he is passionate about putting something back into society.

His own experiences leaving prison in 2008 had served him well. Whilst serving his sentence he, like so many men, ended his relationship with his partner, leaving him homeless on release. Night one was on a friend's sofa. Then, after contacting St Giles Trust, a charity specialising in training and accommodation services for people coming out of prison, he was found a room – which he described as smaller and more cramped than the cell he had just left. Declining the offer, he continued sofa surfing until an encounter with an estate agent who supported him through the housing benefit system into his own flat in Thornton Heath. His analysis of the interactions between himself, accommodation providers and organisations designed to connect the two was reflective and poignant. He saw the charities as primarily concerned with providing clients for landlords rather than providing vulnerable people with places not just to live but to thrive – what he called a 'factory service'. He might just as well have been describing the potential subtext to payment by results, i.e. a target culture of getting people into beds as quickly as possible rather than examining the complex needs of offenders coming back into the community.

Branstaff maintains his operation through housing benefit and jobseeker's allowance. He has managed to garner some support from a small charity based in Kennington called Change Up, of which I am a voluntary director. This gives him a base from which to work plus some business mentoring, IT and support for his day-to-day activities. He gives himself three years to get properly set up. He receives referrals from prison and probation as well as the specialist organisations for which he used to volunteer. Clients receive his contact details and he meets them – very often literally – at the prison gate. He assists them through the financial maze of signing on and crisis loans and does his best to steer away the nefarious influences from people's pasts which can be the unwitting downfall of so many. Breaking away from negative peer groups both geographically and intellectually can be the hardest part of release for many. Building up new and positive peer groups can be even tougher. He has built up his own network of estate agents and will personally support people through interviews and paperwork. He will sort out tenancy agreements and, importantly, ensure that any housing benefit goes straight to housing rather than pub landlords or, worse, drug dealers. He keeps in touch with the most vulnerable but admits his personal and practical limitations in the processes. He estimates he deals with around five to seven people per week and since starting his work has found accommodation for more than 150 individuals. His immediate personal ambition is to pay his own rent and to have an income.

How many potential Branstaffs are out there it is impossible to say. Do they have a future? They have their critics, who focus on results, professional qualifications, ticked boxes and value for money, as does Branstaff. In a compassionate society we would hope that Branstaff could flourish and be seen as part of the solution rather than part of the problem. Just as he may be sucked into a larger charitable body, so too may the larger charitable bodies be sucked into the multinationals. Localism subsumed by commercialism.

Multimillion-pound regional contracts cleverly constructed by corporate lawyers will cleanse local communities of Branstaffs. Will that deliver reduced reoffending or an increased share price for G4S? We will need to be very careful. If charities are forced to live off earned income, as many are currently having to do, they will cease to have a future. If they survive on earned income they will cease to have the primary function for which they were set up. They will in effect cease to be charities. If they are to innovate and challenge they will need philanthropy. Philanthropy needs them as an outlet for endowments. Trustees in some trusts are taking the decision to 'spend out', still according to the terms of the original endowment, and whilst this might have short-term benefit it is unlikely to benefit the respective sectors in the long term. Reasons for such decisions will vary but maintaining an endowment through the vagaries of economic markets has proved very difficult and this, coupled with the effective privatisation of the sector, makes such decisions difficult to criticise. Politicians tampering with charity law do so at their peril. Recent changes effectively making government services charitable services do not augur well. If charities are to function they must do so independently. If the new world removes that independence and if they are forced to become an arm of government they will cease to engage or simply 'bail out'. In the long term income will be lost forever to the sector and the true cost of delivery through large contracts let to large commercial enterprises will not be seen for years to come. It will be a repeat public-private partnerships debacle. Trusts and foundations by their very nature will not threaten or blackmail. They will continue to make long-term strategic decisions. They will try and be the oil in the wheels of change and innovation; but if they cannot then the funds will migrate from criminal justice to churches and paintings and even that will not be forever.

EIGHT

CORRUPTION

Is there corruption in prisons? Is the Pope of a certain religious persuasion, and do bears defecate in the woods? We should ask why wouldn't there be corruption in prisons. After all it is fairly common in many other areas of life and after recent scandals around the complex relationships between politicians, the police and the media one might say that in some areas of life it is rife. In the UK we like to think that it is the problem of other countries, primarily the ones we tend to be inherently prejudiced against such as Nigeria, Russia and North Korea. The list goes on, as indeed does corruption. India most recently has seen hunger strikes, civil disobedience and a government reacting many steps behind public opinion to bring in tough legislation to tackle what the general public are beginning to say is unacceptable.

Corruption comes in many forms. Some we readily accept as criminal and wrong. Others make us more uncomfortable because they are activities that often come too close to home. Transparency International is the world's leading non-governmental anti-corruption organisation. It raises awareness of the issue, promotes legal reform and practical measures to combat corruption, and has set out its own view of corruption's various components.

Bribery is the most obvious and well understood. Rebekah Brooks, former News International chief executive, in her infamous exchange in 2003 with a Commons Select Committee said that she had paid police officers for information. Andy Coulson, her then boss and subsequent media advisor to Prime Minister David Cameron, interrupted and reassured the assembled MPs that they did so only within the law. It took eight years for someone to acknowledge that there are no circumstances whereby a police officer can be paid for anything other than his employment. Transparency International (TI) points out that bribery does not have to be cash and that gifts and hospitality fit easily and logically into the corruption definition. A fine meal in an expensive restaurant or a stay at an expensive health farm would fit the bill if there was a perceived advantage resulting for the donor.

TI also highlights collusion as a form of corruption, where groups of people conspire, often commercially for communal financial gain. Government watchdogs such as the Competition Commission were set up to expose and regulate cartels. Other definitions include something which increasingly characterises Whitehall but receives scant attention: conflict of interest. Former ministers and government mandarins migrate from public sector appointments with considerable influence and procurement power to private sector directorships in related companies. Imposition of three- or six-month delays before allowing such appointments serve only to allow for long vacations before the arduous and well paid new position takes effect. TI defined 'Revolving Door' as a corruption category where officials move between the public and private sectors. They omitted the fact that these days the movement is one-way from public to private as Whitehall is 'slimmed down' and government contracts go out to the Big Society.

TI spotlighted cronyism or nepotism, citing the nation's honours system as being under regular review for evidence of such activity. MPs after the expenses scandal were finally barred from the long-term practice of employing family members as secretaries or researchers (though not for employing the family members of their fellow MPs). Some fell foul of employing their children where there was no evidence of work actually being done. But, hand on heart, how many of us have or would use undue influence were we able to get our offspring employment in the current economic climate?

MPs' untoward activities were also readily included in TI's fraud definition, citing the expenses scandal, which for foreign countries placed
the UK firmly alongside Nigeria, India and Russia in the international
corruption league table. Interestingly, TI identified lobbying as a corruption category, arguing that access and influence can become too high
and too significant. Lobbying in the UK has become a growth industry
and companies presumably measure their success by just how high they
can reach and how significant their influence can be. Three months
before becoming Prime Minister in 2010 David Cameron said commercial lobbying was 'the next big scandal waiting to happen'. He added,
'It had tainted our politics for too long' and was 'an issue that exposes
the far-too-cosy relationship between politics, government, business and
money'. Less than two years later, at the Conservative Party autumn
conference, lobbying companies Bell Pottinger, Fleishman-Hilliard and
Lansons, to name but a few, were all high-profile event sponsors. It is a
difficult circle to square.

Illegal disclosure of information and misuse of information technology was also on the TI list, and fits nicely with phone and computer
hacking, seemingly inevitable components in recent years of 'news' gathering. Vote rigging, money laundering and abuse of authority completed
TI's exhaustive and illuminating list.

It would be fair to say that corruption, like love, is all around. But
do we take it seriously enough or just hide from it on the basis that only
he who is without sin can cast the first stone. Nationally our record of
action is not good. The Serious Fraud Office (SFO), or Serious Farce
Office as *Private Eye* christened it, has an inauspicious record, not least
in its dealings with BAE Systems. The company was accused of illegal
financial dealings with Saudi Arabia with slush funds and bribery to the
value of £60 million. The SFO investigated only to announce in 2006
that it was stop the inquiry, 'to safeguard national and international
security'. There was uproar and allegations in the media of corruption
on a grand scale. A judicial review of the decision by the SFO to drop
the investigation was granted on 9 November 2007 and the High Court

ruled that the SFO 'acted unlawfully' by dropping its investigation. *The Times* described the ruling as 'one of the most strongly worded judicial attacks on government action' which condemned how ministers 'buckled' to 'blatant threats that Saudi cooperation in the fight against terror would end unless the ... investigation was dropped.' The SFO appealed to the Lords and won, leaving a bitter taste in the mouths of many commentators. It had not been the first and was not the last controversy around the business dealings of BAE Systems.

On a smaller scale many members of the public remain confused why some MPs went to prison over the expenses scandal, some paid money back and others were granted the view that their activities, an anathema to the man in the street, were within the rules.

Is corruption merely in the eye of the beholder? If we promote family and friends are we merely offering a helping hand whilst for politicians and multinationals it is nepotism? If we benefit by a small amount of money is it merely a perk but bribery if it is enough for a holiday? Are we in denial, scared or ignorant?

The prison service is most definitely in denial. It would be astonishing if there was not a corruption problem in prisons. Have we not perfectly constructed an environment where corruption could only flourish? Corruption is crime and crime will proliferate where four things come together: opportunity, motive, gain and low risk of capture.

Prisons house many different people: some difficult and damaged, some chaotic and disordered. In terms of clinical analysis by specialists, most agree that 25 per cent of prisoners meet the definition of psychopaths, with some 75 per cent passing the test for having some kind of antisocial personality disorder. If we examine the various definitions of a psychopath we see words and phrases like irresponsible; lack of empathy, guilt or remorse; pathological lying; manipulative; egocentric; and descriptions of people persistently violating social norms. Do not psychopaths and corruption therefore fit hand in glove? Psychopathic tendencies are not unique to prisons and we could all reflect on them and people in our own workplace. How many of us have not worked, or still work, for a raging psychopath? Individuals will not be consistent in the way they behave, changing for better or worse over time and space. But in prison we have very significant concentrations of such people confined for long periods in a total institution – one in which they are completely isolated.

Having brought together an agglomeration of such people in one (often poorly designed, old and dilapidated) environment, we add the toxic mix of drug and alcohol addiction, poor mental health as well as all the components of social exclusion. We then select a workforce to look after them that on the briefest of examinations is highly unlikely to cope with the pressures of such a complex and demanding environment. An applicant for the post of prison officer does not require the basic minimum standard of education, i.e. five GCSEs A–C. He or she, if selected, receives a nugatory six weeks training, gets paid a pittance and is then inculcated into a disaffected workforce as part of a nebulous organisation that no one identifies with. Is it any surprise then if, Houston, we have a problem.

So we should expect corruption in prisons and just 'get over it'. We have ignored it and it has not gone away, quite the opposite. This is not to say we cannot deal with it, minimise its effects, catch and convict the perpetrators and generally improve the safety and security which corruption destroys. But none of that can be done unless the problem is acknowledged. For too long the stone has been briefly turned over and the sight of so many worms has bred panic in political and prison leaders, with the result that the stone has been quickly and firmly replaced.

Given that a prison is a natural breeding ground for corruption, how might it manifest itself behind the secure walls? Escapes are what breed fear in the minds of politicians, officials and of course governors – who inevitably carry the can. One senior official overseeing the corruption prevention policy I was given responsibility for opined that there could not be much corruption around because there were very few escapes and the levels of drugs in prisons was reducing as evidenced by the Mandatory Drug Testing (MDT) statistics. MDT is the prison service's primary test of illicit drug use in prison. Eschewed by practitioners in the drugs field as a worthless and easily fiddled figure, the prison service clings to it like glue. It is certainly true that the prison service record on escapes of the last twenty years has been impressive. Whilst once routine, they are now rare. The higher the security of prisoner the rarer the incidence of escape. There has not been a Category A escape in at least the last ten years, nor has there been an escape from a high security prison over the same period. To what extent such success is about the efficiency of prison service policy and practice as opposed to changes in society and the nature of criminal activity is worthy of debate.

We saw in Chapter 3 that escape from prison is not difficult if you have the will, a few friends outside and a long-term plan to disappear and reinvent yourself – a very expensive business. So what are the disincentives to escape? A ten-year sentence helps. This is the maximum sentence for escaping or aiding and abetting an escape. It is only people looking at very long sentences or indefinite detention who will see 'having it on their toes' as realistic. One major question is where in the digital world do you go to if you do escape? The one place you would want to go to and the last place you can go to is home, if you have one. Going abroad and adopting a new identity is expensive and requires considerable and extensive networks which are beyond the reach of the majority. But even that wore thin for Ronnie Biggs, who eventually came home for a warm pint and the ability to die at home. New passports, and everything that you need to open a bank account, buy a home, gain employment are all part of a digital world that will catch most people out eventually.

What we are reluctant to acknowledge is summed up in the opening to every episode of *Porridge*:

Norman Stanley Fletcher, you have pleaded guilty to the charges brought by this court, and it is now my duty to pass sentence. You are a habitual criminal, who accepts arrest as an occupational hazard, and presumably accepts imprisonment in the same casual manner. We therefore feel constrained to commit you to the maximum term allowed for these offences – you will go to prison for five years.

For many, prison is an occupational hazard and for some, not least in a cold winter, better than sleeping on the street, or in a dilapidated hostel or with dysfunctional friends or family. For many it is a refuge from real life and from personal responsibility, all of which the prison service has manifestly failed to see as necessary to instill in prisoners before they are released.

A chance encounter one day on Brixton Hill, the main approach to the south London house of correction, underlined for me the dilemma we have created with the prison system. I was returning to the jail after a meeting in Lambeth Town Hall where I had been to forge links with local police, education, probation, health and social services. A towering young man with a beaming smile bounded up to me with a 'Hi governor, how are you doing, how's it going?' A massive hand grasped mine and pumped an enthusiastic hello out of my forearm. I recognised him as a recently released young man from the prison's A Wing. Seeing people in the prison one day and on the streets of south London the next was quite common, and to be honest always a pleasure. I never received any animosity. Nevertheless there was always a millisecond of 'shit! – they haven't just escaped have they?' – but I drew comfort from the assumption that an escapee would not greet the governor of the jail he had just escaped from with a warm handshake.

Michael was keen to know how the 'guys' were, how the projects were doing, how the music course was progressing. I assured him all was well and that I hadn't been sacked yet (a common expectation around the jail by staff and prisoners). 'But how are you?' I enquired. 'How's life on the outside?' His enthusiasm instantly waned and his massive chin, a good foot above the top of my head, dropped towards his chest. 'Lost my job, had a row with the girlfriend and she has left with my baby. Probably lose my flat now and will have to go back on the dole.' His voice trembled as he raised his head slowly, looked me in the eye and proclaimed, 'Course I never had those problems when I was with you, did I?'

All but lost for words I mumbled meaningless encouragement,

wished him well and trudged back up the hill wondering what on earth criminal justice was all about. More particularly, I pondered on why the prevention of escape from custody so dominated the criminal justice system. Any correlation between escapes and corruption must be seen as at best tenuous.

Corruption and crime in jail is a very different matter. For Michael Howard and many other uninformed politicians, the media and the public, and for some time the police too, there was a perception that whatever prison did or did not do incarceration provided the community with respite from an individual's offending. Not so. It will obviously stop certain people doing certain things. Burglars will not be able to burgle your or my property. Shoplifters will leave retail premises in peace. And that's probably about it. Some crimes become more difficult inside, some actually become easier, not least drug dealing. There is very little crime that cannot be perpetrated from within a prison: theft, violence, sexual exploitation, rape, blackmail and even the most serious of terrorist offences can be commissioned from within the walls of a prison. Even murder.

In 2008 a Belmarsh prisoner used a smuggled mobile phone to order the killing of a man in Brockley, south London. He was convicted and given a life sentence. Delphon Nicholas, aged twenty-nine, was in prison and should have had the perfect alibi when Andrew Wanoghu was shot. Also found guilty of murder was gunman Trevor Dennie, aged thirty-four, from Deptford. Both men were told they must spend a minimum of thirty years in prison. Dennie and Nicholas made hundreds of calls to each other and exchanged texts as they plotted the shooting. By analysing the mobile phones, detectives established that Dennie was operating under direction from Nicholas in his Belmarsh cell with his smuggled mobile phone. It was never established how he got the phone.

HMP The Verne, a medium security prison on the Isle of Portland in Dorset, once suffered an armed robbery by prisoners within the perimeter of cash being delivered to the establishment. However, in order for any of these crimes to be committed there needs to be some form of corruption to facilitate the criminal. Anything on the TI list of types of corruption will do, and it only needs a vulnerable prison officer workforce responding through fear, financial gain, blackmail or general disillusion with the organisation they work for to enter into the deal.

We should also not delude ourselves that such criminal traffic is one way: prisoners exploiting and corrupting prison staff. There are many proven cases and many more suspicions of staff exploiting their positions of power and authority to perpetrate crime. There are even instances of people joining the prison service with the express intention of perpetrating crime.

One particular officer at Brixton came under increasing suspicion. Only two years into the job, his relationships with prisoners appeared inappropriate and his movement around the jail at times incompatible with his duties. A plan was hatched with my security department to monitor him closely with a view to mounting a surprise search of him.

It is only prison staff going into prisons within the High Security Estate (those holding Category A prisoners) who are searched on every occasion. This emanates from the Woodcock Report in 1996. The rules also require some searches on exit but they are rare and usually intelligence led (some significant items of capital equipment, such as computers, have been known to have been removed from prisons). For the rest of the estate the requirements are minimal and searches may only occur once a month. Searches on suspicion can be more frequent. Searches at the gate as staff enter the premises are easy to spot by the queues of staff meandering out of the building and down the street. Should a prison officer have contraband about him then he is unlikely to wait in the queue to be caught. More subtle methods requiring staff to enter the prison and then be diverted elsewhere to be searched can also be given warning of by accomplices inside making telephone calls outside. So routine searches of all staff coming on shift rarely find contraband. Spot searches tend to be more effective but have to be well planned. On this occasion we decided to conduct a surprise search of this individual on a Sunday as he entered the actual wing on which he was working. The plan worked and 'Mr Roberts' was caught red-handed with an array of drugs and mobiles including nine-bars (9oz bars of cannabis) strapped to his legs. The police were called, 'Roberts' was arrested and everyone felt the usual strange mix of elation at catching a crook but betrayal at the actions of a supposed colleague. It was also proof positive at the time, although I did not need it, that the primary route for significant amounts of drugs was staff not visits where only personal supplies tended to be smuggled.

My satisfaction at a good job done was assuaged the next day when I was telephoned by the police officer dealing with 'Mr Roberts' to tell me he had some bad news. Checks had revealed that our bent screw had served a two-year sentence for theft some four years ago at Wormwood Scrubs prior to his joining the prison service. Not only had criminal record checks missed this significant barrier to his employment, such was his audacity that when at the prison officer training school he had applied to work at Wormwood Scrubs. Sensibly, he had been posted to me at Brixton.

We were only just coming to terms with the ramifications of all this when another call from the same police officer declared that he had more bad news for me. Short of 'Roberts' being exposed as Osama bin Laden I was not sure how much worse it could get. Roberts was an illegal immigrant. So much for all the processes and procedures of identity checking. The icing on the cake was another form of corruption, namely the selling of information to the press. It has been the practice over many years for the media to pay for stories or information from prison officers. Photos of prisoners are especially valuable, and certain tabloids openly advertise in their organs for people to come forward. It is a criminal act and the prison service – and I include myself – has failed to catch such individuals. The fact that newspapers are commissioning crime has never been challenged. Perhaps the hacking scandal will change attitudes. On this occasion I suffered a *Sun* headline the following day of 'Brixton employs asylum seeking thief'. I trudged home forlornly yet again down Brixton Hill that evening, reassured only by the fact that yet another crook in my employ had probably lost his £500 from *The Sun* on the 3.30 at Lingfield.

A much sadder and worrying incidence of staff perpetrating the sort of crime we don't want to acknowledge in the total institutions that are prisons occurred in HMP Downview and came to trial in July 2011.

Russell Thorne was a 41-year-old principal officer at the prison who subsequently became the acting governor of the women's jail near Sutton in Surrey. He was jailed for five years for having sex with inmates. He gave the women presents from the Argos catalogue, cans of Red Bull energy drink, biscuits and day-release passes in return for sexual favours. He particularly exploited a Colombian woman serving a seventeen-year sentence for importing £75 million of drugs into the UK. He demanded sex from the women in a variety of prison settings including the prison library and a store cupboard. Prosecuting counsel told the jury that life inside Downview prison, near Sutton, Surrey, was like a 'real-life version of what twenty or thirty years ago the *Carry On* team might have suggested as *Carry On Inside* ... with Sid James playing the role of the prison officer'. Whilst this was an image the tabloid newspaper readers may have enjoyed, the exploitation of vulnerable women was horrendous and as big a failing of the duties of the prison service as any escape.

It was alleged that Thorne was 'at the heart' of corruption that engulfed the women's prison and only exposed when some of the women who had been exploited came forward, unsure whether in such circumstances they would be believed. One of the women said she had been ordered to climb onto a desk before he performed oral sex on her and revealed she had feared that if she did not comply with his wishes he would cancel a party she had helped to organise for the women prisoners.

In sentencing Thorne at Guildford Crown Court, Judge Michael Addison said:

You were a prison officer in charge of female prisoners and you had a sexual relationship with a prisoner. You had intercourse with the woman on many occasions over a period of more than two years, continuing the intimate relationship with her. She, at that same time, was carrying on with a sexual relationship with another woman. You got the two of them to perform sex acts in front of you and you yourself got involved. You were acting governor at one point and had considerable power. You had the power to issue releases on temporary licence. The prisoners knew that fact and were anxious to be on good terms with you. You abused that power by having a relationship with the woman. The sexual activity was mostly short and hurried and in squalid surroundings and circumstances.

I took into account your good character. You contested the case so I can give you no credit for an early guilty plea and you have shown no remorse for your behaviour. This offence is so serious only a custodial sentence can be justified. I accept that it is unlikely that you will commit further offences.

The sentence for this offence must clearly be one that will deter other prison officers that might be tempted to make sexual advances to prisoners. If they do, they must know they will go to prison for a substantial period. I pass a sentence of five years' imprisonment.

Prisons are unfortunately not crime-free zones; indeed, one might argue they are crime hotspots, which presents a major dilemma for the relationship between the police and prison service. Relationships, for reasons I have never been able to fathom, have tended to be fraught rather than based on the fact that we are all essentially doing the same job: protecting the public. One senior award-winning governing governor (i.e. in overall charge of the prison) once revealed to me that she did not trust the police, they were always 'shafting' governors. My incredulity at such a comment was off the Richter scale. I commented that there were lots of people I didn't trust but I tended to see them as individuals. Not trusting the entire police service was a bit extreme and anyway it was the prison service itself that was most adept at 'shafting' governors.

At a local level there are real issues. My relationships with a variety of borough commanders in Brixton were excellent, we developed mutual support and respect, and I remain in contact with some even today. Borough commander in Brixton must be one of the most difficult jobs in policing, with this part of London having the highest murder rate in the country alongside serious issues of drugs, violence and all the social problems of poverty and exclusion. It must also be said that it spite of all its problems it remains one of the most vibrant and engaging communities I have ever had the pleasure of working in.

From the borough commander's point of view crime in Brixton prison, unless it is major, part of serious organised crime or a threat to the local community, whilst not something to be ignored, will not be at the top of the priorities list. A couple of nine-bars will be small beer in this part of the world. Illicit mobile phones, although now against the law, are not likely to keep the commander awake at night. Part of my job, I saw, was to engage not only with local borough commanders, but with national organisations like the Serious and Organised Crime Agency (SOCA) to determine what the real and potential effect of crime in prison was in relation to wider criminal activity. In that context the prison service has never seen itself as, and nor is it designated as, a law enforcement agency in the way the police, the Border Agency and Revenue & Customs are. Consequently the prison service has not seen and does not see crime prevention as a primary task, rather it sees serving the courts and keeping people in custody as its main function.

Prisons are complex closed communities and whilst corruption supports and promotes criminal activity in them there are other aspects of life in prison which corruption influences but which are invisible to the outside world.

Prisons vary enormously in terms of their physical conditions, geographical setting and what they offer in treatment, education, work and the ability to allow visits home or employment in the community during sentence. Prisoners will be allowed access to these according to their perceived need, length of sentence, time into that sentence and proximity to release. Whilst there should be a direct correlation between a prisoner's need for such help and support and his or her access to it, this is all too often far from the case. Not all prisoners at the end of their sentence finish off in resettlement prisons – there are only two in the country and we release up to 80,000 prisoners per year. Many do not finish off in open prisons which are much cheaper, with more appropriate security for people who will be back on the streets in days, weeks or months. Despite the introduction of the National Offender Management Service whereby prisoners supposedly have their time in custody planned (but not if you are serving less than a year), the lack of sufficient interventions and activities for everyone is a major problem. This is made worse with the recent rise in the numbers of people on indeterminate sentences who cannot be released until they have done something to prove it is safe to do so and who take priority.

Some would argue that there is even an inverse relationship between need and access. Many courses, work and general activities require basic communication skills, sound mental health, the absence of learning difficulties and a certain degree of advocacy from others. Large swathes of the population therefore miss out not by design but by default. In ten or twenty years' time we will be discovering in our prisons elderly prisoners, on indeterminate sentences, with speech and language and learning difficulties, perhaps with low level mental disorders, and devoid of family and friends, wandering the wings or hospitals of local prisons. We will be wondering why they are there, not least because the charities that advocate for such individuals will have been driven out of existence as the Big Society subsumes the Small Society.

We should also worry about prisoners doing things for their own nefarious ends. It is widely recognised but rarely acknowledged and even more rarely proven that prisoners have paid for recategorisation (move-ment to lower security status) so they can be transferred to less secure prisons in parts of the country they want to be. 'Accelerated promotion' of prisoners has been around for years and should be prevented by good management but it simply is not. Some years ago it was known for prisoners to jump from Category A status to Categories C and D and be working outside very quickly into long sentences. In the past some absconded and the occasional investigation would reveal a breach of rules. More recently the practice of working within the rules has been adopted but with the oiling of the wheels so effective that long sentences can become little more than Fletcher's 'occupational hazard'.

As part of one investigation I carried out some years ago, I tracked the movement of one prisoner serving twelve years for drug importation. He spent the first two years as a trustee prisoner working in the reception area of a local prison before transferring to a Category C prison where he received full-time education, finally ending up in a resettlement prison for his remaining two years. Here he worked outside daily on a job he had found for himself to which he drove in his own car. He gained parole on the first day of his parole eligibility halfway through his sentence. Escape was not worth his while.

Ironically, whilst cash for places has undoubtedly occurred, 'accelerated promotion' and 'the good life' can easily be achieved by more subtle but equally corrupt practices, namely conditioning and manipulation. Everyone likes a calm, ordered and hassle-free working environment and no one more so than prison officers. If a particular prisoner is intelligent, articulate and engaging then why not put him in a position of trust or place him on a course you know he will attend and pass, thereby supporting your key performance indicators? Even better if they make good tea and toast and can be relied on to keep the scallywags in order. Far easier to punish and keep behind locked doors those more disruptive individuals struggling with depression, drug and alcohol dependency and lacking the social skills to engage with staff and articulate the reasons for their poor behaviour. This is not to say that this is the underlying premise of the prison service but it is a scenario which must be seen as increasingly likely in difficult times and something which should be tackled however difficult it may be to do so.

So how do people operating corruptly in prison operate on a day-to-day basis? Evidence has shown that it is rarely two individuals, the corruptor and the corrupted, acting alone. If it is a serious organised criminal seriously organising crime then it is likely that he will have one or more individuals at the 'coal face' whilst he attempts to keep out of the spotlight. Indeed he may become the model prisoner, the one to be trusted and the one to be allowed more access to facilities and people around the jail than is appropriate. It is also likely that there will be people outside facilitating payments and the movement of contraband. It may also be the case that corruption inside may be part of the facilitating of crime on the outside. In short, the networks of criminality and corruption may be complex and widespread. Breaking into these networks is difficult and requires considerable time and energy. It also requires collaboration between police and prison services. Such collaboration is rare, but when it does occur it can be very successful.

During my tenure as head of the prison service's Anti-Corruption Unit I presided over the service's first and last such collaborative unit, LPACT. The London Prison Anti-Corruption Unit was set up in 2007 and consisted of up to three prison and seven police staff based in New Scotland Yard. Police resource input far outweighed that of the prison service, which funded it on a temporary and reluctant basis. The remit of the unit was to tackle corruption of prison staff in London prisons. It was a proactive detection unit employing specialists and developing skills which began to reap increasing benefits. One operation in particular illustrated not only what such a unit could achieve but also the scale of the problem that was being faced.

The case centred around Robert Talbot, a 33-year-old man who was serving an indeterminate sentence for his role in what was described as the 'Reservoir Dogs Gang'. The five-strong gang targeted wealthy individuals in south London and Kent and were described by the sentencing judge at Kingston Crown Court as a significant risk to the public. In one of their most brutal attacks, echoing the torture scene from Quentin Tarantino's film *Reservoir Dogs*, they started hacking off a man's ear to make him reveal the code to his safe. In another attack they threatened to cut a man's fingers off and they also told a woman, who was alone at home when they struck, she was going to be raped. The gang carried out the spate of midnight robberies between July 2005 and January 2010, garnering more than £1 million in valuables, including jewellery, plasma televisions and cars.

Judge Charles Welchman told the gang: 'The victims feared for their lives and that of family members. It was clear that the robbers had good intelligence. They also relied on and had personal information about their victims' families as part of the psychological campaign when they had their victims in their power.'

Talbot started his sentence at HMP Wandsworth but despite the nature of his violent and brutal offending, the judge's comments and his effective life sentence he progressed quickly to HMP Coldingley, a low security prison renowned for its industrial work and training ethos.

It was following a year-long, painstaking and exhaustive investigation that on 6 May 2009 police officers from the Metropolitan Police Anti-Corruption Command that we had been working in further collaboration with arrested twelve people after a series of dawn raids on fourteen different locations in London and the south of England. Vehicle documents (the Met's stolen vehicle unit was yet another partner), phones and computers were seized.

The investigation had started as one into a range of individuals believed to be involved in the theft and ringing (swapping plates on a stolen vehicle) of high-value cars and the supply of illicit drugs into prisons across the country. Talbot, as suspected, proved to be the ringleader from within his cells at Wandsworth and Coldingley. Key to his activities was 35-year-old Ian Cooper, a Wandsworth prison officer. Cooper smuggled mobile phones, drugs and other contraband in to Talbot, on some occasions in large cartons of orange juice.

Talbot's business on the outside, the theft and ringing of high-value cars, was led by 27-year-old Thomas King from Sutton in Kent. He was Talbot's 'runner' and acted as the go-between to supply contraband for Cooper. When King's house was searched a package was found containing heroin, cocaine and cannabis worth £22,000. It was almost certainly heading for Wandsworth or another London prison. Talbot worked at the top end of the market organising the theft of Porches, BMWs and Range Rovers from homes in the south of England to the tune of over half a million pounds. His corrupting skills were masterly and his choice of Cooper either very lucky or extraordinarily skillful: Cooper's partner was a serving Metropolitan police officer, Hayley Cloud. Cloud was based at Lewisham borough and was tasked with cloning the vehicles. She would carry out unauthorised vehicle checks on police databases. Talbot would then obtain log books from vehicles identical to those stolen, allowing the vehicle to receive a cloned identity before being sold on to an innocent buyer. On one occasion Talbot instructed Cloud unlawfully to release a Lamborghini Gallardo seized as part of a totally separate criminal investigation from a police car pound in south London, and arranged for King to pick it up. Cloud even went on to corrupt her friend Natalie Ricketts, a civilian worker with the police based in Bexley, south London. The two women helped Talbot by carrying out unauthorised checks on his associates, including another of his runners, Stephen Palmer. Ricketts added insult to injury by also stealing police radios from Bexley Heath police station and passed them on to Cloud for illicit use by the Talbot gang.

Talbot was jailed for twelve years, Cooper five-and-a-half years, King four years, Palmer twelve months, Cloud two years and Ricketts ten months suspended for two years. On 17 August 2010, ten more men were jailed for a total of more than twenty years at Croydon Crown Court after being convicted of stealing high-value cars, ringing them and selling them on. The operation was led by cops from Bromley working with the Met's stolen vehicle unit. The convictions were directly linked to the anti-corruption investigation.

Sixteen convictions, including police and prison officers, forty-five years of jail, cars thefts of well over half a million pounds and contraband into prisons that could not begin to be estimated. And all done from within a prison cell with an illicit mobile phone. All very different to life on planet Howard where prison still works apparently.

If you think Robert Talbot was a busy boy in prison, then George

Moon took us to new heights of serious organised crime, seriously well organised in prison again, aided and abetted by illicit mobile phone technology.

Moon was a career criminal, aged sixty-three; he had been a free man for just twelve weeks in the past twelve years. On previous sentences he had been a model prisoner who progressed rapidly through the system. At the time of his arrest he was finishing off a sentence of fifteen years for conspiracy to import Class A drugs and about to go to open prison. On this particular sentence he managed to import a million pounds' worth of cocaine despite, like Robert Talbot, being locked up in a prison cell. Like Talbot, key to his activities was a smuggled mobile phone which he used to coordinate contacts in several countries to organise the importation of twelve 500g packages of 77 per cent pure cocaine from Panama and Venezuela to the UK and the Republic of Ireland. Powering the phone using a modified electric razor, he made thousands of calls to fellow dealers abroad as well as to the rest of his gang in England. Like all sophisticated and efficient businessmen, he stored the names and numbers of all his contacts as well as the routes of all his 'packages' in a notebook and on a spare SIM card. SOCA eventually picked up on his international activities and after a long-running surveillance operation on members of Moon's gang he was arrested in his cell in November 2008 as he was on his telephone setting up a deal.

At his trial at Liverpool Crown Court he admitted conspiracy to import cocaine into the UK and Ireland as well as two offences under the Prison Act relating to heroin and SIM cards. Detectives believe they smashed the importation operation in its infancy and that Moon could have made millions from his deals.

Moon orchestrated his criminal empire from his cell in HMP Lindholme, a Category C prison holding nearly 1,000 men near Doncaster. One of his contacts was Leo Morgan, who is now in prison in Panama serving ten years for cocaine offences. A SOCA agent involved in the operation described Moon as 'the central hub in the importation ring from Panama into the UK'. The investigation started in 2008 after someone from within the prison tipped off the prison intelligence system, which contacted police and SOCA.

Bill Hughes, Director General of SOCA at the time, was bullish and optimistic. He declared:

> We know that career criminals like George Moon look for any way to continue their illegal activities, even within prison. They are ingenious and determined, but so are we. This was an excellent result for SOCA's partnership with the prison service. Moon was a cynical, complacent criminal who thought he was beyond reach but he was caught red handed. This is a warning shot for anyone who thinks prison won't affect business as usual. We are determined to stamp down hard on criminals – wherever they operate.

Moon was sentenced to eighteen years, whilst four members of his gang admitted charges of conspiracy to import cocaine and a fifth admitted smuggling heroin and two SIM cards into prison.

Moon was not satisfied with being an international drug dealer and was clearly something of a workaholic. He also ran a meat scam from his prison cell, for which he received another two years for fraud which will not begin until 2018. Making full use of his illicit mobile phone he posed as the managing directors of legitimate meat suppliers. Gang members on the outside helped place orders with wholesalers in the UK, Germany and Europe as either 'the northern branch' of Crown Chickens or Scotch Premier Meat. The gang faked letterheads, order forms and financial details from the legitimate companies to gain credit before Moon rang the wholesalers acting as the MD to seal the deal. At a trade show in Paris, a representative for Scotch Premier Meat was approached by a Dutch wholesaler who told him their £100,000 order of rib-eye steak would be with them the following week. But it was Moon who had ordered it and was set to sell it on to fund his drug smuggling. That deal was blocked, but the gang did get £85,000 of meat and cheese in two deliveries from companies in Manchester and Germany. The plot unravelled when one of the gang faxed an order to a company from his local library. The letterhead said Crown Chickens but the top of the fax said Widnes Library. Other companies were suspicious because they thought it strange Moon was not trying to haggle on price for such large orders.

As head of the prison service's Anti-Corruption Unit at the time I discussed with SOCA whether corrupt staff had facilitated Moon's activities. I was informed that no such activity had been detected by them. Not satisfied and having examined Moon's files myself, I made a plea to the head of the prison service that an internal investigation be carried out to examine thoroughly whether any staff had been complicit. One was commissioned. I was later informed that the inquiry had resulted in administrative action against an unnamed individual. I was not allowed to see the report. Moon had initially been made category A but downgraded to Category B shortly after his conviction against the advice of myself and SOCA.

SOCA know there is a problem and tell Mission Control in the Prison Service so every year in its annual UK Threat Assessment. As part of the strategy it has set up a Lifetime Management of Organised Criminals and Prison Programme. It declares: 'Organised criminals operating at a national and international level often enjoy lavish lifestyles funded by a lifetime of crime. These "career criminals" are criminally active throughout their lives, including any spells in prison.'

SOCA goes on:

Prison provides organised criminals with good opportunities to network, due to the concentration of 'experts' in all areas of organised crime. There is clear evidence of organised criminals developing their knowledge and expertise whilst in prison, as well as expanding their networks of criminal associates. For example, importers and distributors of Class A drugs have forged new relationships with overseas supplier networks, and criminals involved in frauds have identified and developed new methods and contacts. The main constraint in prison is the inability to meet associates freely. Prison forces criminals to change their methods of communication and to delegate the day-to-day running of their criminal businesses to those on the outside. The ability to communicate clandestinely with these associates is seen as crucial.

It concludes: 'Imprisonment does not necessarily stop organised criminals from continuing with their criminal activities. Some have shown they are capable of running criminal businesses from prison.'

So if SOCA gets it, why does the prison service not, and what evidence is there that it is in denial of the problem? The best evidence lies in resources. The Metropolitan Police has its own Department of Professional Standards, a highly organised and professional body which saw its origins in the police corruption scandals of the 1970s and 1980s. So endemic was the problem that a so-called 'Ghost Squad' was set up of trusted and experienced officers who were officially posted abroad, retired or seconded elsewhere whilst unofficially they set up their own unit of 'untouchables' to tackle the issue. Their first problem was denial. Today, although the problem has not gone away, policies and practices are engrained in the psyche of not just the Met but every other police force. 'Integrity is not negotiable' is the watch word. The Met has a workforce of some 30,000, the prison service some 40,000 directly employed and a similar number through direct contracts and volunteers. The Department of Professional Standards or Anti-Corruption Command has over 2,000, with a significant number under cover detecting corruption and from time to time organising sophisticated stings based on intelligence and professional detection methods. The prison service has no full-time, dedicated corruption investigators.

Who is trying to corrupt police? Criminals would be the safe reply. Where do those criminals end up or from time to time emanate from? Prison. Police and prison are fighting the same corruptors. For the police their contact with corruptors is spasmodic. It may relate to certain operations, meetings in pubs or discreet dwellings. It is regulated, controlled and well managed. In prisons, staff live with the corruptors day in, day out. They are contained within the same institution. Not for the prison officer the periodic meeting, in prison it is day-to-day contact. Seasoned and experienced as well as budding corruptors living with staff cheek by jowl. At risk are not just prison staff with six weeks' training, only one day of which covers corruption, but also doctors, teachers, drug workers and the plethora of well-meaning but often inexperienced volunteers who receive little more than a criminal record check and instructions on how to use and not lose their keys.

So within this highly toxic environment how many staff might be allotted to the task of rooting out corruption and preventing its tentacles undermining the good work and safety of all those living and working in jails? The answer is: not many. And the history of how the problem has been sidelined is inauspicious to say the least.

The prison service set up a Professional Standards Unit (PSU) some ten years ago. It was a small enterprise housed in the grounds of a midlands jail, with extensive farmland providing fine views and anonymity. The latter was hardly needed as its role was unclear and its impact on anything other than the precise definition of officer's uniform negligible. It began an intelligence-gathering system but it was not widely promulgated. It was no ghost squad and it did not pretend to be combating corruption because there was not thought to be any to worry about.

The apple art was upset in 2005 by Metropolitan Police Commander Gary Copson. Copson was appointed as police advisor to the prison serv-ice in July 2002. The Police Advisors Section, or PAS as it was called, was based in prison service HQ and consisted of seconded senior police officers whose job it was to support the prison service on matters of crime and provide an essential link with the police service. I worked extensively with them over the years, not least when I was at Belmarsh and dealing with Irish terrorism. I found the various incumbents highly professional, a source of considerable knowledge and invariably helpful and supportive.

Copson questioned the role of the PSU and tried to encourage the prison service to professionalise and give it specific focus on corruption prevention. By 2004 Copson had made little progress and the prison service eventually put up the shutters. This did not stop him examining the nature of corruption in prisons, and after reporting directly to the then Deputy Commissioner of the Met, Sir (now Lord) Ian Blair in May 2004. Operation Balios was then set up with the objective of developing a strategic intelligence assessment for the joint benefit of the prison service, the Home Office and the police. The Balios Report was delivered by Blair to the prison service Director General, Martin Narey, in June 2005.

A summary of the report was disclosed under the Freedom of Information Act to the BBC several years ago. It made no headlines. Six of the key findings were:

1. Research indicates significant problems within the prison service in relation to drugs, racism and corruption.
2. The prison service lacks appropriate intelligence systems that might justify police confidence or be capable of withstanding external scrutiny.
3. Whilst the prison service has professional standards arrangements, this paper suggests they lack effectiveness and objectivity in dealing with corruption and criminality.
4. The structure of the prison service undermines its ability to tackle corruption and criminality.
5. Those charged with investigating corruption within the prison service have not been provided with sufficient resources, training or investment to succeed.
6. There is a need for greater police involvement and independent oversight in relation to allegations of corruption and criminality within the prison system. Responsibility for lack of engagement between police and HM prison service must be shared between both parties.

The report caused an almighty row and opposition was so fierce that Copson was withdrawn by the Met Police in Sep 2005 and the size of PAS significantly reduced.

Her Majesty's Inspectorate of Constabulary (HMIC) committed to a six-week review of the role and function of PAS. This was delivered more than two years later but was never implemented.

PSU rattled on with its nebulous role in the shadow of the poor prison–police relationships left in the wake of Copson's de facto sacking. Relationships gradually improved but corruption lay firmly under a stone. The problem of drugs in prison, however, was exercising everyone, not least the media and the politicians. Newspapers were regularly running stories of prisons being awash with drugs. Reports spoke of prisoners first becoming addicted to heroin in prison. Indignant politicians who had never inhaled were indignant and demanded drug-free prisons or at least drug-free wings, both about as likely as sugar-free doughnuts. The prison service defended itself with its remarkable MDT figures – crisis, what crisis? The prison service however relented and under pressure commissioned a former chief constable, David Blakey, to conduct a review of the problem of drugs in prison. Blakey, assisted by only one administrative assistant, got straight onto the task and produced his report in less than six weeks, unencumbered by any research or discussions with prisoners.

Blakey's recommendations were relevant but sufficiently undemanding for the prison service that they agreed to implement them straight away. A Blakey review team was even set up. Corruption was barely acknowledged as an issue and the report provided a perfect cloak of denial. Despite this and somewhat miraculously, one senior official in NOMS pushed for the PSU to have more focus and it morphed into a Corruption Prevention Unit (CPU) in May 2008. A corruption prevention strategy was set up and a memorandum of understanding between the police and the prison service agreed to ensure the better handling of intelligence. The London Prisons Anti-Corruption Unit was set up as part of the strategy and it seemed as if progress might at last be made. The senior manager running the unit transferred to another post in July of 2008 and I was appointed in his place after a routine recruitment process. The CPU I inherited consisted of my post,

a seconded police chief inspector, three middle managers and six administrative staff. The unit was responsible for policy and strategy and had
neither remit nor resources for investigations. Prisons were nominally
required to have a corruption prevention officer (of which there were
ten) and there were also to be regional corruption prevention managers. None was full time nor dedicated to the role. None had anything
other than the barest minimum of investigative resources. Some worked
closely with their local police forces, others had no dialogue at all. At
this time also came yet another review of the structures of the National
Offender Management Service. The result was a cutback in resources
such that the local and regional roles became subsumed in the wider
security and administrative function and their ability to tackle the
issue of corruption was even further eroded. We had some successes.
We promulgated the issues and spoke openly about those we caught.
We had a proactive media strategy, internally and externally. As well as
catching the corrupted I promoted policies for identifying and dealing
with the corruptors. Importantly also, I prompted a discussion on the
vulnerability of staff to corruption and the need for support and training. It was chipping away at the edges but there was relief expressed by
many in the service that at last 'Houston' understood their might be
a problem.

Then in August 2010 I was called into the office of my line manager,
the head of security policy for NOMS. He was due to go on three
weeks' leave that afternoon and I assumed a chat by way of handover.
He informed me that there had been a review of my unit (there hadn't)
and that my post had been removed and my unit was to be subsumed
under the intelligence unit. I was from that moment jobless and was to
be placed on the surplus list – managers for whom there was no job. He
then left for his vacation.

I launched into fruitless protestations about employment policy that
had been ignored. A review was finally carried out towards the end of
2010 and I was again summoned, to be informed that the review had
concluded what had been decided in August. I was further informed 'I

have no work for you'. I packed my bag and went home to worklessness until finally taking voluntary redundancy in March 2011. Remarkably, at this time the only review in the entire security directorate was that of my role. It was also a time before financial savings were required. CPU now sits under the auspices of an intelligence unit. Its nominal staffing has been further reduced and like the rest of the security policy unit in NOMS, it contains no staff who have run a prison and only a tiny number who have ever worked in one.

It is clear from government responses to parliamentary questions over the last couple of years that there is nothing to worry about, that no resources are needed because there is no evidence of a problem, be it organised crime, drugs or mobile phones.

MP John McDonnell asked on 6 April 2010 how many prisoners had been charged with further serious crimes carried out whilst they were in prison. The answer was that the data was not held centrally and could only be found at disproportionate cost. So here was the prison service appearing to have no interest in the extent of the problem at the same time as SOCA in its report of 2010 'Extending our Reach' suggesting organised crime in prison was widespread. McDonnell and fellow MP David Howarth asked questions in March 2010 on the extent of prisoners corrupting public officials in the previous twelve months. The parliamentary answer said that prison service databases do not hold specific information on such offences and that the information that is available does not identify whether the defendant is a prisoner or not.

On 30 March 2010 McDonnell asked how many illicit phones were found in prisons and how many had been found on staff, prisoners and in communal areas. The answer stated that the prison department does not hold centrally the information on location or ownership of seized phones, nor did it have data on which group of individuals brought phones in. The answer did reveal that the phones seized were required to be sent to a central unit in the west midlands for analysis. An answer to Neil Gerrard MP on 9 March 2010 revealed that in the previous year over

9,000 phones or SIM cards had been sent to this unit but it was acknowledged that this was a serious underestimate of those in circulation as not all jails sent in all the phones they found and some went to the police for further investigation. It was also stated that some were not sent because they were not deemed suitable for interrogation – code for the fact that some would have been recovered from body orifices and neither safe nor pleasant to deal with. Tables were issued to Parliament in March that year to show that the number of phones found varied considerably from prison to prison. Some reported zero; HMP Altcourse, a private prison in the north-west of England, reported 700. There was no suggestion that this prison was any more susceptible to illegal trafficking of phones. Data gathering in private prisons is subject to much greater independent scrutiny as fines ensue if the data is not provided properly. No such system operates in the public sector and the parliamentary answer acknowledged the whole process was not audited in the same way so many other things were.

Whilst there is ample evidence that illicit mobile phones are integral to crime in prison, McDonnell must have been surprised with his answer to a further question about whether the prison department had commissioned and evaluated any research into the way in which mobile phones came into prisons. The department stated that they had not commissioned any such research. MP David Howarth was interested in what information came from all the phones that were found and he asked in particular about prosecutions for pornographic or violent images found on seized phones. Minister of State Maria Eagle in April 2010 answered: 'Whilst data are extracted from mobile phones by a central unit action taken as a result of that data is a matter for individual establishments and their partners. This is not held centrally and could be obtained only at disproportionate cost.'

MPs also tried to find out the nature and extent of illicit drug smuggling in prison and whether there were implications for corruption. This was an exchange on 23 March 2010:

Philip Davies: To ask the Secretary of State for Justice if he will make it his policy to collate at national level the (a) quantity and (b) type of illicit drugs seized in prisons in England and Wales?

Maria Eagle: The National Offender Management service (NOMS) collates the number of drug seizures in prisons. The number of drug seizures in England and Wales in 2008–9 is given in the following table. Many seizures are similar in appearance and where not attributable are not categorically identified by scientific analysis. Weight is not recorded and there are no plans to record it.

A table was attached showing 776 seizures of heroin, 262 of cocaine, 1,731 seizures of cannabis and a variety of other small seizures. Nevertheless, there is no record given of the amount of drugs, whether it is a few grams, or several kilograms, or simply a trace of the stuff – leading one to think they neither knew nor cared. There was, however, some helpful some clarification of the figures. Maria Eagle added: 'These figures have been drawn from administrative data systems. Although care is taken when processing and analysing the returns, the detail collected is subject to the inaccuracies inherent in any large scale recording system. The data are not subject to audit.'

Poor Mr Davies was unable to find out what drugs and in what amounts were being found, but he had been hopeful he would find out how they were found. No such luck.

Philip Davies: To ask the Secretary of State for Justice how many and what proportion of illicit drug seizures within prisons was attributed to (a) sniffer dogs, (b) closed circuit television, (c) strip searches, (d) intimate searches, (e) searches of prison cells and (f) police intelligence in each of the last five years?

Maria Eagle: Information is not recorded in the format requested and would require requests for and detailed analysis of data returns from all prisons in England and Wales. To do so would incur disproportionate costs.

OUT OF SIGHT, OUT OF MIND

Our tenacious MPs had one last shot at Ms Eagle. She did not know the quantity of illicit drugs in prison, nor how they were discovered. Surely she knew who was bringing them in?

Shailesh Vara, Member of Parliament for North West Cambridgeshire, had also had a go:

> Mr Vara: To ask the Secretary of State for Justice how many (a) visitors, (b) staff and (c) prisoners were caught attempting to smuggle illegal drugs into each prison in England in each of the last five years; and what steps have been taken in respect of those caught?
>
> Maria Eagle: The data are not available in the form requested.

If MPs were concerned that the prison department did not have a handle on the nature and extent of the illicit drug problem in prison they only needed to go to the NOMS *Annual Report* for 2010/11. Loud and proud in the report of achievement against the service's key performance targets was the Mandatory Drug Testing (MDT) figure. The target for positive tests nationally was 9.3 per cent. In 09/10 it had been a mere 7.8 per cent and for 10/11 it had slumped to 7.1 per cent. That's all right then.

NINE

THE PRISONER'S PERSPECTIVE

All names have been changed.

MICK

Mick uses the word 'lump' to describe himself, not because he is over-weight but because he is the sort of man you would want on your side if things got difficult. More precisely, if you were in prison with him you would make sure he was on your side. Mick doesn't rush. He wears the right gear and moves slowly and deliberately. If you were looking for a good case study for the long-term benefits or otherwise of prison healthcare, a prison diet and regular access to a gym, for free, at forty-four years old and only out of prison for eight of the last thirty years, Mick would be the perfect candidate. He talks of 'coming home' in the same way a soldier might talk about returning home after war. Maybe that's the way he sees it. He has had enough; he is tired of it all. He has grown out of it – the drug dealing, the robbery, the guns. He has taken all the prison courses, but what has set him on the straight and narrow is old age, his mother's death, time with his kids and a word in his ear from a friend. He has chosen to stop offending, inside and out, not because of a failing system but by choice. At my perfect fantasy dinner party I would sit Mick next to Michael Howard and let him tell the former Home Secretary precisely why he is living testimony to the fact that prison does not work.

I asked Mick to tell me, first of all, about drugs and corruption in prison. He was soon in full, unrehearsed flow:

Getting drugs in the prison was pretty easy. It was easy in all prisons, but especially easy in private prisons. You could corrupt officers. I would say four out of ten easily. It would take someone who knows how to assert themselves about three weeks. In private [prisons] you are dealing with less trained officers. In HMP [public sector prisons] they train officers how to conduct themselves. Those in the privates are not really trained on their game enough. And they would come in after just being shelf packers in Tesco. They would get a job as a prison officer but they haven't got the life skills.

In July 2011 Secretary of State for Justice Ken Clarke announced the largest prison privatisation programme in the history of the English and Welsh prison service. The number of private sector prisons could have doubled by mid-2012. Private prisons are here to stay. The new programme is about the privatisation of existing state-run prisons. Previously all new prisons were contracted out to large multinationals like SERCO and G4S but were new constructions on greenfield sites. As such the workforce was newly recruited from the local area. They would receive the same nugatory six-week training programme that those in the public sector received, but the levels of experience across such establishments were always significantly lower than in the public sector. Lower wages and poorer conditions also meant that staff turnover conspired to keep experience levels low.

Mick continued his guide to the conditioning and manipulation of prison staff, public and private:

You would get to know the officer – their name – you get to know what shift patterns they are on – you just basically be friendly. You would set them up. My favourite one was to set up someone to give the officer problems. Then I would come along as the person helping them out. Then they would break down their guard to you.

I had one guy – he was about six foot five – he was a problem on the wing. No one could really talk to him but I had a good rapport with him because I had taken the trouble to get to know him. I would tell him I would give him something if he would cause problems for a particular person today – about banging up [being locked in your cell] *or something and I would come in as the rescuer of that particular officer. So she gets all the attention and all the dairy* [troubles, problems or general aggravation] *put on her. And officers, they don't like that. They don't like confrontation.*

So then I come in. I say, 'No, Jerry, you don't have to deal with her like that – she's all right really.' I'd pull him away and take all the confrontation away from her. And then she's in bed with me – not in bed in that sense – virtually – like, she owes me. She says, 'Thanks – you was very helpful' etc. And then you build a rapport from that.

The next stage, you get to know the person, what they do, what their hobbies are. And if they carry on talking to you and opening up to you – the more they open up to you the more you are getting your foot in the door. And if the progression is good and if they don't cut you off abruptly, you know there's an angle you can get in there. You have to adjust yourself to see how you are going to put 'that' question. So you find out if they have got a boyfriend, if they have financial problems or if they like to go on holiday. You begin to know how to tap them.

So you ask how they would feel about getting a holiday for them paid for – full expenses paid. So if they say, 'What would I have to do for it?' that's your opening. And it does happen – there is human weakness: money. So I paid her £300 to bring an ounce of each [heroin and cannabis] *in every other week. I paid her £300 for every parcel she brought in. Each parcel had an ounce of heroin and an ounce of weed* [cannabis]. *Heroin is worth four grand to me inside. The ounce of heroin could last me four to five weeks and that ounce would be worth £4,000 to me inside. I'd sell it on – it would be a fast turnover. So I would make about three-and-a-half grand out of each ounce. On a good shift you would get rid of it in about two weeks. The ounce of gear would cost about £600 – if you have reasonable contacts. If you have better contacts you can get better gear, cheaper. So it would cost me about a* grand to buy the gear and get it in, sell it on for four – three grand straight profit. And that would be every two to four weeks. Easily done.

But what you had to do was programme the officer to try and make sure they didn't get caught. Once you have the rapport they tend to tell you everything, so you ask them about the security. They wanna be safe. So you ask them, what is it like on the gate? What are the searches like? Are they under any suspicion? So it's like you are schooling them. We look at it as passing customs. Customs is the gate [to the prison]. So you have to school them to pass the customs. Don't keep eye contact – be your normal self – be chatty but try not to be nervous. But eight out of ten, once they have done it the once, it's like you've created a monster because they want to do it more and more and more to get that money – and they get addicted to the money. And you want that – because that's where you have them and control them anyhow you want.

Why it normally comes on top [draws suspicion] is the member of staff gets greedy and tries to do it for every Tom, Dick and Harry and that's when the cat is out the bag. And that's when they get caught. If they was just to work with one person they would never get caught.

In Parkhurst, I was there three years and I worked with one person two-and-a-half years. I ran him for two-and-a-half years until the SO [senior prison officer] was taking me to reception one day and he said to me, 'Mick – don't think you are fooling anybody. We know what you're up to but we have had no burn outs [deliberate cell fires], no one running off the wing to say they are in debt, so that's why we will leave you alone – because you don't run the place like some other prisoners do. We think you are more of a professional.' I've had SOs and POs [senior and principal prison officers] tell me that.

Parkhurst is a structured prison – you've got long-termers [people serving more than four years] there. Me burning out a man over fifty quid is just bringing attention to me and the wing. He can pay me five pound a week. He doesn't have to run or go on protection [prisoners under threat can ask to be segregated from other prisoners for their own protection]. What I'm selling you, you have to come back for because its physical [the addiction] – *so you can't afford for me not to be selling you, supplying you, because you are going to need me two days from now. I understand that side of the game. Other guys would beat an inmate up and write off the money. I didn't see that as an answer to the problem. I wanted my money and I knew how to assert myself to get it.*

If you owed me £100, you would rather pay me off £5 a week and still smoke [heroin] *in between. You are not blacklisted and not sick* [in withdrawal]. *Where you going to go in Parkhurst to get your gear – you can't go round the corner and get it yourself can you?*

Rye Hill [HMP Rye Hill, a Category B prison near Rugby] *was easy; Channings Wood* [a Category C prison near Newton Abbot in Devon] *was ridiculous. And I mean ridiculous – the officer actually approached me! I'd been shipped from pillar to post by then. When you are a bit warm* [under suspicion], *a bit active, they ship you about a bit; they ghost you from here to there* [frequent transfers between different prisons for prisoners seen as disruptive were quite common]. *I had done eight or ten nicks* [prisons] *by then, so they shipped me to Channings Wood – to the end of the world. I'd graduated from B Cat to C Cat. I'd been shipped out of Guys Marsh and Erlestoke* [both Category C prisons in the south-west of England] *for suspicion. So they said, all right, let's send this one to Channings Wood now.*

The officer approached me – no, tell a lie, the officer approached an associate of mine. You know, when you get to a new prison you tend to keep yourself to yourself for a while. So everyone knows you but doesn't know how to tap you. I had a bit of a naughty reputation for selling, so sometimes people would try to rob me and I've had to sort them. If you've been inside a long time your name carries wherever you go. So when I got there, this guy, he knows of me through a friend. Once you get to a new prison you don't keep any secrets for very long – everyone has got a phone [illicit/smuggled in] *and they make a few calls and pretty soon they all know about you.*

This officer was keeping a rapport with an inmate that I knew. I came about a week after they had struck up a relationship, but because Channings was so active I said let me stay the man behind the mirror. Because I wanted to work my own programme. I was enhanced [the top end of the privileges system]. *I was doing a lump* [long sentence] *already. I wanted to stay enhanced. My behaviour was never bad; I was always a good prisoner. I knew how to conduct myself so when attention did come to me people would say, 'Selling drugs? No, not him, he's a nice guy.' That's the flip side of the coin. A lot of inmates selling drugs, they tend to bring a lot of dairy* [trouble] *on themselves. You cause yourself to be noticed. I was a bit shrewder than that. I would be a model prisoner but I would still be doing my thing. You are under the radar and it's better that way. So this officer, he approached my friend and said, 'Do you want to do something?' Before I arrived they were iffing and butting about what they wanted to do. So when I arrived, my mate said, 'Mick, you got experience – what should I say to him?' So I stayed the man behind the mirror and did the programming.*

Cut a long story short, he brings in two 2-litre bottles of vodka. That's after a month of me being there. He sells a litre of vodka for £50. So it's £100 he's making on the big bottles. So I said, 'OK, now get him to bring five phones in for you. You can sell them for two-fifty [£250] *a pop – start making some proper money. You can buy a mobile for less than twenty quid – one of them shit, flip ones. Fold in* [insert] *some shit SIMS and sell them for £250 as they come through the gate.' So he says, 'How is he going to get them in?' I said, 'What do you mean, how is he going to get them in? He knows the procedure at the gate. Let him work it out. He can bring in two at a time – two in the morning and two in the evening – or he can bring in two if he goes out for lunch.'*

So he brings in the phones and two weeks later I had him bringing in two ounces of gear [heroin]. *The whole place erupted, because in Channings Wood you've got Bristol and Gloucester there – all the* [heroin] *smokers. All hell broke loose in the prison because, until I arrived, everyone was relying on visits where all they could get was a little eighth* [of an ounce], *so they couldn't supply the demand. So I saw a way I could supply the demand but still stay out of the picture. They were on one wing and I was on the super-enhanced wing* [wing with most privileges for the most well-behaved prisoners] *– and that's how I stayed the man behind the mirror. When the drugs came in, he would report sick before going to work – so he would* walk past my window and hand the gear over. I could then distribute it to every wing. I was selling eighths for £300. So you have gone from one man supplying the prison through visits with just an eighth to me getting in 2 ounces [56g] and supplying the whole prison. The demand was there but no one could meet the demand. So I arrived and started meeting the demand. I was in that prison eight months and I made £15,000 in eight months – that's how fast it was – until even I got scared.

Normally I would make money but it would be trickling in – one, two, three hundred pound a week. Sitting on my arse in prison, £400 a week is still good money to me. But when you are making £1,200–£1,500 pound a week you have to start reflecting on your bank account. You aren't doing something legal here so you have to start moving your money around. You have someone outside who you can trust managing your money. So when it got to about £8,000, I would transfer the money out of that account. When it gets to about £10,000 they can start investigating what's going on. One time they pulled the girl I had managing my money and they asked her what business she was in. I had already pre-programmed her to tell them she was running an internet business. That was her cover and it worked. I told her to put up an internet page and tell them she was nickel and diming [buying and selling cheaply] crap. They left her alone.

I got to a stage where they eventually had me under suspicion and the officer got nicked. I went into hospital on the Monday and he got nicked on the Tuesday. He had already brought my parcel that week but it was the usual problem – he started doing business with every Tom, Dick and Harry. He started doing business with one person off every wing and that's how it came on top for him. Because you get these little idiots – when you walk down the landing they say, don't worry, I can get you something in an hour. So if it's five o'clock on a Tuesday afternoon and someone says that to you and you know there are no visits on a Tuesday, obviously other inmates are working it out. They sit down and watch – especially the [heroin] smokers, the addicts – they sit down and watch every little movement. Because if they see you slip they will just take it. Then the staff get suspicious – then its Chinese whispers and it all comes on top.

I had a real good rapport in Parkhurst. Officers used to bring me a nine-bar of hash [nine-ounce bar of cannabis resin, usually compressed and tightly wrapped in layers of cling film], *ten phones and 2 ounces of heroin – but that would be over a period of a week. That would cost me £1,200.*

It was £500 a phone. It varies in different prisons. In Parkhurst it was difficult to get stuff on to the island. Visits was difficult. So when something did come on the island it got eaten up. There's a different class of prisoner there. You are dealing with a man doing fifteen [years] *for importing heroin. So you can network and do all sorts of things. There were guys there gambling for half a key* [kilogram] *of heroin and crack. They were gambling and betting half a key! I witnessed that. And when they lost and had to pay at the end of the week, they made a call on the mobile and the half a key would be dropped off at the man's house. He would make a call – 'Did you get that?' – 'Yeah' – 'Is it any good?' – 'Yeah.' So everyone did business. You just had to know how to network. It was serious stuff.*

And then on the flip side you've got kids coming into prison and leaving with habits because of the heroin problem – and HMP and private prisons are not aware of this problem. It's escalating.

The prison service's view on the scale of drug taking in prison comes from its MDT policy. Mandatory drug testing was introduced for all prisons in February 1996. It was aimed at deterring the use of drugs and, theoretically, identifying those to treat and those to punish. It was thought that it would provide information on the level of drug use within the prison and the type of drugs being used. All prisoners are subject to the random selection and testing process. Prisons are required to test 5–10 per cent of their population, depending on the size of the jail, each month. Urine samples are collected from prisoners and sent away to a central laboratory for testing.

The MDT rate in a prison is regularly monitored and results are made public and used as part of the prison service's performance measurement system, which feeds into its league tables. Various performance measures are used and all are weighted according to the level of seriousness they present in the eyes of the 'bean counters', as Sir Alan Beith described them in a Commons Select Committee Report in July 2011. Escape numbers are the most serious and most heavily weighted, unsurprisingly, with staff sickness levels and MDT rates coming second and third respectively. Governors and bean counters therefore have a vested interest in maintaining low MDT rates. Salary bonuses and performance appraisals depend on them. Harmful effects on prisoners, prison regimes and the public are less of a factor.

When I took command of HMP Brixton in 2003 it was officially the country's worst performing prison. It was failing at almost everything, with the exception of MDT. The service's nominal target for prisons was around 10 per cent; the MDT rate at Brixton was only 5 per cent. Under the circumstances, it was a very creditable performance, and not one any sensible governor would want to challenge. For the first few months of my tenure I noted the apparent success and set about all the other 'failures' on my plate. However, as I and my new team gradually got to grips with the nature of Brixton's problems, I pondered on the startling MDT figure and how it could have been achieved. Everything else in the jail – health, drug treatment, levels of violence, general disorder – tended to suggest that there was a drug problem in the jail. I slowly put in place the sort of performance management team required and eventually set them the task of reviewing the MDT process. Within a short space of time the officer running the testing programme took early retirement. We started to test people properly and the MDT rate soared to 50 per cent. All of a sudden I was being asked by the bean counters why, since I had taken over, the prison was now awash with drugs – my protestations that there were potential flaws at best and corruption at worst in the process nationally and that a full investigation was urgently needed fell on stony ground. My assertion that external validation of the process was essential for something the service set great store by was also ignored. The official mantra was that the MDT rate nationally was low and reducing, and the drug problem, therefore, was being successfully addressed.

Mick had his own particular take on the MDT process:

With MDT they have created a monster. It's gone out of control. Before the MDT started we used to just have a puff and the officer would come along and he would say: 'Come on you lot – bloody hell – open the window!' You used to just get on with it. There was no problem or friction on the wing with a bit of a puff. Now there is friction. There are burn outs [deliberate cell fires]. *There is violence going hand in hand with the drug selling. There's people coming in who don't know what they are doing. There are some who think they have a bit of heroin power – there's muscling, people getting beaten senseless for a bit of gear. It's only if you are a bit of a lump and know how to handle yourself that you can get by. When MDT came along, people knew that heroin would be out of your system in three days – with the puff it was fourteen.*

I never took class A [heroin and cocaine primarily], *it wasn't my thing. But plenty of people started. What started as a bit of a monkey on your back became a silverback* [major problem]. *And I've seen so many kids green to it come in, doing a little stupid two years with good family wrapped around, only for this other guy, who's two years down the line, who comes along and corrupts him. They are banged up in a cell together. The experienced guy gets a bag* [of heroin] *– the other guy, he's green, and before he knows it his Mum's sending in £50 a week and she's got to send it cause she knows it's his first time inside and she don't want him to get into trouble. And the man in the cell with him is much more experienced and he transfers that experience. The more money the younger man can get out of his parents, the better and the better life he can live as a smoker. The heroin kills the time – it's a bird* [time in prison] *killer. Then, when he gets out, the young guy has a habit he doesn't know how to manage. It's getting worse and worse and worse.*

I ask Mick how he feels about being the main dealer in such circumstances. Does he worry who he sells to?

You can't have a conscience in that game. If you are selling drugs in prison, you sell to whoever is going to pay you your money, because you are all about money – nothing else. You have to look at it from the point of view of the person who is serving a long sentence. He can either sit down in jail and rot or he can be proactive and make some form of money. So when he gets out he is standing up on his feet at least. You can't expect someone to be in jail and rot. For many, nothing else in jail is motivating and this is the reason why most drug dealers do it – it's just about the money.

If the long-termers doing their sentence had more things for them to do, more for them to facilitate themselves, to motivate themselves, and a structure where they can get to D Cat [open prison] and go out and work and earn a bit of money just before they get out, they would be able to stand on their own feet. Hypothetically, that's how it could work, how it's supposed to work – but it doesn't.

I went to my D Cat after serving twelve years. I'm there for eighteen months 'til I get out and I'm fighting tooth and nail for them to give me home leaves. I got there with big dreams and aspirations. I've got eighteen months left. It can take me three months to get home leave or a job working outside the prison, but it just doesn't happen – there's not enough jobs for all the Cat Ds going outside to work.

Then you have lifers and IPPs [those imprisoned for public protection with indeterminate sentences] – they carry priority. You're in a D Cat doing the same thing you were doing back in a B Cat years and years ago. That's what I was doing. I was working in the laundry in Parkhurst years back in my sentence and I ended up in the laundry in D Cat years later. It didn't make no sense. And there are staff who just want to make life difficult. Leyhill was typical. You got there and you had to do a money management course and an IT course before you could graduate to go outside to work. And you had to prove you had literacy and numeracy one and two [NVQ level 1 and 2]. I arrive there with thirty-five certificates from various courses. The money management course – I've done it three times. They say I have to do it here as well. But then they tell you there are no courses right now so you have to go on the waiting list. How long's the waiting list? It's nine months. Plus lifers carry priority over long-termers. So you just feel like you don't count. So you might as well sell drugs. You try and do it the right way and the right way just isn't working. You *try and be proactive – you do everything you can leading up to this time. Then you see someone who has done less than you, but because he is on a life sentence getting priority. I'm not taking it away from a lifer, but we all have our burden to carry. They go out and mess it up because they have had too much too quick. You say if you had had that space you wouldn't mess up. So it causes unneces-sary resentment in the prison and there is no answer for it. Because unless they address these problems they are always going to have a drug problem. Because you are leaving prisoners like me who have the know-how to make our own way.*

The last Christmas I was there, one particular officer pissed me off. So I said all right, we'll see. My game was to just flood that prison with drink that Christmas. I did it for a laugh. I don't even drink. But because he pissed me off, I said all right, I'll show you. You ain't gonna have a nice Christmas. And he didn't. He was running from one wing to another because there was drink everywhere. And you know how prisoners get with the drink and it was out of control. And I done it just to piss him off.

I was behaving myself and I was not active and he called me in the office and he said, 'Look, I've read your file and if I hear even a whisper out of you, we'll be cuffing you.' I said, 'I've been here six months and you haven't heard a whisper out of me. I'm not active. But if you want to push me I can be. It's only a phone call.' He said, 'I'll know if you are at it.' So I said, 'OK, we'll see.' So the next week I flooded the jail with 10 litres of vodka. It was easy. The fence is that big. [He raises a hand about four feet high.] *It's not rocket science. I phoned my mate in Bristol, it took him 15 minutes to drive down to the jail with two smokers* [heroin smokers] *jump the fence and run it to the window.*

So I ask him how much he has made over the years.

I had a partner [in the drug deals]. *When my Mum passed away in 2009 I went to my Mum's funeral. My partner was there and he said it's time I stopped all this and came home. He said, look, it's not all about money. If you don't want to listen I'm gonna cut off all your links and tell everyone not to deal with you no more. But I listened and he was right. And I had kids and, although I had kept in contact with them, I wanted the time to concentrate on them more. So I started on planning to come home and reinventing myself and focusing in on what to do when I came home. So I stopped for the last two years from my Mum dying in 2009 to getting out in 2011. But I'm not going to lie to you, I did make a lot of money in jail. I had a daughter to get through university; I had to buy her a car. The money was handy. I made about £28,000 on that last sentence, over a period of six years. I stopped over the last two years. That was just profit at the end. You have to realise the more money you earned, the more you spend, and I spent a lot when I was inside. I spent a lot of money on my kids. They wanted this and that and I got it for them. You're not spending it on yourself necessarily, but on your family. When I stopped, I had £28,000 when I came home. That was easy. I had mates who made over £100,000.*

I asked him more about MDT and how you might get round the system.

There is this tablet what sells in Boots – over the counter – when you puff [smoke cannabis] you take the tablet. If you puff Friday, Saturday, Sunday and take the tablet on the Monday, take it again Tuesday, by Wednesday you are clean and can pass an MDT – the tablet cleans your liver. It's not illegal – it sells over the counter. Then you have this new thing – spice. That's what they smoke in D Cat [open prison] now – spice – it's legal. There is no THC [Tetrahydrocannabinol, the active ingredient in cannabis] *in it. If an officer comes in your cell, it's legal so it's not a problem – it sells over the counter. Many a time I was smoking it in my cell, an officer would say, 'Oh, that smells nice, what is it?' And I just say it's a new tobacco I got off home leave. The officer hasn't got a clue and if he piss tests you it doesn't show up.*

For VDT's [voluntary drug testing] I used a tea bag for the last six years of my sentence. They come and tap you and say they want an MDT off you. You have a tea bag on you and you know there is water in the bleedin' toilet. It's so easy it's ridiculous. I think I gave them tea bag for the last six years. You take water out of the toilet, squeeze the tea bag in it – make it dark like piss – and give it to them. Nine times out of ten they just want to tick their box and they are happy – they aren't checking anything. Then when some of them started to do their job properly they would take the temperature of the piss. So when they started to do that I would carry a bottle and my body temp would warm it up. When they come for the test I just give them the warm water, coloured with the tea bag.

Then we used steradent tablets, which they used to sell in the prison shop to clean our flasks out. You would carry a bit wrapped in cling film and hidden in your foreskin. You get an MDT and then you drop it in it, it's all over.

I asked Mick why the lab tests on the urine samples didn't pick up the fiddle.

The voluntary ones don't get sent to the outside lab, they just use a machine test in the prison. I would use steradent for MDT and it was once picked up. I argued that I had simply used it to clean my flask and had made my hot drink in the flask and that it must have contaminated it. It's not my fault there is still steradent in the flask. I am not going to admit that I have administered it 'cause that is tampering with an MDT, and I got off. After that they didn't bother.

I then ask Mick if staff were ever paid to fix an MDT.

I had two friends coming up for D Cat [open prison]. They had an MDT and they had been smoking and they knew they would fail, so they bunged the officer £200. They had been smoking skunk all week – it was going to be a positive. All they [prison staff] do is tear a hole in the bag that it's sent off in and the MDT is written off – it goes off in a sealed bag and if the bag has a hole in it, it's regarded as written off. So all the officer had to do was put a hole in the bag when it's sent off. They won't test it if the bag is damaged – they just write it off. The MDT figures don't mean shit because there's ways round it, like I've just said.

Most C Cat prisoners are using those legal tablets. The tablets will be smuggled in just like drugs and phones. They sell for £10 a pop and they sell in Boots for £4.50 for thirty tablets. You can also get it in liquid form. It's madness. Easy as pie. You can buy spice over the counter in them smokers' shops – £25 for *3 grams and it's selling like hot cakes in jails now, mostly in D Cats.*

But you are getting a lot of heroin users now making D Cats and they can't manage the freedom. They can get the drugs in dead easy. I've seen guys get to open condition try to get help – they just can't get it so they phone their people and say look, I can't hack it here no more, I'm going to abscond tonight. Then they will just go to the police and hand themselves in and say they just couldn't handle the drugs in the prison. I've seen it happen numerous times in open prison because there is a real problem. They aren't getting enough help to get them to come off the drugs. Not getting aftercare – it's just a vicious circle. What HMP [public sector prisons] *need to do is hire inmates like myself who used to be proactive that way – to come in as a security advisor, to watch the prison for a week and advise where their weak spots are and tell them. We can identify the problems and really tell them what's going on in the wings. I could walk into any wing in any prison and within half an hour tell you who the main man is. I could tell straight away. He is the man that everyone is around. The one everyone wants to be friends with. I preferred to be the man behind the mirror – they don't notice who I am but I am creating the most problems in the jail. That's how I used to be, but other people would use brown* [heroin] *power, get a bit leery. You have an ounce, you have the swagger, and then that ounce runs out and you're stuffed. I was consistent. I never ran out 'cause I always had my resources and someone to tap . That became me, became my life – programming people, getting the drugs into the prison. It was like a job to me.*

MICHELLE

Michelle had her own take on corruption. She described how she grew up with her mother and an abusive father. Eventually she moved out and lived with her grandmother, who died when she was thirteen. She began smoking and drinking, quickly gravitating towards cannabis. Sexually abused during her teens by her cousin, her drinking got worse and she describes 'getting into unsafe situations'. At twenty-three she was raped and moved on to crack cocaine. At twenty-five she gave birth to a son, but she had a breakdown when he was six months old. She sought help from social services, but as she was abusing drugs they took her son away from her. Her mother thought that losing the child would be the shock she needed to get her clean. It made things worse. She rocketed out of control. Drugs led to crime and she eventually went to prison for robbery, possession of firearms, wounding with intent and possession with intent to supply Class A drugs. She could no longer look after her son.

I got four-and-a-half for the gun charge and three-and-a-half for the supplying – I went guilty. I was mixing with hardened criminals. I used to do a lot of armed robberies and walk around with guns. I had no idea what I was doing; I just wanted to get involved.

I didn't progress too well in prison because I was still linked and in contact with serious criminals – one got two life sentences. I was still corresponding with my co-defendant. I wasn't allowed to work outside the prison. It held me back.

Before I went away, I used to go and see my son's dad, Jimmy, in prison – he would get nicked quite a lot. He told me that he wanted mobile phones and that I would have to go and meet certain prison officers outside. He wanted me to do it and I thought nothing of it. He asked me to meet particular officers. He wouldn't give me the name of the officer, he just said what he would look like. Jimmy would give me a spot to meet him – one time was in Stoke Newington. Before the meet I would be given an envelope and some packages by one of Jimmy's friends. I knew there was money in the envelope but I never counted it. I knew the packages had drugs and mobiles in them. Jimmy would phone me from prison and talk in code about the meet or he would just tell me on a visit what to do. When you meet the officer there are no names, just 'Hi, you OK?' We would just know each other from eye contact. I'd then give him the packages and he would go off. I knew he was

a prison officer because I was told he was a prison officer. I recognised one
particular guy. He was a visits officer when I went to see Jimmy one time.
I did this for about a year, with about four different officers. I always said
my name – but they were very clever, they never said theirs. I didn't want to
know who they were to be honest. Jimmy kept telling me it was ok and that
it happened all the time – how else would we get phones in? But it didn't sit
comfortable with me.

Michelle described how the system worked well whilst Jimmy was
in Brixton and Pentonville. Jimmy was well used to both jails, being
remanded there on numerous occasions. He formed good relationships
and knew who to deal with.

Jimmy was finally convicted and sentenced and transferred to HMP
Swaleside. This was a jail I governed for over four years in the late 1990s.
It is a large Category B training prison, close to the village of Eastchurch
on the Isle of Sheppey in Kent. It is now part of a cluster of prisons with
neighbouring Elmley (a local) and Stamford Hill (an open) prison. It
is, for many prisoners from London, a second stage for those serving
long sentences. Mainly white staff from Kent preside over an institution
comprising men from outside the area with very different ethnic and
cultural origins. Things were completely different here for Jimmy and
he did not have the contacts to continue with the acts of trafficking he
had mastered so well in London jails.

Michelle was quickly pressurised into trying to smuggle directly into
the prison through visits and failed spectacularly – receiving three years
for supplying drugs.

I was due a visit but was smashed on drugs and felt really pressured. I felt I
had to do it. He hadn't been there long and didn't really know anyone yet.
I had a half-ounce [14g] of heroin, one-sixteenth of crack and a nugget [of
crack] in my purse. I was totally stoned – I'd just come back from raving and
went straight to the visit. When Jimmy realised what I had he went mad and
told me it was all too big to plug [insert into his anus] and that I would

have to go to the toilet, break it up and reshape it so he could plug it. Men can't plug massive amounts – women can – use your imagination. Visits is a route, but only little bits come in on visits – just bits for personal use. The real amounts come in through officers or over the walls – it's obvious isn't it?

Because I was totally out of it the officers got suspicious and it all came on top. When the prison officers went for us, Jimmy grabbed the bag and quickly shook the contents all over the floor and other prisoners started picking up the bits. Other prisoners started grabbing bits and plugging them – there was nearly a riot. They didn't find as much on me as they could have done. But I got three years for the heroin and three for the crack and two for the stone of crack in my purse – all concurrent. I just put my hands up.

Michelle started off her sentence in Holloway and then went to HMP Downview, a women's prison in Surrey. She described how women going to work outside the prison would bring in drugs 'plugged' (inserted into their anus or vagina). She also described how contraband was thrown over the wall and working on the gardens was the best way of retrieving such items. But it was corruption of relationships that she remembered most, and how it was staff using prisoners rather than the other way round that was at the heart of that particular system.

Officers having relationships with prisoners was quite common. It was always talked about openly when I was at Holloway. This male PO would come to my door all the time and he really scared me. Nothing would be said, but you just knew. This guy just wanted something more. He was well known – he had a reputation for relationships with women. He had keys and could open the door and have sex. At first he seemed like a nice man, but he was slimy. You always got that feeling that he was after something. That was a scary time. Women would succumb because they would get free alcohol and free drugs. There was a deal. I know the power of addiction. People will take advantage. Because they have often been working the street they are really open to being used. They want what they want. It is abuse of power by staff – and abuse can be both ways. For many it is just another form of prostitution. For some men and lesbian women, they just want what they want. If you look at the dynamics – addiction is quite powerful. In jail it's worse. For women, the reality of waking up to prison is pretty bad. It's very painful and heroin is a bird [time in jail] *killer. It's a day out. Taking heroin is a holiday – you aren't in reality, you are in another reality. It's quite powerful. People who don't use drugs don't understand the power of drugs, but they understand the mindset of those that do, and they know they are vulnerable and they take advantage.*

I remember one officer in Cookham Wood [formerly a women's prison in Kent, now a Young Offender Institution] *– a man. When he was doing the early morning roll check, instead of knocking he would just walk right in – before opening the flap* [observation hatch in the cell door]. *Girls would be just getting dressed. He knew that – we confronted him but he just laughed. Girls would be naked. I eventually heard he got suspended for a sexual relationship with a prisoner. Usually it's all very discreet but you can see it in people's contact and conversations – you don't see people having sex, but it's all around you. I think people in prison are vulnerable. There was once a real big clean-up at Holloway and lots of officers – mainly women – got moved. It didn't stop it – relationships in prison is massive, you know what I mean? And it can get very serious – too serious sometimes.*

I remember in Downview one of my friends was really cut up. An officer was using her – she had mental health problems and was very vulnerable. We were all showering one day and messing about, laughing and stuff. Then she suddenly started telling us about this relationship she was having with an officer. She said that she thought they had something but now the officer suddenly didn't want to know. It had got real heavy and the officer suddenly told her not to talk to her again. I've seen these lesbian officers – they can be quite brutal – pick you up and then throw you away. She was really tearful and very upset. We then got banged up. Next morning, just as we were being unlocked for breakfast, I heard this scream – the girl had hanged herself. I can't prove anything, but I made the link and so did the others. Nobody spoke to us about her; we didn't hear anything about any inquiry. We were all looking for parole – we weren't going to rock the boat.

PETE

Pete is a gregarious 31-year-old now working hard to support his family, gain qualifications and give something back to society after serving four years for assault and GBH. He served sixteen months in HMP Liverpool, or Walton jail as it is known locally. It is a huge structure holding over 1,100 souls, and it has had a chequered history over the years, seeing executions as late as 1964. With some wings as high as five stories, it is as imposing as any place of incarceration in the UK. It has a complex culture underpinned by an even more complex history. It is one of the most difficult prisons in the country to run, as some of its past governors will testify. The people of Liverpool may well be known for their wit and good humour. Their jail has no such charm.

Pete described working on the 'yards party' – going round the jail sweeping up litter and picking up the parcels of excrement that still get thrown out of windows despite in-cell sanitation.

There was about six of us. One of the lads on the yards party was a very influential guy in the prison. He carried a lot of clout and everything went through him – drugs, hooch, all the contraband. We would be on yards duty. It would be the same officer in charge of us on the yard. We would get to a certain part of the prison – a blind spot for the cameras. The officer would get the nod – he would turn around and walk away, fifteen to twenty yards. Then numerous parcels would start coming over the wall – big parcels in pillow cases as well as small parcels. A couple of the other lads – the runners, never the con [prisoner] in charge – they would get the parcels and quickly pass them through the cell windows on the ground floor. The parcels would be broken up, and in minutes would be all round the wing. We were never short of drugs or mobiles. Then the officer in charge of us would turn round, and when we had formed into a group again he would come back over to us. We would then carry on cleaning around the prison.

I asked Pete how the people on the other side of the wall knew when and where to throw things over it. What was the signal from the prisoner running the operation? 'He just rang them on his mobile!'

TEN

SAVING MONEY

At a time when the economy is barely recovering from the meltdown of 2008 there is no point in expecting the problems of the prison service to be solved by throwing cash at it. That will not happen. Not only will prisons not receive extra cash but they are expected to save money, to reduce expenditure. That process is underway and is being addressed in a manner which underlines both the intellectual and the moral bankruptcy of the service. Perhaps the best example of this was when back in 2008 a decision was taken nationally to close all prisons on a Friday afternoon, thus effectively cancelling all activities for prisoners and enforcing 'bang-up'. That would be, for some, from lunchtime on a Friday to first thing Monday morning – with only limited time out for exercise. This one size fits all approach even permeated to the private sector, which when bidding for contracts for new or existing prisons was required under the tender specifications to follow the same principles of a 'core day'. How much was actually saved has never been articulated. Neither was the financial and opportunity cost of education, drug treatment, employment, training and other work, often externally contracted for Friday afternoons, which had to be cancelled or curtailed. Intelligent and imaginative governors, capable of taking hard decisions about their own jails in their own local circumstances were insulted and, as ever, sidelined.

It is possible to save money in prisons, to be more efficient, but to be so in an intelligent and constructive way which is in line with the aspirations of reformers, the diktats of government and the strictures of the manda-rins. There is perennial debate about the locking up of prisoners: too few or too many depending upon your own particular standpoint. The prison population continues to soar ever higher. The Labour government lit the blue touch paper for the explosion in the prison population, and the Conservative/Lib Dem coalition, after a brief outbreak of commonsense under the direction of Secretary of State for Justice Ken Clarke, decided to ignore it by following the Blair government and ignore any notion of being tough on the causes of crime in favour of just being tough on crime. The city riots of August 2011 finally buried any hopes of a falling prison population as the public mood pushed the judiciary into the most extraordinarily severe sentences rather than what in more rational times would have been fines or community punishments. But the problem of rising numbers has not been solely about the punitive public mood or more and more offences hitting the statute book. Getting people out is as much a part of the problem as stopping people coming in. Keeping them in conditions of appropriate security and the costs that go with it adds to the financial dilemmas faced by the prison service. The management of the remand population is a prime example of an area of prison life compounding all of these issues.

REMANDS

We talk of the remand population in prison but how many members of the public fully understand exactly what is going on?

If you commit a crime or are suspected of committing a crime you will be arrested and taken to a police station where you will be charged with an offence. You may be held in custody at the police station and may not be charged immediately. You may then be released on bail sanctioned by the police. All these events are strictly regulated, not least in terms of time. But at some point you will, if the police so decide, be brought before a court, initially a magistrates' court, where you are required to answer the charge. It may be dealt with, if you plead guilty, there and then. It is very common if you plead not guilty for the case to be adjourned and dealt with at a later date, by which time evidence can be gathered and the defence and prosecution cases prepared. In that intervening period between first appearance at court and magistrates hearing or court trial, the court has to decide what should be done with you: remand you in custody – i.e. send you to prison, or release you on bail. That decision can have the most profound impact on individuals, the legal system and of course the prison system.

The numbers of people involved are very significant. In 2009 over 55,000 people were remanded in custody awaiting trial. A total of 37,000 people were remanded into prison having been convicted but not yet sentenced. At the end of a court case, if you are found guilty the judge or magistrate may take some time, possibly a few weeks, to decide what your sentence should be. Very often he or she will seek reports from probation officers or legal experts that inform the sentencing decision. At the end of September 2010 the remand population, i.e. those on trial or awaiting sentence, was 12,706. That is approximately 14 per cent of the prison population. Nearly 800 of the remand population were women, about 18 per cent of the female prisoner population. This figure of 12,000 prisoners is the equivalent of fourteen Brixton prisons. Brixton costs approximately £20 million a year to run. So keeping that remand population behind bars costs about a quarter of a billion pounds.

It is worth reflecting on the fundamental principle that an individual is innocent until proven guilty: we spend a quarter of a billion pounds keeping innocent people in prison. Obviously, some of these will be violent and dangerous individuals from whom the public needs to be protected. But the law emanating from the Bail Act of 1976 is quite clear on how we should differentiate between those remanded to prison and those released on bail. The law says that there should be a presumption of bail for all people except those awaiting trial on charges of murder, attempted murder, manslaughter, rape or attempted rape. The legislation goes on to require bail with various conditions for all others unless there are strong reasons not to let people out pending their trial.

The reasons are all very obvious: if the offence is particularly serious or an individual has previous convictions for similar offences, they might run away, commit further offences or interfere with witnesses. Being shown to be abusing Class A drugs through testing on arrest can also cause bail to be refused. A court opinion on whether an individual is able to comply with any bail conditions will also be a factor. But whilst the law appears quite clear on the matter, we are dealing with some of the most chaotic and often socially excluded in society. At a very practical level, if someone appears before a court on what might be a relatively minor charge but they are living rough, with drug and alcohol addiction and mental health problems there is a good chance the court will see them as too chaotic for bail and send them to prison. We should ask therefore, are they sent to prison for criminal or social reasons? In fairness to the court, for such an individual there are few options it can consider. Bail hostels do exist as a halfway house between custody and community but there are too few and they lack the support mechanisms to deal with the plethora of candidates with their innumerable health and social care issues.

Secretary of State for Justice Ken Clarke, in the summer of 2011, attempted to address the problem by proposing that those facing a charge that was unlikely to lead to a custodial sentence should automatically be given bail regardless of other circumstances. To most informed observers this was little more than the 'bleedin' obvious'. Having talked about the scheme to a Tory conference in 2010, the proposal was included in a government Green Paper. Clarke's proposals also included other very sensible ones regarding sentence discounts for early pleas of guilt. The proposals survived an initial onslaught by the usual suspects in the form of the tabloid media, magistrates and Labour politicians keen to out-tough the Tories on crime. Clarke eventually had the rug pulled from beneath him by Prime Minister David Cameron following one of a series of U-turns last year as the coalition fought a wider political battle for popularity. Savings of around £40 million were therefore scuppered, to be sought elsewhere as part of the required £2 billion for Clarke's department.

But there are three components to the costs of the remand population. There is the cost articulated by Clarke in terms of prison numbers.

Reducing the numbers will always be a holy grail for all but the most rabid of right wingers. There are also human costs to the remand population which have knock-on effects both socially and economically for wider society. The average waiting time before a suspect in jail goes to trial has risen from ten to thirteen weeks over the last decade. Conditions in prisons holding remands, inner city local prisons, tend to be the most spartan and the least suited to supporting access to information, legal counsel and every other form of advocacy. Although only 14 per cent of the prison population, remands accounted for 43 per cent of all self-inflicted deaths in 2008. A quarter of all men and about half of all women receive no visits whilst on remand. It is also worth remembering how disruptive remand in custody can be to an individual, how it can make a life that is difficult considerably, and unnecessarily, worse.

Imagine yourself at home, at work or simply walking through your local town. You are arrested and taken to a police station where you will be allowed contact with a solicitor and a call to a friend or relative. You are then taken to court and remanded in custody. You are now in prison. You will be processed through 'reception', as the welcoming process is called and be allowed to make one phone call. You may be one of the fortunate few who memorise phone numbers or be like the majority and rely on the memory on your mobile phone. This will have been taken off you, and don't assume access to it to find a number will be straightforward. Over your first week in prison you may be able to get yourself a visit and perhaps another phone call. Neither will be easy, not least the phone call which will require you to buy a phone card with money you may not have, only to have to queue up on the wing for access to one of the very few public phones, behind others desperate to contact home, in the short time the prison regime and the paltry amount on your card allows. Prisoners pay more per minute on phone calls than anyone else on the planet. You will have left behind a whole social infrastructure of family, friends, work, home, pets (or for some, none of the above). You may need to collect benefit, pay rent or most importantly turn up for a job you may have only just got. There is a real chance that if you have just managed to acquire a stake in society, a period on remand may just blow it all apart. One young remand prisoner approached me in Brixton to protest forlornly that he had parked his car legally but for a predetermined time immediately before arrest, that he had the only keys and that by now it would have been towed away incurring a spiral of penalties he could not afford. Another was desperate because his dog was now locked in his flat.

A natural response from the general public may be that this is something the individual should have thought of before getting themselves into a position in which they were arrested. But if we put aside, as we too often do, the pure humanity of the situation the facts should cause us to pause and think. In 2007, 11,400 people were remanded into custody, 21 per cent were acquitted, 30 per cent went on to receive a non-custodial sentence. Three-quarters of those under eighteen locked up pending trial with a judge or magistrate were either acquitted or given a community sentence. Bear in mind that if as a defendant you are acquitted after a period of remand, which can be months or even years in some cases, you are not automatically entitled to compensation. The chances of compensation in all but the most exceptional cases are virtually zero. You may lose your job, your home, friends, benefits, car or cat, but the system simply says 'tough'.

If defaulting to remand in custody with adults is expensive and retrograde, then to do so with children is, in the eyes of the United Nations Children's Fund (UNICEF), unlawful. In a report in October 2011 UNICEF was scathing in its criticism of the UK judicial system for locking up children allegedly involved in the riots of the summer of that year. It saw the UK legal system's punitive approach as likely to be in breach of children's rights under UN obligations.

UNICEF and the World Health Organization have always regarded anyone under eighteen as a child. Jurisdictions incarcerating such young people have always been reluctant to use the term child, preferring 'juvenile'. During my time with the prison's inspectorate where I led on the inspection of prison establishments holding 'juveniles', I was exhorted to 'stop calling them children' in my reports by a very exasperated and very senior prison official after yet another damning report about the treatment and conditions in one particular children's prison. I declined and the matter was wisely not put to the then Chief Inspector of Prisons, Sir (now Lord) David Ramsbotham.

Britain was a signatory in 1991 to the UN Convention on the Rights of the Child and UNICEF was of the view that the actions in the courts following the riots of August 2011 were a breach of the convention. Of all the under-eighteens detained after the riots, 45 per cent had no previous criminal history. Ministry of Justice figures that year showed that more than 40 per cent of the 269 children whose court hearings were not completed by mid-September were remanded in custody. Remand rates for the previous year had only been 10 per cent. Of those on remand, 60 per cent had no previous convictions and 45 per cent had had no contact with the judicial system at all, including official reprimands or warnings.

Article 37 of the UN convention was in line with what the courts should have been doing anyway as part of all court processes, namely using remand only as a last resort. In a country which already imprisoned more children than any other European country, the number increased by 8 per cent after the riots.

The inequity of it all was illustrated by wide regional variations. Only one of the fifty youths awaiting sentence in Manchester was remanded in custody, whilst in London the figure was 85 out of 219.

UNICEF's UK branch said in a statement:

The UN convention on the rights of the child [CRC] is clear in article 37 that the detention of children should only happen as a last resort in criminal proceedings. The fact that 45 per cent of the children detained on charges of rioting and looting are completely unknown to the UK's criminal justice system is, therefore, very worrying.

People who were assaulted, mugged or whose property was destroyed by the rioting will have been scared and know that their rights have been badly violated. However, our justice system must not violate the rights of children in response to these terrible events. It is vital that it adheres to the CRC when considering the punishment of children who commit crimes.

The statement continued:

> We believe that society needs to understand the deeper causes behind the involvement of children, not simply blame them. Far from being a cause of antisocial behaviour, we believe that respecting rights builds strong societies, strong values and citizen engagement.
>
> We must also make sure that following any criminal punishment the children concerned are helped and supported to return to their communities and develop into adults who contribute to our society not become repeat offenders.
>
> The riots are a concern and responsibility for us all. We urge those in charge of responding to the riots not to blame children's rights, but to respect them.

The UK is therefore remanding people in custody in flagrant breach of UN conventions and UK legal guidelines. We are incarcerating people by a process that is at best misinterpreted or at worst redefined. We can deal better with the remand system by simply using it for the purpose for which it was intended. Those who do have to be held behind bars can be accommodated more efficiently and cheaply.

Outside the categorisation system of A to D, all remand prisoners are given the category 'U' for uncategorised. Categorisation is designed to be implemented after conviction and sentence. The category will depend upon the sentence length, previous convictions and a host of other criteria brought together after trial. Whilst in trial, the individual is uncategorised, despite the fact that they could be looking at a sentence of forty days or forty years. The only exception is that if they are seen as particularly dangerous and likely to be a Category A after sentence, they may then be treated as a potential Category A and treated accordingly. All the U category remands, however, are held in local prisons which are effectively secure Category B status – the second highest and the second most expensive at £35–£45,000 per prisoner place per year. Clearly this is an expensive place to hold someone who has a high chance of being acquitted, receiving a non-custodial sentence or one so short as to require release a brief time after sentence. Reconfiguring the prison estate, looking again at the function and role of prisons, is long overdue and likely to present considerable savings. Categorising remand prisoners would be a logical and sensible first step.

ELEVEN

OPEN PRISONS, TAGGING AND PAROLE

t the other end of the categorisation system, i.e. where people are
leaving prison as opposed to coming in, are open prisons. There are
six open prisons holding adult men. Together all six can hold up to
2,900 men. For women there are only two, Askham Grange in Yorkshire
and the beautiful country house of East Sutton Park in the gentle Kent
countryside. Together they hold 250 women. For young offenders there
are two establishments, Drake hall and Swinfen Hall in the midlands,
with a combined capacity of 800. So for a total prison capacity of 88,000
and counting, the capacity of the open prison estate is barely 4,000. Open
prisons cost significantly less to operate than closed prisons. The average
cost of imprisonment is £41,000 per prisoner per year, the average in an
open prison is £30,000 per prisoner per year. At any one time there are
nearly 8,000 prisoners serving less than twelve months. With sentencing
laws, whether you like them or not, stating that anyone serving under
twelve months will be released automatically at the halfway point then
there are 8,000 prisoners spending less than six months inside. If you add
to that figure the 21,000 serving twelve months to four years, most of
whom will also only serve half their sentence, then we have nearly 30,000
prisoners confined for less than two years. If we then look at what people
have been sentenced for, we find half the population have been sentenced
for offences other than violence against the person, sexual offences or
robbery. Finally, if we add the fact that we release up to 80,000 prisoners
per year for all offences and sentences, it is hard not to conclude that

we are overplaying the security aspects of imprisonment. No one would argue that serious, violent and dangerous offenders need to be kept in secure custody for long periods and in some cases (although currently only about forty) forever. Yet huge swathes of the prison population are serving short sentences for non-violent offences or moving towards the end of longer sentences. Only a handful have been told by the courts that they will never be released and whilst that number will be increased by those who prove during their sentence that they remain a danger to the public, the vast majority of prisoners will be released at some stage. So if open prisons are much cheaper why are there not more of them? Why do they scare the public, the media, the mandarins and the politicians, at a time when cost reductions are unavoidable?

Absconds are fear number one. Anyone escaping from within the secure perimeter of a prison is said to have escaped. If you walk out of an open prison you are said to have absconded. Absconding is clearly very easy because by definition there is no secure perimeter in an open prison. There are on average 150 absconds a year from the open estate, 4 per cent of the open prison population. The numbers are few but media interest is always intense and the term escape rather than abscond is almost invariably used to add to the hype. In 2009 East Sutton Park hit the headlines when Jane Andrews, the Duchess of York's former dresser for nine years until 1997, absconded. She had been jailed for life for murdering her boyfriend at their house in Fulham, west London, in September 2000. Andrews, who had attempted suicide on at least two occasions was found just two days later, covered in mud only nine miles from the jail after sleeping rough in the surrounding countryside. Prisoners like Andrews who have commit-ted homicide and abscond as they are being prepared for release into the community invariable invoke the 'Killer on the loose' headline. Do they, and did Andrews, really pose a major threat to public safety?

The majority of those who abscond from open prison, murderers or fraudsters and all those in between, tend not to do so with any sophis-ticated plan. Many will abscond because they cannot take the pressure of living in an open environment after years of control and restrictions.

Some do so by way of escape from bullying and harassment. Others after domestic arguments or disasters. Some will do so in a fit of pique because they were not allowed home leave or work in the community. Many, particularly young offenders, do so on impulse. There is very little research into the reasons why people abscond or what they do when they are free and the figures for those who have gone and never been recaptured are imprecise. High-profile absconders are usually quickly recaptured simply because the police go looking for them and urge the public to help. Many are recaptured because they go home and get arrested within days for petty offending. Many simply wander off aimlessly like Jane Andrews. One young man absconded from HMP Stanford Hill on the Isle of Sheppey in Kent, walked to the nearby railway station at Queenstown and waited hours for a train, not realising that there were no trains from that station on a Sunday. Foiled in his plan to get to London, a passing prison officer from the same jail spotted him on the way to work and gave him a lift back to custody. It was hardly *The Great Escape*.

But can open prisons offer anything constructive to the rehabilitative process? The evidence is clearly that they can, but because of the pejorative perception of this part of the prison estate the positive is subsumed by the much more interesting negative. This was amply illustrated by the riot at Ford open prison on New Year's Eve 2010. Ford is perhaps the most well known of Britain's open prisons. Near the picturesque town of Arundel in affluent west Sussex, Ford's notoriety has come from its famous inhabitants, including footballer George Best, and its holiday camp image perpetrated by stories of what came into the jail in the form of drugs, alcohol and women rather than who got out. Sadly it is now synonymous with riots after forty prisoners high on illicit alcohol burnt down four buildings. There had been warnings from HM Chief Inspector of Prisons and the establishment's own watchdog, the Independent Monitoring Board. The riot has put back the cause of open prisons despite the efforts of reformers like Juliet Lyon of the Prison Reform Trust pleading that the baby should not be thrown out with the bath water. Also part of the debate was that the 'wrong people' were being sent there. This was reference to the allegation that people not ready or suitable for such trust and freedoms were finding their way there due to the pressure on prison numbers nationally. So is Ford an illustration of the ineffectiveness of this type of institution and an argument against the principle of open prisons, or simply an example of the principle being managed badly.

HMP Kirkham, housing nearly 600 souls and the largest open prison in Europe, is proof that well-managed open prisons can work. Formerly RAF Kirkham and built between Blackpool and Preston in 1940, it was a prestigious training centre for troops not only from Britain but from many other allied nations during the war. By 1945 it had trained over 70,000 troops. It was a demob centre after the war and eventually closed in 1957. Kirkham was one of a number of former military encampments that were inculcated into the prison estate during the 1960s and became an open prison in 1962. Some new buildings were constructed to form prisoner accommodation but many structures of Second World War vintage remain, including some very dilapidated hangars. Like many prisons, open or closed, it has had a troubled history. In 2003 figures were produced showing that there had been 911 absconds since 1998. In 2004 the Prison Reform Trust highlighted the jail as having the worst record on drug misuse in the English and Welsh prison system, with 355 prisoners testing positive for illicit substances.

But at the end of 2009, a report from the Chief Inspector of Prisons, Anne Owers said:

Kirkham was a very purposeful and active prison, with plenty of good quality work and education. The numbers of prisoners working towards qualifications was much increased and achievements were high. There were also good library and PE facilities.

The strategic management of resettlement and delivery of related services had continued to develop. Offender management and public protection were well managed. Release on temporary licence was thoughtfully and appropriately used as an aid to resettlement. There were some good services available along all the resettlement pathways. The one missed opportunity was the underuse of the impressive Next Steps Centre – the old intermittent custody facility – and this resource needed to be better utilised.

Kirkham is an impressive open prison. It manages its risks well, focusing on safety, setting appropriate boundaries and confronting poor behaviour. Prisoners respond well, feel safe and the level of absconding has fallen significantly. Staff–prisoner relationships are good, supported by some of the best personal officer and prisoner-led advice work that we have come across. The prison is also very purposeful and active, with a wholly appropriate focus on resettlement. The governor and staff deserve considerable praise for what has been achieved.

It was not just the chief inspector heaping praise on the jail. Getting the local community on board with a prison rehabilitative agenda is the holy grail of some visionary governors, and the indomitable John Hewitson, governor of Kirkham, may just have managed this, as a letter to the *Daily Telegraph* in August 2011 demonstrates:

Prisoners at work

SIR – Ted Shorter (Letters, July 28) writes of prisoners' idleness. Kirkham and the rural Fylde in Lancashire have an excellent working relationship with HMP Kirkham, which does not believe in idleness.

Rather, we are in very grateful receipt of a regular workforce to tackle every job possible, including grounds clearance and maintenance, decorating the community centre, maintaining street furniture and spot litter picking.

Very importantly, in the worst of the winter weather, they have come out to clear the pavements of snow and ice for residents and businesses, not only in the town but also around doctors' surgeries and sheltered housing schemes.

The prison makes top-quality garden furniture and sells produce from the home farm at the prison shop. The prisoners are a pleasure to work with.

M. D. Barnes

Town Clerk

Kirkham, Lancashire

There is little to add to what was one of the most impressive reports ever produced by the inspectorate of prisons at a time when some prisons are still receiving damning reports and all are struggling with increasing numbers and financial cutbacks. So here is an effective and cheap prison being well managed by an effective and far-sighted 'governing governor' who has been in post for over three years, a relatively long period given that the average tenure of a governing prison governor is less than twenty months. Kirkham also has the benefit of extensive grounds around it, much of which is given over to farming, animal husbandry and a nature reserve. Here, if we need to expand the prison estate, is a place with land and, given its relative remoteness, little likelihood of local objection. It has the ethos, the leadership, the track record and the room to expand. Alas the expansion plans for the estate remain within the closed estate or in new constructions which are designed and run as secure Category B establishments, regardless of the pressing need for facilities of less and cheaper security status.

HOME DETENTION CURFEW

There are many other processes in prison which, if they operated efficiently would get more people out of prison and reduce costs without changing the law.

One such process is Home Detention Curfew (HDC), or tagging as it is often known. The scheme came into force in January 1999. It had two functions: to reduce the size of the prison population and to prepare prisoners better for release into the community. The prison service in its own rule book states: '[Prisoners] will normally be released on HDC unless there are clear grounds to indicate that they are unlikely success-fully to complete the period on curfew.'

The time released on HDC depends upon the length of the sentence ranging from fifteen to thirty days for very short sentences to ninety days if serving over twelve months. It involves being tagged, having an electronic ankle bracelet which monitors the primary condition of the release on licence, namely that the prisoner stays at home or at a desig-nated address in the evening and overnight.

There is therefore a clear presumption in favour of the scheme, not least because it is aimed at those offenders serving sentences of between three months and four years for offences that do not include serious violent or sexual offences. In other words non-serious offenders serving relatively short sentences. The scheme is not aimed at rapists and murderers. It does not apply either to anyone under eighteen, whom it is assumed (wrongly) will have a family to go to. The two stings in the tail of the scheme are: 'However, prison-ers must pass a risk assessment and have suitable accommodation approved by the Probation Service before they can be granted Home Detention Curfew.'

When looking at risk assessment we should first remind ourselves of the nature of the offenders we are talking about. They will have undoubtedly created victims but the law has decreed that these offences are not at the serious end of the spectrum. They are only being let out between two and twelve weeks early. They will therefore be out soon in any event. But in the current climate of risk aversion there is every reason for the governor of a prison making the final decision to find reasons not to release a prisoner. If a governor releases someone early on HDC and they go on to commit crime he will invariably receive opprobrium in the media. If however he insists as a result of perceived risk that the prisoner stays to the end of his short sentence and he then offends the day after his release, the criminal justice system is seen not to be blameworthy. A governor will be measured by his failures. He or she will not be measured by successes. Releasing no one and having no one offend on licence is the best option for a governor considering his career and the size of his mortgage. This is reflected in the fact that it is very difficult to find statistics on the rate of release of those eligible for HDC. There are approximately 40,000 prisoners per year eligible according to their length and type of sentence. Only about one-third will be granted such release and the rates vary considerably across prisons of similar types with similar populations. Some prisons release as many as 50–60 per cent of those eligible whilst others manage less than 20 per cent. The differences are not explored or accounted for in any way. But in terms of a prison's performance HDC failures will move it down the prison service performance league table and potentially ruin a governor's promotion prospects. The absence of HDC failures or effecting successful reintegration through the scheme count for nought.

The other element considered is accommodation. Unless an individual can find suitable accommodation, not least somewhere with a telephone line with which the electronic tag can be linked, then he or she stays in prison. Given the statistics of homelessness for those coming into prison and the further social exclusion to which a prison sentence adds, accommodation can be a major problem. 'Suitable' will not include sofa surfing or moving in with friends who are also in and out of prison, both of which are the most common 'accommodation' for prisoners immediately on release. Very often, therefore, people will stay in prison because they have nowhere to go and live. A few weeks later, however, they leave anyway, whether they have anywhere to live or not. You might assume that in the period between housing being identified as a barrier to early release and eventual release that all the stops would be pulled out to find someone a place to live. Not so. In a busy local prison where many of these short-termers find themselves or in a prison miles from home it is unlikely that anything other than somewhere for the first couple of nights, a hostel of some kind, will be found. So people remain in prison not because the law says they should as part of their punishment, but because there is nowhere for them to go. Hardly the best use of expensive incarceration.

PAROLE

A constituent part of the prison system is parole. Often referred to and often misunderstood. The origins of the word parole are French; the terms means voice or the spoken word, referring to systems in the Middle Ages where someone would give their word to abide by certain restrictions or to behave in a certain manner. Parole is very often referred to as serving your sentence in the community. Essentially it is a system whereby someone is released into the community before the end of his or her sentence under certain restrictions which if violated will cause them to be returned to prison. There are a plethora of rules and regulations around the many types of sentences that have evolved over the years. The likelihood and length of parole is greater the shorter and the less serious the offence. There is an obvious reticence on the part of the decision-making authorities and a more elaborate process for the most serious and dangerous offenders. At the far end of the spectrum are those sentenced to life imprisonment. If released, it is under the term 'life licence' rather than parole. 'Life should mean life' is the retort of many, particularly in the context of murder. It does indeed mean life, in that the licence on which someone is released remains in force for the rest of that individual's life. The conditions of the licence may vary but the licence itself remains.

The Parole Board is the independent body that makes the decision whether to release someone. Established in 1968 under the Criminal Justice Act of 1967, it makes decisions about those on all types of indeterminate sentence as well as determinate sentences for more serious offences, normally those of four years or more. It is a body under increasing pressure without a commensurate increase in resources. It will examine as many as 25,000 cases per year and does so either as part of an oral hearing or as a paper exercise. It currently makes a decision to release only about 18 per cent of those it considers, a figure which is slowly decreasing. Of equal concern is the rate at which those released are recalled to prison for breaching the conditions of their licence. In 1999 the figure was 1,200. In 2010 it was 1,500. So not only are fewer and fewer prisoners being released on parole, but the number of those coming back for 'failing' are increasing.

'Recalls', as they are called, are not just a statistic that increases the prison population. As a group they are difficult to manage. They tend to be somewhere between angry and bitter to sadly resigned to the fact that they cannot cope in the outside world. I met and spoke with many at Brixton. Some recalled disputes with probation officers and blamed their recall on a supervising officer's over-zealous approach to the terms of the licence. Tales of recall for being half an hour late for an appointment abounded. The truth was invariably more complex but the bitterness remained. Some admitted to breaches of rules and regulations with which they had no hope of complying. Chaotic lives were not being reordered by paper licences. Others found themselves ill prepared for life outside and were resigned to incarceration until the system finally threw them out 'time expired'. As a whole they would be subject to reviews and hearings to determine their future which was, more often than not, no second chance. Engaging them in any meaningful aspects of the prison regime was virtually impossible as many would have a relatively short time to serve or were too demotivated in a scenario where competition for education, treatment and training was already intense. Like those refused HDC, they were a part of the prison population for whom the system was ill-designed to respond to their complex needs. It was, arguably, also not capable of responding to the fact that offending is a chronically relapsing condition. Many people stop offending eventually but they start by offending less and for less serious offences. Often referred to as desistance, the gradual reduction of offending, as opposed to stopping all offending immediately, is progress not recognised or measured. Making analogies with giving up smoking, drinking or dieting may not please many, but a life of habitual offending where norms of society are as little understood as they are complied with is the background of many and difficult to ignore. Even if the wishes of the individual are sincere and resolute, those of influential negative and nefarious peers groups will be in stark contrast.

I noticed a young man one day on G Wing at Brixton. He caught my glance but quickly looked away and sought to dodge my advance. With nowhere to go he turned and looked at me forlornly and said, 'Sorry, Gov.'

I recalled Alan as a disturbed, young habitual offender who had progressed from the young offender to adult system. With a typical background of care, school expulsion and social exclusion, he had shown promise in jail on his last sentence, engaging in arts and charitable projects. Typically serving yet another short sentence, he had left with warm wishes and high hopes. Here, less than six months later, he was seemingly back where he had started. He relayed to me the familiar story of so many young men in south London, a life in and out of crime since the age of fifteen. He was down but not out, underlining to me at the end of his story that on this occasion he had been out for six months whereas before he hadn't lasted six days. As far as the system was concerned he was a negative key performance indicator, a statistic I thought best not to share with him.

TWELVE

LIFE SENTENCES
– A NATIONAL OBSESSION

Perhaps the biggest single contribution to the problem of prisoners failing to get released has been Britain's national obsession with the life or indeterminate sentence. Whilst the UK has devised ever more reasons for imposing it and increased the offences to which it implies, in some countries it does not exist at all. These include Spain, Portugal and Norway as well as a number of South American countries such as Brazil, Bolivia, Colombia and Ecuador.

The modern approach to dealing with the most heinous of crimes came with the abolition of capital punishment in 1965. Since then an offence of murder has carried a mandatory sentence of life imprisonment. It is only applicable to defendants aged twenty-one or over. Those aged between eighteen and twenty are sentenced to 'custody for life'. The term for those aged under eighteen is 'detention during Her Majesty's pleasure' (often simply referred to as HMP) for murder, or 'detention for life' for other crimes.

The life sentence has two components. The first is the tariff or minimum term to satisfy the requirements of retribution and deterrence (the punishment part). Then, once the tariff has been reached, a prisoner will only be released if he or she can satisfy the Parole Board that the risk to the public is acceptable. A court may set a whole life tariff, i.e. to stay in prison for the whole of a person's natural life (although not for those under twenty-one) but in 2011 there were fewer than forty of those in the entire prison estate.

Before 2000 for young offenders and 2002 for adults, the tariff was set by the Home Secretary. After trial a tariff document would be circulated to the trial judge, the Lord Chief Justice and then the Home Secretary. In a short paragraph they would set out the tariff and their reasons for it. The final entry and the final decision would be that of the politician not the judiciary. This power was eventually challenged in the House of Lords, which ruled that it was incompatible with human rights, and the decision was later upheld by the European Court of Human Rights. It was the frequent increase of the tariff by the politicians at odds with the view of judges that prompted the appeal. For many years there was concern that politicians with a propensity to waver under political and media pressure should not supersede the decisions of those presiding over the case and any legal appeal. The Attorney General still has the power to petition the Court of Appeal if the tariff is seen as particularly lenient. The change also ensured that defendants would receive the tariff as soon as possible after conviction. Under the old system considerable delays were common and transparency over the reason almost non-existent.

As with every other sentence, guidelines for how long murderers should spend in prison before being considered for parole were set by the Criminal Justice Act of 2003. The guidelines established criteria for the possibility of whole life tariffs and indicated a minimum of thirty years where there were multiple murder victims. Minimums of thirty years were also recommended where there were sexual or racial motives, or where there were firearms involved or police officer victims. Fifteen years was the starting point for most other murders. Judges are not obliged to follow the guidelines, but have to give reasons if they depart from them. The 2003 Act represented a significant push upwards in the average time a lifer could expect to serve. From around nine years in the 1970s the average increased steadily to around twelve years at the start of the twenty-first century. That is set to go even higher as the system fails to cope with the numbers and responds to the risk aversion of the public and media pressure.

Yet whilst the abolition of the death penalty was seen as enlightened legislation, what followed has been seen by some as a legal mess which did not serve the interests of the public and was the starting point for an obsession with indeterminate prison sentences which represents one of the prison service's most significant problems and which should bring shame on the country.

The point was made adroitly by Lord Lloyd in a House of Lords debate in March 2007: 'Murder is too important a subject to be considered by the lawyers, as it has been, and by civil servants, as it is about to be. It is a subject in which the public are involved.'

In the same year the Law Commission went further: 'The law governing homicide in England and Wales is a rickety structure set upon shaky foundations. Some of its rules have remained unaltered since the seventeenth century … others have been constantly changed to the point that they can no longer be stated with any certainty or clarity.'

Various reviews of the law relating to homicide had taken place since the abolition of the death penalty. Much of the legal world was unhappy with the relationship between murder and manslaughter. For the general public it was less about happiness and more about bewilderment. Terms like provocation, self-defence and diminished responsibility abounded in many famous and more routine cases. Many saw these partial defences to a charge of murder as ways to 'escape' a murder verdict. As ever with the legal system, the more money you have, the better your legal team, the greater your chances of 'escape' from murder to manslaughter. Many saw the legal dilemma as emanating directly from the intransigent mandatory life sentence for murder. Lord Lane, the former Lord Chief Justice, commented: 'The judges at present find themselves having to pass a sentence which in many cases is patently inappropriate and does not mean what it says. That does nothing to enhance their standing and nothing to enhance the authority of the law.'

All the reviews ran up against or sided with the overriding political view across all parties that it was the mandatory sentence of life for murder which gave the public confidence in the criminal justice system. Others would argue that it is a key factor in the public's confusion and disillusion. What research shows is that the public are strongly in favour of sentences that reflect the gravity of the crime, and that they are disillusioned with and confused by the current system. The term 'life' promotes anger, with the assertion that 'life' does not mean life for all but a few at present. Being on licence for life with the potential to be brought back into custody for relatively minor offences does not engender sympathy in the general public. Sympathy does come very often with mercy killings: when a husband kills a wife in great pain through terminal illness; or where a wife brutalised over many years by a drunken and vicious husband finally 'snaps' and kills him. In such cases the life sentence is all that a judge can impose.

The case of Francis Inglis, a 57-year-old mother, in January 2010 is typical. She gave her 22-year-old brain-damaged son, Tom, a lethal heroin injection to end his 'living hell'. She was sentenced to life for murder. Tom had suffered severe head injuries when he fell out of a moving ambulance. Mrs Inglis gave a tearful and emotionally charged account to jurors of how she had 'no choice' and had done it 'with love' to end his suffering. The judge, Brian Barker, the Common Sergeant of London, expressed some sympathy but underlined the law relating to murder: 'We can all understand the emotion and the unhappiness that you were experiencing. The fact is that you knew that you intended to do a terrible thing. You knew you were breaking society's conventions, you knew you were breaking the law, and you knew the consequences.' Mrs Inglis believed that her son would not recover following his accident in July 2007, and the judge accepted that her view was 'sincerely held'.

Judge Barker described her as 'a devoted mother and highly regarded for your work in the community'. He added:

This is a highly unusual and very sad case. I accept that his life and yours were changed on July 7. What you did was to take upon yourself what you thought your son's wishes would have been, to relieve him from what you described as a living hell. But you cannot take the law into your own hands and you cannot take away life, however compelling you think the reason. You have to take responsibility for what you did.

The judge said that because of the circumstances of the case he was able to 'make a reduction well outside the usual limits' of the minimum term she must serve – for which the starting point was fifteen years. He set a tariff of nine years.

Abolishing the life sentence would allow judges to take all the circumstances of the case into account and to graduate their sentences accordingly, passing determinate sentences where appropriate, and reserving life sentences for the most serious cases. It would also reduce the numbers in prison serving indeterminate sentences.

The retention of the mandatory life sentence and the 2003 Act which has ratcheted up tariffs have been but two small stages in the inexorable rise in the numbers of those in prison who do not know if or when they will get out. It was the introduction of the indeterminate sentence of imprisonment for public protection (IPP) which was the masterstroke in the abuse of human rights and a fatal blow in attempts to reduce the prison population.

The IPP was created by the Criminal Justice Act of 2003 (CJA) and was a new form of indeterminate sentence. Like a life sentence, an IPP has a minimum term, or tariff, to be served in custody; thereafter release can only be authorised by the Parole Board. It differs substantively from the life sentence only in that it does not necessarily entail a lifelong licence period and is available for a greater number of offences.

Prior to the introduction of IPP indeterminate sentences were only available for the gravest of offences. The introduction of IPP marked an increasing emphasis by government on public protection as a goal of sentencing. Since the onset of criminal justice in society the principle of proportionality has prevailed, in other words the idea that the severity of punishment should match the seriousness of the crime. Now it was

'dangerousness', a person's likely future behaviour, and not just the gravity of past behaviour, guiding the sentence.

It was hard-line, uber-populist New Labour Home Secretary David
Blunkett who created the indeterminate sentences and who, character-
istically, blamed judges for misusing them. In a counter-attack the High
Court said the sentences were unlawful because many prisons cannot
assess whether inmates are safe to be released. This meant prisoners staying in prison, which the court ruled was 'unlawful'.

Blunkett had 'previous' from his three years as Home Secretary to
2004, in which the open-ended incarceration of foreign terror suspects
without trial was also declared unlawful. Mr Blunkett rounded on the
judges then, too. The government steamrollered the new sentence
onto the statute book in a measure designed to persuade the public
that dangerous people would be locked up for longer. However, unlike
the US criminal justice system, which Blunkett was reputed to admire,
the legislation did not create truly lengthy set sentences of thirty, forty
or fifty years, and it did not build a new generation of prisons to put
the criminals in. Instead, it left the whole thing open ended – with
judges, officials in over-crowed prisons and the Parole Board given the
responsibility for setting minimum 'tariffs', assessing the risk posed by
prisoners and deciding when to release them. It also failed to deliver
the resources to allow these processes to work adequately and caused
existing resources to be hijacked to tackle the chaos.

The IPP also marked a fundamental shift in the principles of
sentencing. The IPP is available as a sentence for the ninety-six
offences in Schedule 15 of the Criminal Justice Act 2003 that have a
maximum sentence of at least ten years' imprisonment. The number of
cases for which an IPP sentence was mandatory turned out to be much
larger than the Home Office had originally envisaged. Changes were
subsequently made in 2008, such that the sentence could no longer be
passed, with some exceptions, for offences with a tariff of under two
years – equivalent to a four-year determinate sentence. As a result of
these changes, usage of the sentence by the courts declined, but not to

the extent that had been expected by the new Ministry of Justice, which became responsible for the ensuing debacle. The IPP has swept up huge numbers of offenders as courts have abdicated their responsibility, taking safe and risk-averse decisions faced with individuals coming before them as chaotic and disordered as before but now able to lock them up potentially for ever – just in case. As a sop to perceived public pressure to be protected IPP has failed miserably. The press invariably fail to describe it properly and the public to understand it at all. Its consequences will be around, quite literally, for a lifetime. In the early days sentencers wallowed in their ability to 'protect the public' and in 2008–09 prisoners sentenced to IPP were appearing in prisons at a rate of about seventy-five a month. Fortunately the initial rush of blood to the heads of sentencers declined and a mere 1,001 people were given an IPP sentence in 2009, a decrease of 35 per cent from 2008.

As with sentences generally, IPPs marked a new era of unintelligibility, especially for those receiving the sentences but also for families and the media. Politicians did not show much interest lest they be seen as soft on crime. A high proportion of prisoners have lower than average educational attainment levels and higher than average mental health issues, learning difficulties and speech and language problems. None of these affects the language of courts and sentencers and I have experienced many a newly sentenced offender unaware of what has just happened to him. Lawyers move on swiftly to their next case, families and friends are as bewildered as the convicted, and prison staff will resort to 'computer says ninety-nine years' as it actually does with a life sentence. In their brief brush with training prison officers gain scant understanding of the huge complexities of sentences in favour of being able to handcuff someone properly and the invariably favourite part of training – control and restraint, the very good but overused system of controlling violent and refractory prisoners. Consequently prisoners wander prison wings dazed and confused asking questions of the uninformed. The tariff quickly becomes the fixed sentence in their minds until that tariff is passed. At the end of 2010 there were 6,375 prisoners serving an indeterminate IPP sentence; half were being held beyond their tariff expiry date. Since 2005 just 202 people serving IPP sentences have been released from custody. Many of those had short tariffs sentenced before the amendments in 2008. Initially a third of IPP prisoners had tariffs of two years or less. After the amendments of 2008, 18 per cent had tariffs of two years or less; 24 per cent had tariffs of five years or more.

By the end of 2009 over half of those IPP prisoners who were over tariff were still awaiting a Parole Board review of their case or a decision from a review. Approximately 10 per cent of the entire prison population will be serving IPP sentences by 2015 at the present rate.

Whether Blunkett was a fan of the Czech novelist Kafka is not clear but he has added Kafkaesque to the prison lexicon. As with all life sentences release is dependent on proving to the Parole Board that you are safe to be released back into the community once you have completed your tariff. The public prefer the term 'no risk' but there can only be 'acceptable risk' in reality. Unfortunately, in a risk-averse world we have crept towards the former and drifted away from the latter. For the Parole Board to make a decision it has first to hear your case, which is easier said than done. Whilst the time by which the Parole Board is required to hear your case may be specified, there is no recourse to law or the board if that date is passed. Pressure on the Parole Board and government's failure to meet its resource needs has meant that hearing dates and subsequent decision dates are often missed. The board's decisions are based on a lot of information, including interviews with the prisoners themselves, psychiatric reports, medical reports and most crucially a report from the National Offender Management Service reflecting on all aspects of the period of incarceration. This will include reports on behaviour, attitudes, training, education, and involvement with drug, alcohol and offending behaviour courses.

Back in the halcyon days of the mid-1980s, when there were 2,000 lifers in the system, my first role at a junior governor grade was as lifer liaison officer. It was my job to organise the report writing on the more than 100 lifers serving in HMP Maidstone, my first jail. Reports were written annually on a prisoner's progress, with more substantive reports provided if parole reviews were imminent. I would act as secretary to the lifer review board. The governing governor would chair the meeting and the whole event was conducted with a gravity I came to expect and admire. We were determining the future of someone who had committed the most heinous of acts and doing our duty to protect the public and the human rights of individuals. Attendees were many, including the prisoner's personal officer, whose role it was to keep close day-to-day contact, the principal officer in charge of the wing and the wing governor, although that was also often my joint role. In addition there would be the senior medical officer, principal psychologist, education manager, workshop instructor and a member of the Board of Visitors, an independent watchdog now called the Independent Monitoring Board. There would be long deliberations over a range of reports, some professional and technical, some more straightforward relating to day-to-day life on the wing. At the end the prisoner would be invited in to hear the thoughts and views of the panel and to be offered a chance to say his own piece. Reports would be sent to the Lifer Management Unit at prison service HQ where there were a dedicated series of case workers who got to know everyone. A visit there always underlined the huge task being undertaken. Lifer files, some going back many years, were often up to a metre high and so large as to require transport on a trolley. Most prominent on the files were the prisoners numbers. A quick glance revealed those who had been in longest. Numbers only represented the longest servers when mere numerics could encompass the lifer population. A and B prefixes were later added. This was well before word processing of evidence and typewriting abounded. Meetings at lifer HQ were punctuated at lunchtime by a trolley bearing sandwiches and a choice of red or white wine. Unfortunately one women's prison went through a brief period of making its own – officially. It was an impressive and rewarding training ground for a young governor, demonstrating a thoroughly professional approach to a complex task.

Today the Parole Board is grateful if it gets just one timely report from an offender manager, the designated case-worker for a prisoner. These reports give what information they can and a crucial element will be attendance on so-called 'courses'. Seen as the holy grail of risk reduction, about which more later, they are what lifers will pin their hopes on. Sentence plans – the document which purports to be integral to the management of an individual's incarceration (but not if you are serving less than a year) – define the need to attend such 'cures'. But a combination of the general rise in prison numbers, the inexorable rise in the number of indeterminate sentence prisoners and the reduction in prison regimes has meant that many are called but few are chosen. On 19 January 2010, of the 2,468 people being held beyond tariff, 466 had completed no accredited offending behaviour programmes. The prisons inspectorate in which I worked for over three years, and which has the task of monitoring the treatment of and conditions for prisoners, stated:

> The current situation is not sustainable. IPP prisoners now constitute around one in fifteen of the total prison population ... even with the recent changes in legislation, these numbers far exceed the capacity of the probation service and the prison system [and the Parole Board for that matter] to deliver the necessary quality of service.

HM Chief Inspector of Prisons described those serving IPP sentences as 'prisoners with many and complex needs, including mental health, learning disability and a risk of self-harm'.

The backgrounds of many IPP prisoners are startling. Nearly one in five have previously received psychiatric treatment, whilst one in ten is receiving mental health treatment in prison and one in five is on prescribed medication. One IPP prisoner in twenty is, or has been, a patient in a special hospital or regional secure unit. They are seen as a high-risk group for suicide and self-harm. Three people serving IPP sentences took their own lives in 2009. Nearly 80 per cent of IPP sentences for women were for offences of arson, which is often an indicator of serious mental illness or self-harm. On 5 July 2010, 2,120 people serving an IPP sentence 'had not completed at least one course'.

Not only is there a woeful shortage of offending behaviour programmes for IPP prisoners, especially in local prisons, many prisoners whom staff consider to be unsuitable to participate because of mental illness or emotional instability are often excluded from taking part in programmes entirely. Research by the Prison Reform Trust found a vast tranche of prisoners with a learning disability or difficulty excluded from most aspects of the prison regime. A report jointly by HM Chief Inspectors of Prisons and of Probation described this predicament, prisoners being unable to access the interventions they needed to secure their release, as, again 'Kafkaesque'. In that context the Joint Committee on Human Rights found, that 'people with learning disabilities may serve longer custodial sentences than others convicted of comparable crimes.' They went on to say that 'this clearly breaches Article 5 ECHR (right to liberty) and Article 14 ECHR (enjoyment of ECHR rights without discrimination)'.

For once a prisons minister got it spot on. According to the prisons minister Crispin Blunt, 'we inherit a very serious problem with IPP prisoners'. In a debate in the House of Commons on 15 June 2010 he said: 'We have 6,000 IPP prisoners, well over 2,500 of whom have exceeded their tariff point. Many cannot get on courses because our prisons are wholly overcrowded and unable to address offending behaviour. That is not a defensible position.'

During the Kenneth Clarke 'spring' after the Conservative/Lib Dem coalition came to power, ministers began to float the idea that there would be a presumption of release at the end of tariff, with the need to make a case for someone to be held beyond that date. This evaporated under wider political pressure on an administration forced into a series of U-turns. The situation with IPPs had suddenly become defensible.

A former long-term prisoner, Barry, had his own view:

It's a monster. The IPP position is just making things worse. Imagine you've just been sentenced with IPP and you go into the office and say to a member of staff, 'can you explain this IPP to me?' He goes on the computer and he says it looks like you're doing life like everyone else because on the computer it says ninety-nine years. That's not an answer. The officers don't even know how to explain what an IPP is. [The sentence has a minimum tariff set by the judge. Prisoners are released if after this time they are considered by the Parole Board to be an acceptable risk for release]. There's people with two years' IPP [i.e. started with a two-year tariff] been in six years. There are people in with eighteen months [tariff] IPP who started off with great expectations they would be out in those eighteen months. Seven years down the line they are still in jail. They are walking round in limbo – they are frustrated – there's no information – everything is broken down – the staff can't tell them what IPP means – and the lawyers still struggle.

Combining the IPP shambles with the pre-existing life sentence policy and the strictures of the 2003 Act makes for a prison population not to be proud of. There were 13,587 people serving indeterminate sentences at the end of March 2011, a rise of 11 per cent in the past two years. The proportion of the sentenced prison population serving indeterminate sentences (life sentences and IPPs) increased from 9 per cent in 1995 to 18 per cent in 2010. As of 1 September 2009, England and Wales has by far the highest number (12,521) of sentenced prisoners serving indeterminate sentences in Europe. The average tariff given for those sentenced to a mandatory life sentence has increased from 13.2 years in 2002 to 17.5 years in 2009.

On 27 October 2011 Ken Clarke finally got to grips with IPP sentences. He told the Radio 4 *Today* programme, referring to those on IPP: 'We've got 6,000 people languishing in prison, 3,000 of whom have gone beyond the tariff set by the judge and we haven't the faintest idea when, if ever, they are going to get out. It's a gross injustice, a bit of a stain on our system.'

Apart from the fact that he made no mention of what might be done with existing IPP prisoners this was the good news. All thoughts of the nation losing its obsession with life sentences however went with his next phrase: 'I'm going back to long, firm, mandatory sentences.' He added: 'Under a "two strikes" approach anyone convicted of a second serious sexual or violent crime in England and Wales would get an automatic life sentence.' The plan was for 'ultra-serious criminals': 'It is a big step and I didn't take it lightly.'

He had accepted all the arguments at long last against the nonsense of IPP, but ignored the entire debate around the mandatory life sentence for murder and added for the first time mandatory sentences for offences other than murder. It was totally at odds with comments he had made only a few days earlier when Clarke told MPs that judges should have discretion over sentencing. He had added that mandatory sentences were 'not the British way', which led to a game in which judges would look for any excuse not to hand down the set terms. Clarke also announced mandatory custodial sentences for sixteen- and seventeen-year-olds who threaten others with knives. Convicted teenagers would face a four-month detention and training order under the plans.

He went even further and adopted the policy of the Blair years: when in doubt bring in a new sentence. This time it was the EDS (the Extended Determinate Sentence). Under this new sentence all dangerous criminals convicted of serious sexual and violent crimes would be imprisoned for at least two-thirds of their sentence, ending the regime which allowed the release of these offenders at the halfway stage. Offenders convicted of the most serious sexual and violent crimes in this category will not be released before the end of their sentence without Parole Board approval and criminals who complete an EDS will have to serve extended licence periods where they will be closely monitored and returned to prison if necessary. In addition courts would have the power to give up to an extra five years of licence for violent offenders and eight years for sexual offenders on top of their prison sentence.

No one would argue against serious and dangerous criminals being dealt with severely to protect the public but, as Clarke himself said, judges should have discretion. They already have plenty in their sentencing armoury as the exploding prison population and its ever increasing sentence lengths attest. Any mention of the consequences for the prison system in having to deal with yet more lifers was missed. Another clear case of prison being out of sight and out of mind.

THIRTEEN

WORK AND PROGRAMMES

nother aspect of prisons where money could be saved, prison conditions improved and prisoner prospects of resettlement greatly enhanced is work. Of the 88,000 prisoners incarcerated, very few work forty hours a week, many do not work at all and of those that do, a four-hour working day with a two-and-a-half hour break in the middle is not uncommon. The average working week for prisoners reduced between 2007 and 2010 from 12.6 to 11.8 hours. Wages of around £5 per week are typical but of greatest concern is the quality of work, which is often unskilled, mundane and not relevant to the outside world. Folding paper, manufacturing prison clothing and putting tea bags, coffee, powdered milk and sugar into individual bags for distribution in prison is still common. Less than a third of prisoners, according to official figures, which the Chief Inspector of Prisons has regularly highlighted as unreliable (or optimistic), are in work. Work is vital to the reduction of reoffending that we all aspire to. Prisoners with no work or accommodation on release reoffend at a rate of 74 per cent compared to a rate of 43 per cent for those who have worked. Despite popular perceptions, prisoners like to work. Meaningful employment passes time. Heroin may be a 'bird killer'; work can kill bird too – with somewhat better outcomes.

The prison service over decades has failed miserably to provide work for prisoners. It may boast of being self-sufficient in milk and underpants but with a workforce of 88,000 who are happy to work for five to ten pounds per week one might expect the service to make some money and provide some relevant work-based skills training. The service has flirted with outside commercial companies, some large multinationals, and some smaller local companies. Cisco, Travis Perkins and Network Rail have provided work places and a National Grid scheme is trotted out perennially as a major success. There are some nuggets but real work for real wages – the basic minimum wage at least – remains outside the grasp of the system. Even the successes have been seen to wither on the vine: a prison I visited recently has its very own derelict railway line with prisoners asking why they can no longer work for skills and qualifications in track laying. The employment potential of high speed rail may, just like the Olympics, evade prisoners as an employment opportunity.

Providing real work in a real environment is not easy and there are many hurdles to cross which do not exist in the real world. During my tenure as governor of Swaleside in the late 1990s I embarked upon my own search for the holy grail of quality prisoner employment. HMP Swaleside is a large Category B training prison on the Isle of Sheppey, a flat and featureless chunk of marshland at the mouth of the Thames. One of three prisons in the Sheppey cluster, alongside Elmley and Stamford Hill, they are effectively managed as one, accommodating nearly 2,500 prisoners. It is like Alcatraz without the charm. Sheppey has claims to fame other than as an island prison. It has considerable geological significance as well as being the home of a number of different nature reserves. It is also significant in aviation history with links to pioneers such as the Wright Brothers, Sopwith and Lord Moore-Brabazon. The original hangar from which the Wright Brothers first flew on the site of Stamford Hill was said to have been demolished by the prison service to erect a pig-sty. Sopwith gave his name to the occupational health suite for staff I constructed at the jail, helped in part by profits from work carried out in the prisons.

Swaleside had been a very troublesome jail accommodating long-term prisoners, mainly from London and the south-east. There were an increasing number of lifers as the range of types of life sentence began to proliferate. I erected two additional wings during my tenure and there have been another two built subsequently. There was some industry in a purpose-built industrial unit away from the residential wings, but it was uninspiring and provided little for prisoners or the jail. I had the good fortune to have on my staff a tenacious and exceptionally clever industrial manager whom I had known from my days at HMP Belmarsh. He was dispatched to find the prisoners real work and was masterly in the process. Within a short space of time we had three workshops buzzing with activity. One was initially repairing and eventually manufacturing webbing for cranes – the webbing which is wrapped around objects in order to lift very large items – so high quality and safety were paramount. Another packaged nuts, bolts, washers and screws for national DIY stores. They would come in bulk from China in large articulated lorries and prisoners would sort them into the expensive bubble packs that we all feel the desperate need for at weekends as our projects unravel for the want of a 2-inch No. 10 screw. Another packed passenger goodie bags for airlines – the bright red freebie we grab on Virgin flights packed with socks, toothpaste, toothbrush and those headphones that never seem to work.

The basis on which the workshops operated was simple as a concept but very difficult to deliver. Normally prison industries will have in-house employees managing the prisoners, the workspace and the production. They would also be responsible for any training that was delivered. My arrangement with the Swaleside private companies was that this would be provided by the companies themselves and at their expense. For my part, the agreement was that prisoners would be available for a forty-hour week with only thirty minutes for lunch. This meant difficult and protracted negotiation with the POA and other unions representing staff at the jail. A normal lunch break in the prison for staff would be 12.30–1.30. In order to facilitate that and in common with the rest of the service, it became necessary to bring prisoners back to the wings if they were working or participating in other activities elsewhere in the jail. Very often that process would begin from 11.15.

Prisoners would then be served lunch from 11.45, with the objective of them all being locked behind their doors, counted and the count checked across the entire jail, for staff to be off duty for 12.30. When staff came back on duty at 1.30 the process would be reversed (without the food), and it would be an achievement for prisoners to be back at work by 2 p.m. With staff having a working day ending at 5.30 after serving prisoners an evening meal at 4.45–5.15, the afternoon work session would be similarly curtailed.

The new Swaleside workshop housed up to 100 prisoners, who although confined to a secure workshop were not deemed to be in their more secure cell locations. The term 'unlocked over lunch' was therefore the phrase that lay at the heart of negotiations with the unions and how best to ensure the safety and security of the establishment. The unions in general and the POA in particular have frequently been cited as barriers to change in prisons and whilst this has undoubtedly been the case in some instances it is in my view a ready excuse for poor management and inappropriate dialogue. We reached agreement and prisoners made do with a thirty-minute lunch break. They made a cuppa on site, had a fag (as they could in those days), the kitchen sent over a baguette with a range of succulent and nourishing fillings and then they went back to work. Not unlike the rest of the world.

Prisoners earned between £50 and £100 per week. They were required to save for their release and or send money home to their families. There were a number of foreign nationals at Swaleside at the time and a number of small Columbian villages prospered on the back of Chinese nuts and bolts for B&Q. Controversially I could not charge for a prisoner's keep and we were coming perilously close to the problem of taxation. As well as the prisoners earning money I insisted that there was also profit for the prison and this ran into hundreds of thousands of pounds. Those at HQ responsible for prison industries remained as unhelpful and unreliable as they had been in the whole 'real work' programme. Profits, they insisted, had to go back to the Treasury. Undaunted, I made my own approaches to the Treasury where I discovered enormously helpful and constructive individuals who assisted in me in using the system to best advantage and profits for the benefit of the jail.

Prisoners were queuing up to get work in the 'shops', as they were termed in prison. Selection required good behaviour and a range of other mutually beneficial components. Not only were they earning money and doing their 'bird' more quickly, they were provided with work-based education and training so they learned to drive fork-lift trucks and develop skills around stores management, computer as well as basic and key skills: B&Q wanted packs holding twenty screws, not twenty-four or seventeen. The lunch period was not the only security problem. These industries required the regular flow of large vehicles through the gate, some of which barely fitted. I had to ensure that only raw materials came in with them and no prisoners went out in them. I also had to ensure that they went straight in and out with no hour-long delays because we were closed for lunch. I always had a feeling that the vultures were hovering were there to be a security cock-up. Fortunately there wasn't and the jail settled down to a work routine that calmed and motivated the entire prison.

So it was with a wry smile that I watched the new coalition government launch its plans to bring real work to prisons some fifteen years later. The rehabilitation revolution would place work at the heart of the prison regime. Clarke revealed plans to pilot one large-scale working prison at the 2011 Tory Party conference, in which private sector employers might pay higher wages, as part of a commercially viable industrial model to raise money for victim support. He said:

I want to revive a policy of John Major's last Conservative government and make deductions from the earnings of working prisoners to provide compensation for victims of crime. In order to raise those funds, we need to instil in our jails a regime of hard work. Most prisoners lead a life of enforced, bored idleness, where getting out of bed is optional. We have to try to get these people who have the backbone, to go straight. To handle life without crime when they have finished their punishment.

In September 2011 Clarke brought in plans for prisoners in work to pay reparation to victims. The Prisoners' Earnings Act, until then only discussed, was implemented. The result was that prisoners can earn up to £50 per week and keep it all. Thereafter 40 per cent of all earnings is taken straight out of their earnings to go to the charity Victim Support. This applied primarily to prisoners in open prisons working in the community on a daily basis alongside 'normal' workers. Few in prison industry are paid more than £20 per week.

Few would argue with the principles. There was little discussion and the action was effectively retrospective; those already in outside work (estimated at 500 prisoners) faced an immediate 40 per cent wage cut. How much of a disincentive it turns out to be for prisoners, who face enormous hurdles anyway in getting into work after sentence, let alone during it, remains to be seen.

In terms of the general principle of working prisons there were informed voices of concern over the needs of those with severe mental health, drug and alcohol problems as well as those with learning, speech and language problems, all of which can be easily forgotten. The public wants prisoners to work, so do the politicians and the prison service. Prisoners are pretty keen on the idea too. However, in order to achieve this laudable aim it will be necessary to overhaul completely the working practices and shift systems of all prison staff and to manage security in a totally different way. It is perfectly possible with good management and innovative thinking. There is, however, a long way to go. In the summer of 2011, over a year after the Clarke declaration on real work, prisons minister Crispin Blunt visited a prison to remark on its innovative workshop: 'This is the first real workshop I have seen in fifty prison visits.'

Some work still to do then.

OFFENDING BEHAVIOUR PROGRAMMES

Offending behaviour programmes, seemingly crucial to the prolonged incarceration of lifers, are worthy of examination when looking at how money in prison is spent. OBPs, as they are referred to, provide one of the main components of the prison regime and access to early release for all. They are what are often quoted when we talk of risk assessment – they purport to provide an indication as to whether or not an individual will reoffend or be a danger to the public. A key to unlock an individual is not a meaningless cliché. But what are they and who is responsible for developing them, funding them and rationing them out? There is a department but its name remains a mystery to all, including those working for it. Windscale became Sellafield in the early days of 'changing the name to protect the guilty'. In recent years the ad men turned British Steel into Corus and business takeovers morphed it to Tata Steel Europe. The prison service once had the OBPU – Offending Behaviour Programmes Unit. Whilst the latest incarnation on the Ministry of Justice website – the prison service website has been closed down – still refers to OBPU the organisation has had at least two identities since, and as NOMS has undergone reorganisation after reorganisation. Whatever its name, it remains accountable only to itself and remote from prison governors, who remain an inconvenience to it.

The Ministry of Justice describes its programmes thus:

… Programmes [are] designed to identify the reasons why prisoners offend and reduce and monitor these factors. As well as reducing risk, programmes support risk assessment and the risk management of offenders. The prison service, through the Offending Behaviour Programmes Unit (OBPU), currently provides thirteen different Offending Behaviour Programmes (excluding Drug Treatment Programmes) which have been fully or provisionally accredited by the Correctional Services Accreditation Panel (CSAP). The target for 2005/6 is 7000 offenders completing these programmes.

This was on the website in 2011 – there is no mention whether or not the five-year-old target was met.

The programmes are listed and described. Enhanced Thinking Skills (ETS) is a relatively short programme which addresses thinking and behaviour associated with offending. The Cognitive Skills Booster Programme is run by both the prisons and probation service as a follow-up to ETS. We then have a course over which derivation of the acronym must have created much satisfaction: Controlling Anger and Learning to Manage It (CALM), aimed at negative emotions such as anger, anxiety and jealousy.

Violent and sexual offenders are targeted with Cognitive Self Change Programme (CSCP). Sex Offender Treatment Programmes (SOTP) are available for sexual offenders, as is the Healthy Relationships Programme (HRP) for men who have either been convicted of, or admit to, abusive and violent behaviour in the home and who have been assessed as at risk of being violent in their intimate relationships.

Then there is Chromis, which

> aims to reduce violence in high risk offenders whose level or combina-
> tion of psychopathic traits disrupts their ability to accept treatment and
> change. Chromis has been specifically designed to meet the needs of
> highly psychopathic individuals and provides participants with the skills
> to reduce and manage their risk.

Then we have FOR. What it stands for no one knows, but it is more motivational stuff at the end of sentence. Women in jail can be offered Choices, Actions, Relationships and Emotions (CARE). The course aims to foster a positive self-identity that will 'enable participants to live the kind of life they would like to on release'. It is not known whether or not CARE is available in the community. There is a pilot programme on 'how to get where you thought you were going'. Wouldn't we all like that one? And for juvenile prisoners (fifteen- to seventeen-years-old) we have the amazingly named JETS Living Skills. We are told very helpfully that the programme is being piloted at HMYOI Wetherby and has been provisionally accredited by CSAP. One would be seriously concerned if JETS were not being piloted: that would make them Drones perhaps!

The principle behind these programmes, and indeed anything that is provided in the way of education, training and interventions, is the phrase 'what works'. The connotations are obvious. The term began life in the 1990s in the probation service and was slowly adopted by the prison service. In 2003 the prison service became very prescriptive, sending out amongst its plethora of rules and regulations a diktat that activities were only allowed if there was evidence they worked. Underpinning the ruling was the very reasonable expectation that we should do no harm. The problem was how to prove such a thing. This was a small hurdle for the prison service to leap as it set up the previously mentioned CSAP (Correctional Services Accreditation Panel). Its rule was law. If the panel declared it worked, then it worked and prisoners could be subjected to their duly authorised accredited programmes. To governors like myself, who constituted the panel was a mystery. We knew it contained a lot of psychologists who had developed programmes for prisons but that set no alarm bells ringing. We were told it was responsible for research and evidence. The Emperor had no clothes but he ruled over us for many years and continues to do so.

Few governors, and I certainly include myself, spend long evenings reading research papers and the evaluation of random control trials. Getting through the day without a crisis or admonishment from above was about as good as it could often get. Sleep was also a luxury, but on one occasion I did try reading an evaluations paper of one programme by way of inducement to slumber. Buried deep in the academic prose were some startling facts. If the programme made a difference, it was slight. The number of prisoners in the survey was very small. And we all knew that we would choose those prisoners most likely to be willing and able to complete any course. Course completions improved our performance figures. There was certainly no cost benefit analysis. In other words, how much did it cost to deliver the programme and how might the money have been spent on other things? The emperor of evaluation remains as naked as ever. In a parliamentary question in February 2008 it was revealed by the government that fourteen out of fifteen offending behaviour programmes had not been evaluated. The ETS programme was the exception and a report on it came out a year later. (I commend the following link as an alternative to drug-induced sleep: http://www. justice.gov.uk/publications/docs/report-on-the-implementation-of-a-randomised-controlled-trial1.pdf.) I was once informed by someone responsible for the delivery of programmes at HQ that the absence of evidence is no evidence of absence. If only that applied outside the hallowed portals of CSAP.

There are problems not only with the content and nature of the programmes but, as I have implied in the context of life sentences, their availability. For 2010/11 NOMS claims 10,000 programme completions. That is not to say 10,000 prisoners have completed an accredited behaviour programme. Some prisoners will complete more than one per year, occasionally the same one. Yet 10,000 is still less than one each for the 13,000 indeterminate sentence prisoners.

Jerry was a career criminal having served numerous sentences for violence and drug dealing. He knew the system well and had his own views on courses in prison based on years of experience:

When I started ETS they tried to analyse me. They do some questions and answers to see if you are suitable for the course. One question was: what would you do if your next door neighbour was playing music too loud? I said to them, I live on Broadwater Farm [a housing estate in north London], why would I question it? I would probably knock on the door and go and join the party! They were looking for me to say that I would knock on the door and ask them to turn it down or else. But everyone doesn't think like that. Just because we are criminals and in prison we don't all think like that. Some of us do know how to engage our brains you know. Some of the questions were very silly. Another question was: what would you do if you walked into a pub and saw your girlfriend with an ex-boyfriend? Only someone with pretty low esteem would question his girlfriend talking to an ex. Any girl you're with now would have an ex so why would you question it? Anything could have happened. I think the

*ETS course is for people with low self-esteem. They said I wasn't appropri-
ate for the course because I questioned everything. They said I would be
more of a distraction. That suited me fine. I'd already done the course four
years ago when I was on a six-year sentence so why would I do it again – it
didn't work that time – cause here I am back again doing a twelve* [year
sentence]. *It didn't bloody work did it! – you understand what I mean?*

Course like PASRO [Prisons Addressing Substance Related Offences], *when it first came to* [HMP] *Parkhurst I was involved in the first pilot. It
did help in the beginning because it asked you all sorts of questions about
yourself, but there was no follow-up to the course, that was the weakness –
the course was actually good but because they didn't follow it on and actually
try and see where it went – it didn't have no use. Good concept but they
didn't follow it through.*

*I had all sorts of different tutors on the courses. Some officers, some
psychologists. I had one woman who got really stuck because she didn't know
all the terms. She knew the professional terms but wasn't getting across to the
group. They wasn't understanding her professional terms. So I translated it
into layman's terms for her.*

I asked Jerry his views on how people were selected for the courses and
whether they were long enough to help people.

If you was enhanced [the top level of privileges, awarded for good behav-
iour] *and ticked all the boxes you would get on the courses. If you had someone
who gave trouble on the wing and got* [disciplinary] *warnings or was on basic*
[lowest level of privileges resulting from bad behaviour] *or was a problem
communicating with staff, they wouldn't have him on the course ... To me
the course would probably really help that person, because that is the person
it should be doing something for. It would help that person grow and mature.*

*ETS was scheduled for six weeks and you do them four days a week, every
day for four days morning and afternoon. For the inmates doing it, it got
too much. They could have crammed it into four weeks and they would have
learned more. But because they dragged it out, in the last week or two weeks*

people couldn't be bothered no more. They wouldn't turn up. You can't keep banging it into people's heads, you have to give them time to process it and put it into action.

But even when you did … I tried, I did one that had assertive skills in it. So one day they asked me how I had used my assertive skills. I said I woke up late one morning and was too late to make an application [a formal written request to an officer – to access some of his property for example, or cleaning materials]. *So I spoke to the officer and friended* [befriended] *him up – I started on a good note and talked about the football scores. I knew his team had won – I just wanted to get him in a good mood so he would take the application, so I explained that that was how I asserted myself. They said no, I didn't assert myself, and that I just conned the officer. But I got what I wanted so as far as I'm concerned I asserted myself. They said I had just conned him. I said no, I just used the skills I had learnt on the course. So I got no accreditation for it. I couldn't win.*

The more I educated myself, the more problems I had. Staff that knew me were fine but staff that didn't saw me as a threat because I would challenge things. The more I learnt, the more I questioned, the worse it got. I would question staff if they did something that was not in the rules – like they would stop association early and I would ask why, or they wouldn't do things on time – and I would argue that I shouldn't suffer or just ask why – so I got into trouble for it. They would see me trying to undermine their authority and I wasn't. I was just asking why.

Jerry went on to describe his newly acquired skills and the problems he and others had in getting out of prison:

The system is not working. I can only tell you what I went through but there are a lot of prisoners going through the same thing. You do your courses and you do your sentence plan – you get your D Cat. When you get to your D Cat you got a new OMU office [the Offender Manager Unit designated staff member to monitor a prisoner through his sentence]. *They have never met you but they have read your file and for someone like me they make all sorts of assumptions. You know what they are reading about you ain't nice – they form a picture of you. I meet them and talk to them and I contradict every conclusion they have reached. You read about me as a monster but then I'm in front of you and I'm a human being. He sees that I know how to conduct myself and that I've achieved a great deal. So why can't we assess him for what he is now and not what he has done before. And that's the problem I and a lot of other inmates had, especially IPP and lifers* [prisoners with a life sentence for offences such as murder] *because they had no voice. Because if they did and a few have, then they would get cuffed and carried out.*

Very often they would make a relevant point and be within their rights but if the governor didn't want to know then he would be shipped out – get rid of the problem. What I done so they couldn't ship me out – I had a good prison lawyer. I would get into trouble for speaking my mind sometimes because I wasn't prepared to be another victim. I started to go into the library and find out what I was entitled to. I would get to know all the PSOs [prison service orders], *rules and regulations and then challenge. So the OMU woman got not to like me. So I told her I wasn't there for her to like me. She was there to do a job.*

And she wasn't doing it very well. My Oaysis [offender assessment system] *assessments were out of date and my parole answer was eighteen months late. She was not going to let me go on home leave. I had done a six – been out for eighteen days and back in prison for a twelve* [year sentence]. *I done a six and a twelve* [year sentence] *back to back and she said I needed a hostel* [supported and supervised accommodation in the community run by the probation service, although increasingly now by private companies]. *I said I have had an address for the last twelve years, I have somewhere to go. She insisted I was a danger to the public and I needed to go to a hostel. I went there – but what they were doing was giving me something to fail. Curfew all over the place. So I try and be proactive and set myself up a job interview for the next date I was due a home leave. I tell the OMU officer and check with her everything is OK for me to get home leave on that date. I tell my outside probation officer as well. I make sure everyone who should know does know. And then a week before, I'm told the home leave hasn't been approved by my outside probation officer. I phone her and she says of course she has. It turned out my application hadn't even left the OMU officers' tray. So I put in a complaint to the governor. The governor tried to defend it but it was all just wrong and prisoners who are getting to the end of a sentence, they can't get what they are entitled to. In the end I missed my job interview and I said, look, I got ten months left and I don't want no more home leaves. I don't want no more – I don't want the stress and the reasons to fail. I refused my Christmas home leave.*

Whilst the OBPU and CSAP have ruled the roost regarding offending behaviour programmes, the world of drug treatment has a wider and more influential context. Drug treatment in the community has evolved over the years and been subjected to a wide-ranging, open and constructive scientific debate around effectiveness. The drug treatment community has found itself in conflict with the prison service. This is best illustrated in an examination of the way in which the budgets operate. Clinical drug treatment in prison has been routinely funded, as with all matters of physical and mental health, by the Department of Health.

Throughout the twentieth century health in prison was 'in-house'. The senior medical officer has been part of the ruling triumvirate of prisons alongside the governor and the chaplain since the development of the modern prison system. Large Victorian houses in London still exist (now sold off) that were the designated residences of one of the triumvirate. Some are still within prison grounds, converted in the case of HMP Maidstone into an education centre. It was early in the twenty-first century that debate around responsibility for healthcare in prisons was initiated by Sir (now Lord) David Ramsbotham, former HM Chief Inspector of Prisons. Under his auspices a document was produced entitled, 'Prisoner or Patient'. The outcome was that in 2003 commissioning for prison healthcare services was transferred from the Home Office to the NHS. For many it was more a forced marriage than one made in heaven and some serious marriage guidance has been needed since. But this was without doubt a major and highly appropriate step forward and is still the best opportunity we have had to emphasise that there is no such thing as prison health, merely public health concentrated in prisons. Other jurisdictions still wrestle with the issue and in 2008 I was part of an inquiry into whether the same transfer of responsibilities for health in prison should be made in the Northern Territory of Australia. A positive recommendation was eventually accepted.

Detoxification (about 50,000 prisoners a year require detox on coming into prison), methadone maintenance and all associated prescribing and treatment therefore comes under the auspices of the local Primary Care Trusts (PCTs) or whatever will replace them under the coalition governments's NHS reorganisation. With the transfer of responsibility in 2003 went the cash. But the amounts transferred at the time and the amounts required since have been the source of much controversy. In prisons such as Brixton that controversy was relatively minor. Many prisoners in Brixton came from and returned to the borough of Lambeth so Lambeth PCT had a vested interest in the health of Brixton prisoners. This is much less the case on the Isle of Wight where three prisons, Parkhurst, Albany and Camp Hill, hold almost 2,000 prisoners, very few of whom emanate from the small holiday island.

However, whilst the clinical money was with the Department of Health, all the other money for drug treatment lay with the prison service, initially in a dedicated drug strategy but later in the infamous OBPU which became responsible for the provision of assessments and drug treatment programmes.

The drug assessment process is called CARAT (Counselling, Assessment, Referral, Advice and Throughcare). The work is contracted out to a range of third sector organisations that provide teams to undertake assessments of need for drug services and provide one-to-one motivational support and group work for problem drug users. It also undertakes a case management role to help prisoners access a wider range of services, both in custody and upon initial release. It is often referred to as 'signposting'. There are around 10,000 CARAT assessments per year. Prison governors are funded for prescribed numbers of assessments per year and delivering the said amount is a key performance target. Which prisons receive what levels of funding to deliver what numbers of assessments can only be described as random at best and chaotic at worst. The service has spent some £150 million on CARAT assessments since its inception over a decade ago.

The OBPU is also responsible for drug treatment programmes, which are again delivered under contract by third sector providers. These include 12-step treatment models such as those provided by RAPt (Rehabilitation for Addicted Prisoners Trust) of which there are around 1,000 per year. Then there is cognitive behavioural therapy, for instance FOCUS and STOP. Around 350 of these a year are delivered. Short Duration Programmes (SDPs) are four-week programmes for short-term prisoners (around 6,000 per year). And finally there is P-ASRO (Prisons – Addressing Substance Related Offending), an offending behaviour programme for drug users (around 4,000 per year). As with the CARAT work, where and why the programmes are provided is a strategic mystery.

An attempt to pull all the drug-related work in prison together came with the introduction of the Integrated Drug Treatment Service (IDTS). Initiated by the Offender Health Division, a body operating across the prisons and health service, it attempted to break down the barriers between Primary Care Trusts, community drug services and the OBPU by exposing the latter to the drug treatment policies and practices across the community which had evolved over many years. More effective and widespread methadone maintenance programmes were introduced along with psychosocial therapies and, most importantly, it acted to link properly drug treatment in prison with that in the community. This schism was exposed in a legal case brought by a group of prisoners alleging ill treatment because they had been refused the continuation of specific treatment they had been receiving prior to arrest when they entered prison. They won their case and received massive compensation payments, much to the ire of ministers.

IDTS fundamentally aimed to make the issue of substance misuse a health rather than a crime issue. Unfortunately the split between the types of delivery remained despite a review commissioned by the Offender Health Division from management consultants Pricewaterhouse Coopers (PwC) which drew the obvious conclusion that the set-up was a mess and wasting valuable resources. It also tackled the issue of evidence and quoted the work of the UK Drug Policy Commission which accepted that there was reasonable evidence to support the effectiveness of the 12-step programmes but that 'there are no evaluations of the effectiveness of: CARAT interventions; drug-free wings; programmes based on cognitive behavioural therapy, such as short-duration programmes and ASRO (Addressing Substance Related Offending) programmes'.

The PwC report of 2007 was effectively buried by the prison service, only for virtually the same analysis to be commissioned from Lord Patel, a Labour Peer and one-time government whip. Not surprisingly he reached much the same conclusion and the recommendations in his report for a more strategic and cost-effective approach are finally under way. All aspects of drug treatment now fall under the auspices of the Department of Health. Whether this fully moves the issue of drugs from being a security problem to a health problem remains to be seen.

You may wonder where alcohol treatment fits in this complex mix of health, addiction and offending. You might assume that given the public furore around drug-related violence, public disorder and domestic violence that tackling offenders with alcohol problems is a high priority for the prison service. Not so. Alcohol detox does take place, not least because unassisted alcohol detox (cold turkey) is often fatal and far more risky than going cold turkey from such substances as heroin. Thereafter the sorts of support services provided in the community by a range of charitable organisations does not take place in prison. Alcohol treatment is the poor relation. Warsaw prison in Poland contains a 150-bed alcohol treatment facility. There is no such facility in England and Wales.

FOURTEEN

THE INVISIBLE PRISON GOVERNOR

The Prison Act of 1952, which, apart from some modifications in 1964, has yet to be superseded, states very helpfully: 'Every prison shall have a governor, a chaplain and a medical officer and such other officers as may be necessary.'

If we are to have a prison system operating effectively and efficiently and, above all, one having the confidence of the public then the role of the governor is vital. I would strongly contend that it is the diminution of the role of the governor, its isolation from policy and strategy and its enforced silence that has held back positive developments in the system.

This is not to say that there were halcyon days of the prison governor when all was well with incarceration. The walls of older prisons are adorned with roll boards listing former governors, going back in some cases to the turn of the nineteenth century. They list mostly men and many of military origin. Modern prisons tend not to bother with such histories, reflecting the reduced significance of the role in the eyes of many. The roll boards would also be rather large, the current length of tenure of a governing governor being around twenty months according to the last time the question was asked in the Commons.

Whilst the Prison Act requires prisons to have a governor, the civil service is much less sanguine and managerial titles have crept in to the extent that the civil service grade of 'governor' has been abolished, and been replaced with that of senior manager with suffixes from A

239

downwards to reflect the importance placed on the actual job and to blur the distinction with mainstream civil servants.

In the 1950s to 1980s prisons would have a governor, a deputy governor and a range of assistant governors. The governor and his deputy would rule the roost alongside the chaplain and senior medical officer. The uniformed ranks would be headed by the fearsome chief officer with a chief 1 out-ranking a chief 2. Three ranks of prison officer served beneath the chief. The chief would accompany the governor on his daily rounds of the prison, opening doors and standing by the governor's side as he listened to prisoner applications – requests for everything from tooth-paste to phone calls, and general complaints. The applications would be duly written down in a large ledger. The term 'prisoner advised' was the most common entry and chiefs would pride themselves on ways to say no. The role of the assistant governor in this ancient feudal process was to do the joined-up writing. AGs, as they were termed, would write reports for parole, lifer reviews and anything else the criminal justice system required. In terms of authority, they had none. Prison officers answered to senior officers who in turn answered to principal officers who answered to the chief. Given that this was a period when overtime was such that some officers spent almost as much time behind bars as prisoners, uniformed staff of all grades earned significantly more than AGs. These were days without budgets and audits. There were however regular inspections and escapes. Prison numbers were less than half those of today and management was about accurate counting, timely reports and above all answering ministers and MPs' questions. A prison version of *Foyle's War* or *Inspector George Gently* would have fitted neatly into the culture.

In 1986 there was a major reorganisation called 'Fresh Start'. Chiefs were abolished to the delight of AGs and the chagrin of senior and prin-cipal officers aspiring to be one. Officers were quietly relieved at the removal of the *Upstairs Downstairs* approach to staff discipline. Overtime too began to be phased out, to be replaced by improved salaries and time off in lieu. As a newly arrived assistant governor I saw my salary double in one year. With it came line management of officers and the yet to be understood stresses of the task. We grinned all the way to the bank, not knowing what was to come. All governor grades became amalgamated into a single structure from governor 5 (incorporating AGs and chief 2s) through to governor 1. A governor 1 would be responsible for large and high security prisons such as Wormwood Scrubs and Parkhurst. A governor 2 would be responsible for a large training prison or smaller inner city local prison. A governor 3 would run a small establishment, often looking after women or young offenders. Deputies would usually be a couple of grades below the governing governor.

The system worked well for a number of years. It was simple and transparent. The lament 'bring back the chiefs' hung around for many years, but began to evaporate as new staff came in without knowledge of the history. Officers were in uniform and aspired to become a 'suit'. There were regular debates about putting governor grades into uniform and many a bar-side chat amongst aspiring young governors would revolve around styles of three-cornered hats, Kenny Everett-style epaulettes, and swords. It would keep us amused for hours. The official debate came to nought and the Marks & Spencer suit department still benefits. What pleased everyone most, especially those not actually a governing governor, was the ability to call oneself 'governor'. You might be a wing governor, activities governor or security governor. It didn't matter, you were a governor. No one really minded. The governor in charge was always 'Number One' and the deputy was the 'Dep'. Most aspired to be a Dep, then a Number One. For those who didn't or who for various reasons abandoned the ship, the system of nomenclature proved very useful. Once a governor, always a governor, not least to a public who were not too interested in the nuances. There are official curriculum vitaes on various web sites describing individuals as having significant pasts including governing various jails. The term 'Governor, Wormwood Scrubs' or 'Governor, Woodhill', for example, is impressive to the reader, but may simply mean was 'a' governor (probably governor 5 or 4) rather than 'the' governor.

The problem with terminology came from the civil service. As the modern prison service grew alongside the ever increasing prison population, there was a natural desire for operational governors to move into non-operational roles at headquarters and for ambitious civil servants to try their hand at governing prisons. Some moved seamlessly into operational roles, others found it beyond their capabilities and reverted to roles at the centre telling governors what to do, having failed miserably to be able to do it themselves. Likewise some operational governors got out quickly before their mistakes could catch up with them or when the going got too tough. Others took time out of operational roles for rest and recuperation – officially career development – before returning to the fray.

For the civil service the complexities of grade relativities, salaries and line management responsibilities were too much to cope with. Outside a jail the term governor, though comfortable for some, was incongruous to others. So out went governors and in came the managers and senior managers from A to F both inside establishments and at HQ. There was some resistance from the Prison Governors Association (PGA) fighting a rearguard action to retain tradition. By this time the onset of privatisation had provided directors of private prisons rather than governors on largely legal grounds and the basis on which they were managed. With the terminology came the managerial methodology. Managerialism had sneaked in when no one was watching. A new era in prison management had been born. The canter toward headquarters bureaucracy became a stampede. Governors became an inconvenience in the daily declaration of new strategies from the centre but they remained the scapegoat for any failure. The increasing layers of management they became accountable to saw to that.

The term 'penal managerialism', which sounds rather painful, came to be coined by academics looking to analyse the change from old to new. The best and most continuous analysis has been under the auspices of the Institute of Criminology at the University of Cambridge and in particular by Professor Alison Liebling along with fellow academics such as Ben Crewe. They acknowledge, as would I, a British prisons system between 1970 and 1990 as one not to be too proud of. Escapes were common; healthcare was haphazard and at times scandalous. There were controversial deaths in custody and allegations of mistreatment from a workforce often seen as quasi-military, macho and at times racist. Before the 'Fresh Start' reorganisation there was little accountability for money generally and overtime in particular. It was said that no one knew where the money went. There were some notable riots, not least the infamous one at Strangeways prison which lasted for many days and resulted in death and massive damage. Research acknowledges exceptional governors as well as idiosyncratic ones. The Prison Officers' Association (POA) was seen as a major problem by former Director General Derek Lewis in 1997: 'Its stubborn defence of restrictive practices, coupled with its belligerent and often threatening demeanour, resulted in deep prejudice against prison officers and an image of the service rooted in the past.' The POA was to Lewis a 'malevolent force'.

That the service was in need of 'managerial grip' is not in dispute. What is, is how far managerialism has spread and whether it has spread at the cost of innovation and rational debate. Professor Liebling identifies a range of professional styles for governors. Some are described as highly skilled operational governors. Others are seen as focusing on performance management, with younger governors particularly uncritically focused on performance targets. Some she saw as acting as entrepreneurs, with another group as simply alienated or complacent. Interestingly, she saw little difference across the public and private sectors. Most importantly she saw this diversity of styles, although largely unintended, as having major effects on prison life.

Whatever style has been adopted or however it may be described, the net result is a body of people that has become buried in bureaucracy to the point where a group of people whatever their strengths and weaknesses possess a body of knowledge and experience which should make them part of the solution rather than part of the problem. That burial is best illustrated by the position in which the governor of HMP Swaleside found himself early in 2011. Being one of three prisons close together, the decision was made in 2007 to put the Sheppey Cluster under one chief executive. The individual in charge of the day-to-day running of Swaleside, and indeed those running Elmley and Stamford Hill, the other two institutions, found himself answerable to the chief executive of the cluster. He in turn was answerable to the regional custodial services manager who had a number of prisons in Kent Surrey and Sussex in his bailiwick. He in turn was answerable to the director of offender management for the south-east, who answered to the operational director of NOMS, who answered to the chief executive of NOMS. There was even a brief period of further insanity when there was a 'super dom', a more senior director of offender management in charge of the director of offender management. Cost-cutting has seen two layers removed but those responsible for the prisons also find themselves subject to a phalanx of audits and inspections. I counted a total of fifteen during my three-and-a-half year command of HMP Brixton. There are also the many policy directorates at HQ moving the goalposts as quickly as they change their names. There are so many opportunities to fail it is not surprising that many do or give up trying. And yet despite all this scrutiny various chief inspectors of prisons seem to have a knack of creeping up behind the bean counters to expose a failing prison the service has missed. The service has nevertheless adopted a strategy in the gap between inspection and the publication of the report in thanking the inspector for noticing all the good things and reassuring everyone that since the inspection everything has been put right.

The managerialist culture and its associated costs, which are impossible to elicit accurately either from official figures or parliamentary questions, contrasts with the management processes for privatised prisons. A private prison is managed on the basis of a contract, often over a period of ten or fifteen years. Locally the establishment will have a 'monitor' and 'deputy monitor' employed by the prison service to ensure the contract is being delivered and that variation from it is dealt with, by prescriptive fines if necessary. There will be annual contract review meetings and whilst there may be contract variations over time, total renegotiation is unknown even in the rapidly changing criminal justice landscape. One such establishment still operates on an original ten-year-old contract. Whilst a private prison is still subject to the strictures of inspection and some of the old audit regime, the management of the establishment is left to those managing the contract, which gives the prison team charged with the task the benefit of knowing that if more resources are required they are likely to follow. For the public sector prison manager the task will always be open-ended, as illustrated during the August 2011 riots when there was a need to serve the courts throughout the night and make room in already overcrowded jails.

Not only have the demands of the new 'penal managerialism' kept governors in their place, but a culture of required silence has kept governors out of the debate on how best to deal with the ever increasing demands on the system. Attendance at external conferences has long been frowned upon. Organisations seeking to develop ideas and thinking on many issues of incarceration, from drugs and alcohol through to mental health and restorative justice are unable to obtain the views of governing governors: they can never attend conferences and rarely are they allowed to speak. They may write in the service's own *Prison Service Journal* but articles must be submitted in advance for censorship. Internal conferences have evaporated on the rationale of cost efficiency and the belief that all events outside the prison perimeter detract from the work within it. The concept of prisons serving and being part of their community has been traduced. In my early days as an assistant governor there were conferences for governors at various levels. They were valuable professionally and socially and a good training ground as well as opinion-forming. Attending the annual governing governor's conference was an aim for all junior governors and attending one's first as a governor in charge was a proud moment. They were brief affairs but good opportunities to have ministers before us. There were discussions on key issues as well as the chance to say goodbye to retiring and occasionally fallen comrades. Conferences gradually became shorter, more orchestrated and simply no fun anymore. The aim became to avoid the three-line whip to attend which became necessary to force those who would rather stick needles in their eyes than be told by our leaders that yet again 'it was going to be another tough year'. They ceased to be governors' conferences as the civil service joined in and they became service conferences – and on one brief and surreal occasion was held jointly with the probation service. As of 2011 they have ceased completely. Apparently there is nothing to say.

As the opportunity to speak publicly at a conference was gradually removed, the ability to speak elsewhere was too, especially in the media. The rule was that governors could speak to their local newspapers without authorisation but nationally they would need to go through the infamous press office. Nick Cohen of *The Guardian* once made reference to some of the people he encountered in the prison service press office. He described them as having the charm of Malcolm Tucker mixed with the intellect of Vicky Pollard. In reality all responses went to the press office for fear of saying something that was not officially sanctioned. I have alluded to my own personal chequered history in this context in Chapter 4 in relation to *Channel 4 News*. My elastic interpretation of the rules made me few friends in the press office. I did however find journalists and the media simply curious for more information and almost invariably interested in the issues. I was nevertheless wary, having fallen foul of the tabloid media when they received illicit stories about my establishments, as in the 'lunatics have taken over the asylum' incident with Charlie Bronson.

On a more positive occasion at Swaleside I was approached by a local journalist after a cell fire in one of the wings. Cell fires, often deliberate 'burn outs' as part of retribution around disputes and drug deals, were very dangerous and a threat to life but sadly not uncommon and always well handled and bravely so by staff. This particular one was no exception. After four or five calls from the same journalist which I had been too busy to take I finally asked my secretary to invite her in. A bright, ambitious young Irish reporter from the local gazette arrived not believing her luck. Armed with notepad and pen in true 'scoop' style, she approached me with a look of steel, anxious to prise out of this thuggish governor all his dark secrets. She started with the fire, anxious for tales of burning flesh and acrid smoke. I genuinely couldn't remember the detail. It had been a lively few weeks for reasons I could only attribute to the phase of the moon. I simply said, 'shall we go and see?' Her astonishment level hit the stratosphere as I led her onto the wings and to the site of a blackened cell already being cleaned ready for the next occupant. I asked the officer in charge to explain the details. Her interest waned as she looked around but she began asking questions on just about everything, which I, the staff and the prisoners were happy to elucidate on. She became a firm ally of the prison and subsequently wrote some interesting and informative pieces. We have lost contact since but I hope she has retained a constructive interest in prisons.

A more embarrassing and higher profile brush with the press took place when I was at Brixton. At the many arts events I hosted we would do our best to obtain publicity to promote the projects and to raise funds for more. We played it by the book, submitting media invitees to the press office. We invited many and only a few attended but some serious journalists did write supportive pieces over the years and ruffled no feathers. I pushed a staunch reducing reoffending agenda which was invariably picked up. After one particular event I was approached by one of the journalists, who had come sanctioned by the press office but who wrote for the 'lads' mag' *FHM*. He wanted to do a piece, came in the next day with a photographer, then proceeded with an interview. He wanted it for the profile section of the magazine, with which I was honestly unfamiliar save for a visit to the barber. I had picked up that previous interviewees had been Fernando Alonso and Bruce Willis. Well, would you have said no?

The interview did not go well. It was clear he was after blood and gore, sex, drugs and rock 'n' roll. Yes, I know I should not have been surprised. I attempted to give the whole thing a serious edge. In endless emails later when I was pushed to be more revelatory I held what I thought was a sensible and reasonable line. I was conscious that this was an educated and affluent readership and there was an opportunity to make valid points about prisons but would not do so at any cost. I held the line, the magazine held its and nothing went to print. A year later and without warning the magazine came back to tell me it was publishing my version. Next thing I knew it was on the news-stands across the world (my secretary's son found it in Thailand). My daughters and their boyfriends loved it and across the jail it was also popular. If anyone bothered to read the text it made some valid points. A few days later my area manager sidled up to me to proclaim that the director general had seen it and was not amused. 'Fancy him being into pornographic lads mags,' I exclaimed.

The invisible nature of the prison governor is not only amply illustrated in the media, conferences and the academic world, it becomes glaringly obvious at times of crisis. Fortunately there are few, but one of the most notable recent ones was the riot at HMP Ford on New Year's morning 2011. Prisons minister Crispin Blunt stood outside the wrecked jail and commented, as did a member of the POA's national executive committee. Then the chair of the Independent Monitoring Board gave his opinion as did the Chief Inspector of Prisons. Some former prisoners gave their view. Where was the governor? Indeed who was the governor? The silence was, and remains, deafening.

FIFTEEN

PATHWAYS TO SUCCESS

So if prison does not work, can it work? Can it serve the public better? Can it protect communities? Can it reduce reoffending? Can it do all the things it says it wants to, what politicians demand of it and what the public expect of it? It can certainly do it better than it does now.

In the aftermath of the riots in August 2011, Ken Clarke said in a *Guardian* article:

> The general recipe for a productive member of society is no secret. It has not changed since I was inner cities minister twenty-five years ago. It's about having a job, a strong family, a decent education and, beneath it all, an attitude that shares in the values of mainstream society.

Such views are not new and have been widely articulated across the criminal justice system by everyone from chief inspectors of prisons, through voluntary organisations, to offenders and ex-offenders themselves. What has not been challenged is the failure of the prison system to put such fundamental aims at the heart of prison policy. The system needs to demonstrate some imagination in using prison effectively and minimise the damage done by short sentences or unnecessary periods on remand.

A report from the now defunct Social Exclusion Unit went further and highlighted key problems that ex-offenders experience on release. This report identified seven 'pathways' to reduce reoffending:

accommodation (top priority); education, training and employment; health; drugs and alcohol; finance, benefit and debt; children and families; attitudes, thinking and behaviour. None of these are counterintuitive and all have resonance with every one of us at some point in our lives. A period in prison can be a convenient way for someone to abdicate responsibility for all of these things, so it is incumbent upon the system not to collude with such an approach, but rather to go further and not only challenge those who shy away from such individual responsibility but equip those who have lost or never had the skills to discharge that responsibility.

A STRONG FAMILY

There is ample evidence for the benefits of dealing with all of these issues proactively and the problems of ignoring them. Issues around families are a case in point. In 2007 a number of charities, led by the Prison Reform Trust, reported to the Inter-Ministerial Group on Reducing Re-offending. Their findings were that 'prisoners who received visits from their family were twice as likely to gain employment on release and three times as likely to have accommodation arranged as those who did not receive any visits'.

The group also highlighted the problems faced by children with parents in prison. At any one time some 160,000 children a year will have a parent in prison. More children are affected by prison than divorce. The vulnerabilities of such children were shown to manifest themselves in greater than average mental health problems and low achievement at school. Without the brave work of charities such as Kids VIP (Kids Visiting in Prison), PACT (Prison Advice & Care Trust) and Action for Prisoner's Families the issues would not be heard. There is no statutory requirement for NOMS to make provision for children, and data collection around the issue is virtually non-existent.

It is inevitable that prison will challenge family relationships and it would be disingenuous not to acknowledge the damage that some offenders inflict upon their families by their own actions. Much offending is carried out within the family, not least sexual offences and domestic violence. In terms of violence against the person, the likelihood is that the perpetrator will already be known to the victim. With such offending it may well be essential not to foster family ties; it may even be appropriate to support the severing of links with families and impose restrictions after release specifically requiring offenders on licence to keep away from ex-partners and children. For other offenders it may simply be that after years of irresponsibility within a family unit involving theft and drug use, the family members may want to give up, for the time being, on a son, daughter or partner. It would be unreasonable of the prison system to impose upon any family the requirement to act like a cohesive unit. On the other hand, there are many cases in which, whilst time in prison will inevitably affect the family financially or in terms of relationships, supporting the unit and helping it weather the storm by making an offender take greater personal responsibility for both the family and their own actions may serve everyone better. I have seen more families want to fix things than abandon all hope of reconciliation. In my experience, it has been women who have been the most determined to carry on with relationships. I have seen female partners of male offenders experience the most extreme adversity, travelling the length and breadth of the country, spending money they haven't got, to take children to visit an errant father in prison – and all the while enduring visiting conditions less than conducive to a repeat of the experience. Male partners of female offenders are notorious for managing little more than an initial visit before finding greener pastures.

So if families are part of the solution, what does the prison service do to support them? Prisoners are allowed phone calls, visits, letters, occasional family days and, if they are lucky, the benefit of an innovative programme from charitable organisations.

In June 2008, there was, after many years of futile lobbying, an action by the National Consumer Council supported by the Prison Reform Trust challenging the excessive costs to prisoners of telephone calls to families. The problem was not only the cost, almost seven times the standard rate, but the fact that prisoners were often held a long way from home, had little cash of their own, could earn little in prison and access to phones on wings was highly restricted and subject to routine bullying and intimidation. The costs remain higher than for anyone else in the country. The problem is made worse because access to official phones is reducing as prison regimes become more restricted following financial cutbacks. For many the illicit mobile phone is crucial to outside contact more for social than nefarious reasons. One distraught mother once contacted a senior headquarters official concerned that she had not heard from her son for a number of days. He normally called her to say goodnight on his mobile.

Visits in prisons will seem familiar to the general public, exposed to them as they are through TV and film. From the raucous in *Porridge* to the intimidating in *Prison Break* via the fanciful *Bad Girls*, everyone will assume they have had a taste. The reality is, as ever, far more complicated. Before getting to the visits room itself there is a need to negotiate a complex series of hurdles that conspire to deter all but the most loyal of family and friends. The first is to determine in which prison your loved one is held. The earlier in the sentence, the more difficult the problem. Such is the level of overcrowding and the need to keep space for a court system that cannot predict how many it will incarcerate at any time, there will often be short notice 'overcrowding drafts'. This may mean at short notice – i.e. now! – going from one side of London to the other or out from a city into the wilds of Suffolk, Kent or Northumberland. You may leave the night before your scheduled visit the next day. Do not expect a phone call yourself or one to be made on your behalf, or indeed reimbursement of costs for the abortive visit.

The frequency and length of visits as well as the booking of them is another jungle of process and procedure that will vary between prisons and over time within the same establishment according to regime changes following cost-cutting and reorganisation. Generally visits are better in length and physical conditions in open prisons and ironically, in the High Security Estate. They are at their worst and briefest in crowded local prisons. As a general rule the better behaved you are the better your access to visits. All prisons adopted in the early 1990s a system known as incentives and earned privileges. There are three levels: basic, standard, enhanced. Basic are barred from having TVs in their cells and allowed only the statutory minimum visits. Enhanced will allow for extra visits, occasionally in a more pleasant physical environment. Standard lies somewhere between the two. Some prisons operate family days where prisoners can spend the whole day with their families. It may only be a mass gathering in the gym with biscuits and juice laid on but for many it is a privilege not to be abused and one that can transform relationships.

The unintended consequence of the system is that if you behave badly, possibly because you are still dealing with drug and alcohol problems, are having difficulty coping or because you have strained family relationships, the one thing that may assist you is denied – greater family contact. I was blessed with a courageous prison officer at Brixton who would run family days with the express intention of seeking out those who might benefit from such a day on the basis of having problems which such a day would help solve, rather than concentrate on those for whom it would be a direct reward. Some establishments allow prisoners to book visits themselves, in others the visitor has to negotiate call waiting either at the prison itself or via a call centre.

Charitable organisations have battled against the odds for many years to support prisoners and their families. They have succeeded most effectively in the introduction of visitors' centres. Prisons can be located conveniently in urban areas, others in more remote rural environments far from railway or bus routes. Occasionally, and only occasionally, the prison may provide some transport or the local bus company will see an eye for extra income. Getting to the jail is one thing, getting in is another. Timeliness has never been a prison virtue and visitors arriving at the behest of unreliable prison transport or long car journeys will err on the side of being early. Too late, no visit. Providing somewhere to wait, with toilet facilities, nappy changing facilities, refreshments or simply somewhere warm and dry has fallen to charities, sometimes with government money, sometimes not. Often the outside structure is provided but not the facilities. Without them there would be little more than car parks. In urban areas even they are absent. Long crocodile queues of frightened, confused or tired and resigned regulars are still not uncommon outside austere prison gates, but more comfortable visitor centres have been brought kicking and screaming onto the agenda. Along with the physical facilities have come advice and support networks: how to get financial support for the visit, how to deal with a family member with drug addiction and a range of counselling services. Alongside such support are dire warnings of the consequences of smuggling contraband and newspaper cuttings detailing those recently caught, as well as advice on how to deal with the drug-sniffer dog, lists of what you cannot have with you and a miscellany of forbidden actions. Of crucial importance is the process of getting from the visitor centre across no man's land to the prison gate (separate entrance of course to anyone else). Some years ago at HMYOI Rochester some wag had decided that the best way to link visitors with prisoners was a numbering system. This entailed visitors being given a large plastic plate with a number crudely painted on it which the hapless visitor would be forced to carry from the prefabricated building that served as the visitor centre through the prison gate and into the visits hall. It was like a scene out of *Schindler's List*.

Once at the 'point of entry' x-ray machines and rub-down searches kick in as well as the ubiquitous drug-sniffer dog for which you should be well schooled if you have spent your time in the visitor centre valuably reading the literature wallpapering the grey walls. There is no doubt of their value as a deterrent, though detection rates are less well understood. One service-wide evaluation early in 2000 never saw the light of public scrutiny so one can only speculate. Olfactory surveillance, as dog-sniffing is scientifically and technically known, is widespread not only in prisons and airports but at bus and railway stations and anywhere deemed necessary by law enforcement agencies. For a challenging exploration of the science and the law I would recommend 'Drug Detection Dogs and the Growth of Olfactory Surveillance: Beyond the Rule of

Law?' by Amber Marks. Like many things in our surveillance society olfactory surveillance has come in with little scrutiny or legal challenge.

My first encounter with these canine wonders was at Belmarsh, where I purchased a fully trained animal from the RAF at a considerable cost of over £50,000 exclusive of the cost of its new prison service handler, kennel and lifetime supply of Chum and vet's bills. On day one of active duty it bit a small child. On complaining to my supplier I was informed that it used to bite its trainer. I invoked the Marks & Spencer principle and got another one. Subsequent attempts to invoke a cost–benefit analysis of the beasts on the basis of their purchase, training, handler and kennel costs against detection rates did my career no good and I have yet to see such a study. HM Revenue & Customs proudly announces the number of kilograms of various drugs their dogs find. No such information is forthcoming from the prison service. There is some information on 'finds' but these can range from burnt foil used to smoke heroin to a nine-bar strapped to an officer's leg.

What prison dogs have a great reputation for is a 'knock'. This is the point at which the animal will get excited or sit stoically in one place, often in front of a trembling visitor. Technically the knock is supposed to indicate the current or recent presence of a controlled drug – or at least those of the relatively few controlled drugs it is trained to detect. A knock will elicit a request to the visitor for a further body and baggage search. A refusal may trigger a call for police assistance, a refusal of entry or a closed visit, i.e. one behind glass as witnessed in most American prison dramas. A subsequent search that finds nothing is likely to have the same response as a refusal. A successful search will invoke police action. One of the problems is the ratio between 'knocks' and finds. The figure is neither known nor wanted. HM Chief Inspector of Prisons frequently comments on the matter when it examines local data and often comments unfavorably on the huge numbers of visitors turned away after a knock but no find. Should you have arrived at the prison gate hot-foot from a student party where everyone other than you has been smoking dope then it might be reasonable for a dog to articulate an olfactory response. There are however many stories, apocryphal of course, of the ability of a dog handler to illicit a knock with the undetectable tug of a lead. From the hound's perspective a knock means a treat. So why wouldn't it? A case of opportunity knocks perhaps?

The searching of staff by drug-sniffer dogs is relatively rare. It should not be. Almost the same principles apply – almost. If the dog knocks and nothing is found after a variety of searches then the member of staff will be questioned. A reasonable explanation such as sitting next to a student on the bus will normally suffice. Few are uncomfortable with such double standards.

So if you can't access or afford a phone call, your granny keeps getting knocked by the dog and you are worried about your baby being put through the x-ray machine, you can write a letter. The paper and the format for a prison letter haven't changed since the inception of Egyptian vellum; name and number at the top and A5 lined paper. Unmistakable and unfriendly. For the many young offenders who have never written a letter in their lives such an act is truly daunting and likely to be eschewed without consideration. For the majority of adults, offender or not, who have not written a letter for years the task is equally difficult. This is presupposing you can read and write and that the same applies to the recipient, if they have the good fortune to be of fixed abode. A first-class stamp is no small matter either at 46p; it is the equivalent to 9 per cent of the typical £5 weekly income of a prisoner. That is the equivalent of £38 per stamp if you are earning £400 per week on the outside.

Has prison service policy in relation to family contact changed over the last two decades? Hardly a jot. Even charities trying to lead the way on improvements, raising their own funds through trusts and foundations, have seen the goalposts move. PACT (the Prison Advice & Care Trust) has delivered invaluable visitor support services, especially in London. Early in 2011 all the services for London prisons were amalgamated into one regional specification which PACT assisted the prison service in drawing up. They then had to take part in a competitive tendering process in which they lost out to an organisation called Spurgeons. Whilst it may become an admirable supplier of services, no one had heard of it before and it had no track record of work in prisons. One assumes it was the cheapest. Not only did PACT lose 30 per cent of its work at a stroke, trusts and foundations that had passionately supported the work of PACT in the past are no longer able to support what is now a commercial enterprise.

Whilst the rest of the world communicates through email, text, mobile phone and the full panoply of social media, communication by prisoners with their families is locked in the age of the quill pen. The reason for not moving forward is the one most often quoted for maintaining the status quo: security. If prisoners were able to text and use social media then the whole prison system would surely come crashing down. After all weren't the 2011 riots orchestrated primarily through BBM (BlackBerry messaging)? The reality is that such contact is already in place. The prison service acknowledges that it finds at least 8,000 illicit mobile phones every year. That number is a gross misrepresentation, as any governor knows. The true figure is considerably higher. With illicit mobile phones we are quickly into Donald Rumsfeld territory. We don't know how many are found and we most certainly don't know how many are not found. Of those that are found there is no data on how many had, or have had, internet access. The data is there but there is too much to analyse with the resources available. There are therefore more unknowns than knowns. What is being done with the internet access is equally unknown – unknown unknowns. If we accept the actual finding of 8,000 and another 8,000 in existence not ever found, then that is one mobile for roughly every five prisoners. In other words if you want access to a mobile in prison you can, although many will eschew them, as whilst the chances of being caught are low the consequences are draconian.

There are two notable flowers in the desert that is family policy in prisons. One is emailaprisoner.com – a testament to dogged persistence against a short-sighted bureaucracy. The architect and now managing director of this project is Derek Jones, who had himself experienced the problem of family contact in prison. It is very simple. Friends and family email a dedicated website. He prints the message and faxes it to the prison. Some prisons are beginning to allow him to email the prisons, which then do the printing. He charges 30p per message to cover costs, which include the provision of paper, envelopes, printers, faxes and ink to participating prisons. Prisons have yet to charge for the labour but don't hold your breath. His idea was first introduced at Guy's Marsh prison but it was then a long battle to persuade other governors to take it on. In 2009 the prison service finally agreed to do a security evaluation of the project – in other words seek a reason not to allow such a technical revolution. I happened to be part of the email trail of views and opinions in my security role at the time. I had already encountered it in my role as a member of the Longford Prize panel as it had received a nomination. It only lost out to innovations of greater longevity. There was nothing to fault it. The emails were easier to read than handwritten material (10 per cent of correspondence is required to be read to intercept escape plans), and they were less likely to get lost, and if they did there was a paper trail by which they could be re-found. There was some staff time involved in terms of delivery, albeit no more than for the distribution of letters. There was arguably staff time savings in censorship and storage and retrieval. It was also an important gesture to prisoners that there was an attempt to improve communication with families. Perhaps it was because the idea was that of an ex-prisoner but the review of the initiative was as negative as it was possible to be without actually anything being found to fault it. The prohibitive cost of paper and ink was mentioned. The conclusion of the review was that it posed no threat to security. With that conclusion I ventured to suggest to the other email recipients that we should therefore actively promote the scheme as it was of clear benefit to prisoners and their prospects of resettlement. I received not one single reply, and there was no active encouragement of the system from HQ – it was up to individual governors whether or not they took it on. More and more eventually did but it was only the dogged persistence of Derek Jones who made it all happen.

Another individual initiative to enhance prisoners' contact with their families is Story Book Dads. It was founded in 2003 by prison tutor Sharon Berry. She managed to overcome the usual prison security concern around audio recordings and trained carefully selected prisoners in audio editing in a derelict prison cell. Mothers and fathers in prison record a personalised story for their children. The recording is edited and digitally enhanced with music and sound effects. A final CD with a picture and written message is sent to the children. Parents who cannot read or who simply struggle with the written word can take part by repeating the words of the story after a teacher, whose contribution is edited out. Repeat 'takes' ensure that the final product is highly professional and very personal. I have attended many conferences where there have been demonstrations of the final products. Many in the audience are moved to tears.

The idea spread amongst prisons, with Dartmoor providing the base and oversight of the project. Other prisons involved in the project send recordings to Dartmoor where staff, volunteers and trained prisoners edit the recordings. Others are now setting up their own editing suites. Training on the software can lead to nationally recognised qualifications and, ironically, the idea has been taken up by the armed forces with Dartmoor providing the editing. Prisoners at Dartmoor are producing stories for serving personnel in Afghanistan. Please don't tell *The Sun*.

A JOB AND THE REHABILITATION OF OFFENDERS ACT

One of Ken Clarke's other three components for success was a job. Employment is important to us all. Whilst there will always be those who prefer not to work, the numbers are few and the reasons usually much more complex than simple idleness. Work is about self-worth, having investment in oneself, family and community. It is at the heart of a properly functioning society. In this context I have found prisoners no different to people in the outside community. The majority want to work. Indeed the yearning in a recently released prisoner is greater than most. Much is said about instilling in prisoners the work ethic. Little is said about the prison service's failure to provide prisoners with the opportunity to prove that they have it. It is true that qualifications-based training is available in prison, often in the form of NVQs, but research around such qualifications in the outside world has questioned their real value and currency in the job market. The implications for such qualifications in prison are even more profound. So if prison provides limited work experience and questionable qualifications, surely it will facilitate a prisoner on his way out seeking something in the job market? Yet again there is a proliferation of small charities trying to help prisoners find work. They will meet, greet and mentor provided they can raise funds from trusts and foundations. Probation officers, or offender managers as they are now called, should provide some help but if you are serving under twelve months you don't get one, and if you are to have one in the community on release they may have contact with you before release if you are in a prison close to home, but otherwise it's start from scratch with your first probation appointment on the day of release. Your offender manager inside may help but will more likely do so if you are a long-termer and release via parole may be dependent upon a home and a job. The figures say it all. Around 80 per cent of prisoners will be unemployed on release, yet having a job will reduce the likelihood of returning to jail by between a half and a third. You might therefore expect all the stops to be pulled out by the prison service to get ex-prisoners into work. The stops are hardly touched, not least because employment rates on release do not materially affect the league table position of governors. Even the simple act of searching the internet for jobs whilst still in jail is forbidden. It's security you see.

But the biggest hurdle of all is the Rehabilitation of Offenders Act. The last one was in 1974 and an amendment act is working its way through Parliament at the moment, albeit at a glacial pace. The Act is all about whether or not you have to disclose the fact that you have a criminal conviction, required in many circumstances, not least when applying for a job. It is often said, and rightly so, that deprivation of liberty is the punishment, yet the vagaries of the ROA and the failure of politicians to update it mean that past imprisonment is a millstone for many years and sometimes life. It may technically only keep a prisoner out of the job market for a prescribed period but in the current economic climate any time out of the job market for any reason may mean worklessness for the rest of one's life.

The 1974 Act enables some criminal convictions to be ignored after a defined 'rehabilitation' period. It tried to ensure that people did not blot their copybook for life, especially for relatively minor convictions. The 'rehabilitation period was set according to and dated from the original conviction. The conviction was regarded as spent if there was no conviction for another offence during the period. With some exceptions an ex-offender need not therefore declare a spent conviction when applying for a job, insurance or during civil proceedings. Although the Act was a recognition of the problem it was still pretty unforgiving. For adults, the rehabilitation period is five years for non-custodial sentences. For prison sentences of up to six months, it is seven years, and it is ten years for prison sentences of between six months and two-and-a-half years. Prison sentences of more than two-and-a-half years can never be spent. For a young offender (under eighteen) the rehabilitation period is generally half that for adults.

The Act goes even further, with exemptions covering a range of jobs and professions where a declaration of a criminal conviction is necessary however long has passed. These include work with children and vulnerable adults, jobs with key financial responsibility, jobs with the security services and, last but not least, jobs in criminal justice agencies. Campaigners over the years have persuaded politicians of the need for change and a number of reviews have been carried out. The former Home Secretary and Secretary of State for Justice in the last Labour government, Jack Straw, commissioned a report published in 2002 called 'Breaking the Circle'. The working group that produced the report consisted of representatives from government departments, criminal justice agencies, employers, and campaigning organisations such as UNLOCK which represents reformed offenders. The report examined whether the Act brought the right balance between public protection and the rehabilitation of offenders. It concluded that the balance was wrong and that convictions should be regarded as 'spent' more quickly. It drew comparisons with jurisdictions abroad and observed that in most European countries the provisions were far more generous and far-reaching than those of the ROA in this country. The report made a series of recommendations bringing the UK more in line with the rest of Europe.

Straw's official response came a year later in 2003 and he accepted most of the recommendations, albeit with some modifications and amendments. He accepted that the current rehabilitation periods should go. Those who had received a non-custodial sentence would have the offence become spent after the end of the sentence plus a 'buffer period' of an additional year. Offenders receiving a custodial sentence of less than four years would have the offence become spent after the end of the full sentence, including any post-release supervision, plus an additional buffer period of two years. For more than four years the buffer period would be four years. However, despite the common sense of the proposals and the consensus that had been reached, the proposals were never implemented. This reluctance reflected again the lack of political will to take forward initiatives with prisoners for fear of being seen as soft on crime. Despite all the evidence of the positive benefits of work and the potential cost savings fear of the tabloids and potential voter fury prevailed.

In January 2010 the baton was picked up by Lord Dholakia. Currently the Chair of Nacro, he is a Liberal Democrat and Deputy Leader of the House of Lords. He has put a Bill before Parliament amending the 1974 Act. It effectively seeks to implement the proposals from 2003. The Tories supported it in opposition and it continues its progress through Parliament. Whether it makes the final hurdle remains to be seen.

A DECENT EDUCATION

Few people come to prison having had what could be described as a decent education. The statistics are stark and often quoted but many are historic and do not form part of a comprehensive or regular reappraisal of the needs of prisoners by the prison service. One of the most common statistics relates to literacy and numeracy. It is said that 48 per cent of prisoners are at, or below, the level expected of an eleven-year-old in reading, 65 per cent in numeracy and 82 per cent in writing. Half of all prisoners are assessed as not having the skills required by 96 per cent of jobs and only one in five are able to complete a job application form.

Amongst prisoners 41 per cent of men, 30 per cent of women and 52 per cent of young offenders were permanently excluded from school. The source for such information is often cited as the Social Exclusion Unit Report of 2002 or eminent people quoting it. This is not to say that the information is wildly off the mark but given that it informs education programmes and the consequent significant expenditure on education contracts it is reasonable to argue for regular reappraisal. Prisons have, as a result of this data, concentrated education programmes on basic literacy and numeracy and they regularly produce statistics that proudly advertise that prisons produce more basic skills qualifications than the outside education system. Whether this takes into account double counting, prisoners taking the same test in different prisons or on different sentences, and prisoners taking the test who are clearly already literate and numerate, no one knows or is prepared to find out.

Education in prison is provided by external contractors, usually further education colleges which tender for contracts every three years. Some colleges have been awarded large contracts covering a number of different prisons. It is a big industry for such colleges, providing potentially large income. The curriculum is set centrally but precise responsibility for prisoner education has been dogged by the plethora of reorganisations within NOMS and government departments. Assessing the effectiveness of education in prison rests, as does education in the community, with Ofsted (the Office for Standards in Education, Children's Services and Skills). Ofsted inspections routinely take place alongside inspections by HM Chief Inspector of Prisons which take place approximately every three years on a pre-arranged basis. Smaller, unannounced inspections can take place between full pre-announced inspections. Juvenile establishments are required to be inspected annually by Ofsted. The conclusions of such inspections are less than flattering. The 2010 annual report on education in England expressed serious concern at the worsening performance of learning and skills provision in prisons. Five out of the twenty-seven prisons and young offender institutions inspected were judged to be inadequate for learning and skills compared with two in 2008/09. In addition, no prisons were judged as outstanding for the overall effectiveness of their learning and skills. In 2008 the Chief Inspector of Prisons reported that only half the prisoners in training prisons felt that their education would help them on release, and even fewer (42 per cent) felt that they had gained useful vocational skills.

Delivery of good quality education will always be hampered by the fact that prisoners can move between prisons at short notice and in the middle of a course. Many will lack the motivation to return to the classroom, not least because they have had bad experiences when at school as a child (a high percentage of prisoners have been expelled from school). Time in classes can be as inconsistent as it is in work, with long lunch breaks and interruptions for visits, court appearances and even going to the gym. But it is the curriculum and how it is delivered that militates significantly against a decent education. The curriculum tends towards a one-size-fits-all with basic education dominating the delivery. Those who are educated to basic level or beyond will struggle to access something more motivating. GCSEs can be taken, as can A-levels and degrees, but the hurdles in terms of cost and access to learning materials will discourage all but the most persistent. Distance learning has often been talked about and in some cases delivered – it is an obvious innovation for a transient body of people who represent as mixed an ability range as it is possible to imagine – but it too suffers from an almost luddite attitude within prisons.

Education in the modern world would be regarded as inconceivable without ICT (Information and Communication Technology) yet education in prison operates at arm's length from it. As a serving prisoner you will be able to access a computer as part of a prescribed course. It will have prescribed software on it and it may be part of a small intranet within the establishment. Access even to this if you are doing distance learning or studying for a degree on your own is either unlikely or sufficiently intermittent as to denigrate its value. Communicating through any digital network is wholly forbidden and seen as a likely threat to security.

So, Ken Clarke, what chance of a job, an education and a strong family?

SIXTEEN

CONCLUSION

We are a nation of 'incarcerholics': we have a national obsession with incarceration. We lock up more men, women and children than most countries in the rest of the world. We are out of step with what anyone might define as the civilised world. Like an alcoholic, we know deep down that it is not good for us, but regular doses of incarceration make us feel happy and comfortable. We have a best friend across the Atlantic who is even more addicted than us, but we simply follow that friend unfailingly. We don't recognise the effect of this behaviour on people and economies; we refuse to see lives being wasted. We believe our sober friends in places such as Scandinavia, where they have coined and follow a doctrine of 'decarceration', to be woolly-minded liberals who don't know what they are talking about. And like all addicts, we are in danger of rapidly incarcerating ourselves to death.

The pride of our bingeing friend is the state of Alabama. In October 2010 it passed HB 56, a new anti-immigration law that effectively criminalised all migration and was described as the harshest and most abusive in the nation. Under this new legislation, anyone lacking the proper immigration papers is considered to be committing a crime – as is anyone entering into a 'business transaction' with such an individual. This would include not only employing them, but also buying something from them or, arguably, even teaching them. Cash-strapped cops and government officials must now enact these draconian measures despite confusion as to when, how, where and to whom to apply the law.

Panic set in immediately, with migrant workers and schoolchildren fleeing the state and services such as water and electricity being cut off from households, as well as the inevitable incarceration of innocents who could not immediately prove their status. So much for a nation claiming the banner of rights and liberties. But what of the consequences?

Liberal application of this oppressive legislation will undoubtedly lead to the imprisonment of large numbers of people, and in Alabama that means in detention facilities run mainly by CCA (Corrections Corporation of America) and the GEO Group, which have a combined profit of more than $5 billion a year. CCA runs the largest facility in the nation in neighbouring Georgia and has its eyes on the lucrative new market in Alabama, worth $200 a night.

But it doesn't stop there. The astute Alabama commissioner of agriculture & industries, John McMillan, has proposed that the farm work left behind by immigrant workers be taken on by the burgeoning prison population. Decatur, a private detention centre 50 miles to the north-west of Alabama, which had been unable to find jobs for its residents, is now providing up to 150 detainees a day to local farmers. Herein, then, lies the perfect solution to the economic crisis. Pass a law, lock up more people in private prisons and provide the same people, at minimal cost, to do the work they were doing before they were incarcerated. Racism rules again in Alabama: profits all round and happy days – except for the 'migrants'. That wouldn't be slavery would it? No, of course not.

It couldn't happen here, could it? In so far as prisons in the UK have traditionally been incapable of letting prisoners out to work or providing work inside prison, probably not. The government is, however, rightly pushing the work agenda in prison and the prison service will struggle to organise itself sufficiently to deliver government desires, but at a time when jobs are scarce and private sector involvement increasing we need to watch carefully for conflict of interest. With that in mind we might want to keep a ready eye on community payback.

Offenders have been undertaking unpaid work as part of a court sentence for over thirty years. It began as community service and is now called community payback. It is an element in many community sentences, and both crown courts and magistrates' courts can make orders. The Courts can order an offender to complete between 40 and 300 hours within a twelve-month period, and anyone not attending is likely to find themselves back in court and can end up in prison. Assessments are made so that the offender can be found a suitable work placement. Some are found suitable to work in an individual placement and are supervised by an agency providing the work. That agency can be a probation service or a private company.

Community payback (CP) has received a lot of attention in recent years. There are debates about its effectiveness but universal recognition that it is cheaper than prison. It is also seen as potentially providing reparation which prison does not. Naming and shaming has been high on the agenda with politicians insisting that people on CP wear high visibility vests so that the public can see their punishment in action. There are real potential benefits to it if handled constructively. CP could provide education and training. With the right levels of supervision by trained and motivated supervisors, communities could get real work done and the work could lead to proper employment. But that takes investment and like everything in the criminal justice system the aim is to drive down costs through competitive tendering. There is a lot of money in CP and companies such as SERCO and G4S are ready to step into a new market. Some probation services are even partnering with these commercial giants to tender for the work. Therein lies the danger. Some of the private contractors are already commissioned to do a range of council services such as street cleaning, gardens management, refuse collection etc., just the sort of menial work deemed ideal for payback. Would we care if already poorly paid SERCO employees were 'let go' in order to provide work for offenders on CP doing it for free? Arrest and conviction might of course get you your job back.

The involvement of the private companies through competitive tendering across the entire criminal justice system is here to stay and we just have to get used to it. The largest single privatisation programme in the history of the prison service in England and Wales was announced in the summer of 2011 following the privatisation of HMP Birmingham, the first ever existing public sector prison to be handed over to a private company, in this case G4S. The contract began in September 2011. Eight public sector prisons and one private prison are to be subject to new competitive tender.

Many of the arguments around 'private good and public bad' remain uninformed and ideological. Private prisons have been built on green-field sites and comparisons with inner-city Victorian edifices are futile. Instead, we should be asking what kind of prisons we need and whether competition will improve the quality and efficiency of the prison service and deliver the rehabilitation revolution the government has promised.

In 2003, early in my tenure as governor of Brixton jail, the then prisons minister Paul Boateng, frustrated by a series of disasters at the south London jail, invited bids from the private sector. Companies declined to tender; Brixton's infrastructure had seen no investment for years and was deemed too hard and too expensive to turn around. But over three years we did turn it around, through what is now called localism – staff working with the local community and the third sector for mutual benefit – not through a brutal and demoralising competition process.

The Secretary of State for Justice, Kenneth Clarke, should learn from these examples and demand innovation. Tender specifications have begun to embrace payment-by-results but the emphasis has been on size and cost: build them big and run them cheaply. Innovation has been driven out by risk aversion and restrictions in the commissioning process. The last series of bids, for example, demanded adoption of the state sector's 'core day' – which means no activities on Friday afternoons, a cost-saving measure. This goes against Clarke's advocacy of real work and introduces unnecessary restrictions.

Innovation and rehabilitation must be at the heart of new tenders, where there is already competition, as well as in the rest of the prison estate where (for now) there is not. For example, prisons need to do more to tackle the digital exclusion of prisoners, something which is vital if we want prisoners to obtain employment on release. It is estimated that 8 million people in England and Wales are digitally excluded: that includes every prisoner.

Homes, jobs, education and positive relationships all reduce reoffending. We search and apply for jobs online. We look for homes online. We learn online. We keep in touch with family and friends by email, text and social media. Yet prisoners have to do all of this by pen and paper, with stamps and envelopes – that's if they can read and write. The official line is that digital inclusion threatens security. Given the thousands of mobile phones that are found in prisons, many with internet access, it is likely there is nefarious digital inclusion going on. Better to make the case for why it is so important and manage it.

Security in prisons is there to be managed, not hidden behind. The success of the prison service cannot be measured simply against the level of escapes. The overemphasis on security and the failure of the service fully to understand its real risks has seen opportunities to make prison effective and efficient wasted. A future strategy should include secure colleges, treatment and training centres where prisoners can turn their lives around. It must break from the bureaucratic inertia that has dogged progress.

The government also needs to understand that good prisons do not run on coercion. We incarcerate 88,000 people and prisons run on the basis of relationships and cooperation between staff and prisoners. The current emphasis is on size and cost – which usually means driving down staffing levels – against a backdrop of redundancies and worsening terms and conditions. This does not augur well for relationships or safety. Prison staff do a job that is little understood, and even less appreciated, and is low paid with little training.

Prison staff are at the heart of any reform but have little incentive but to keep their heads down and hold onto their jobs. The POA has finally been defeated. The tide of privatisation has overwhelmed it and it can do nothing but fight a rearguard action. Officials and ministers may be punching the air in jubilation but a defeated workforce is not a motivated one. Motivation through fear of losing your job in a complex social environment such as a prison will not go far in promoting a positive and constructive culture. It may well be that prison officers will take pride in a G4S or SERCO uniform, there is little at present working for an organisation called NOMS that few understand and to which no one feels a sense of belonging. A good prison requires good leadership. That leadership needs to be visible and straightforward, not swamped in bureaucracy and endless reorganisation.

A demotivated workforce is one thing. A demotivated prisoner population too makes for a very toxic mix. For prisons to work prisoners need to have a stake in their environment. There needs to be something in it for them. It needn't be much but it needs to be something. It may be education for one, a job for another, getting clean of drugs for many. Deprivation of liberty is the punishment in a prison system. Using custody to extract revenge by insisting on austerity and demeaning activity or no activity will cost dear. Add to that prejudice and impossible hurdles in the search for work or housing when you get out, and the boiling resentment at being part of a permanent underclass becomes palpable.

The most toxic combination of all is that of a demotivated workforce and a demotivated prison population. The result is poor staff–prisoner relationships. We are already there and the evidence is before us.

March 2011: 'HMP Ford was failing in its resettlement role, and its security was undermined by poor staff–prisoner relationships' said Nick Hardwick, Chief Inspector of Prisons, publishing the report of an announced inspection of the West Sussex open prison.

July 2011: HMP Moorland – 'Relationships between staff and prisoners were very poor at HMP Moorland' said Nick Hardwick, Chief Inspector of Prisons, publishing the report of an announced inspection of the south Yorkshire jail.

August 2011: HMP Wandsworth – the treatment of inmates at Wandsworth prison in London was 'demeaning, unsafe and fell below what could be classed as decent' said Chief Inspector of Prisons Nick Hardwick. He 'did not detect sufficient willingness' in the prison to acknowledge and address concerns.

In October 2011 a study published annually revealed the experience of detainees in youth prisons and Young Offender Institutions across the UK, including their experience when they are first detained, educational background and relationships with staff. The report was compiled by the Chief Inspector of Prisons, Nick Hardwick, who said the study highlighted some 'deterioration' in the experience of young people in custody. Juliet Lyon, the director of the Prison Reform Trust said in response to the report:

> Teenagers in prison are far more likely than other children and young people to have spent time in care, been excluded from school, suffer from a mental health problem or learning disability and to have children themselves.
>
> Yet despite such high levels of vulnerability, this survey reveals worsening relationships between prison staff and youngsters and shows the isolation and fear many feel particularly those experiencing their first time behind bars.

If evidence from across the entire young offender prison estate, an open prison, a training prison and a local prison were not enough to cause concern, then we should go back to where this book started: HMP Whitemoor. Yet another report by Chief Inspector of Prisons Nick Hardwick in 2011, following an unannounced inspection was bleak. He revealed inspectors were told one in three prisoners felt unsafe and that poor relationships with officers were to blame. Hardwick also found 'poor staff attitudes about race and religion'. Many prisoners said they had been victimised, threatened or intimidated by staff, particularly if they were black, of an ethnic minority or Muslim. Muslim prisoners said many staff were unsure how to relate to them without resorting to assumptions about extremism.

Hardwick continued:

> Too many [60 per cent of prisoners] told us they had felt unsafe in the prison and almost a third, significantly more than in other

high-security prisons, told us they felt unsafe in the prison at the time of the inspection.

In my view, this reflected relationships between staff and prisoners which, although improved, were still not what they should be. I witnessed some good interactions between prisoners and prison officers but also some that gave cause for concern and helped to explain why some prisoners were fearful.

The report told how prisoners referred to 'discrimination, aggression and bullying by staff' in interviews with inspectors. The inspector said managers should develop a clear strategy 'to deal with the underlying negative staff culture and improve relationships between staff and prisoners'.

This report came three years after an even worse one and prompted a request for the help of the Institute of Criminology at Cambridge. A research project was commissioned by the Home Office following the HM Chief Inspector of Prisons report which described distant relationships between staff and prisoners. It was a follow-up to a similar project conducted in the same maximum security prison in 1998. Since the original study had found positive relationships at the establishment, this was a matter of concern. The study was exhaustive and involved observation; a weekly meeting with a regular group of prisoners; long interviews with 52 prisoners and 36 staff; and quality of life surveys with 159 randomly selected prisoners and 194 staff.

The report itself is yet to be published despite the fact that the work was completed early in the summer of 2010. Prison service tactics with all criticism has been to delay publication until sufficient time has passed to be able to say that since the report everything has been put right. This tactic has worked successfully for responses to prison inspectorate reports for many years. Some of its findings however are referred to in the institute's 2011 annual report. Prompting interest at all levels of government was the statistic that 60 per cent of prisoners in the jail were Muslim. The report found high levels of fear and tension relating to 'extremism' and 'radicalisation' in the prison. It found many prisoners converting to Islam in the establishment. Twelve of twenty-three Muslim prisoners they interviewed were in-prison conversions. The reasons discovered for such conversions were particularly interesting. The main motivations for turning to faith included: 'dealing with the pains of long-term imprisonment; seeking "anchored relations" and protection; searching for meaning and identity development; rebellion; and coercion.' Implicitly there was nothing about extreme political ideology and the desire to wage war against the West. It appears to be far more straightforward and little more than the desire to belong and be protected that most of us desire. The institute found that the problem was compounded by staff who kept a distance from some prisoners because they lacked confidence, information and training. Poor leadership was implied but carefully omitted. The result was an atmosphere of distrust. The report said that there was a 'risk of faith becoming the new no-go area'.

Put further pressure on a demotivated workforce, a prisoner population with little hope on the inside and even less on release, and we should not be surprised if serious problems arise. If the relationships between staff and prisoners are not seen as the important security tool they are then the consequences for the safe running of prisons may not be escapes but there almost certainly will be corruption, crime and violence. Any attempts at education, employment, work, drug, alcohol and health treatment will be undermined. Lives and money will be wasted.

A THIRD WAY

As we move inexorably towards a greater percentage of private prisons than anywhere else in the world we should be concerned not with which is better, public or private, nor how one can drive down the costs of the other, the debate should be about what we want from prisons and how best we might achieve it. In previous chapters I have examined what we do badly, where we place inappropriate emphasis and where things could be done better and at less cost. But if we want a real 'rehabilitation revolution', as the coalition government has proclaimed, then we should consider new types of provision for all those we incarcerate. We have for hundreds of years been locked into the concepts of custody or community; in prison or out; on the inside or on the outside. We have ignored the most difficult component, namely the transition between the two. We are very good at the transition from the community to custody – we have a national obsession with it. Yet even though we are sending more to prison for longer, we still release tens of thousands of people a year, many to uncertain if not impossible futures, and we are failing in the transition from custody to community. Getting into prison is easy, getting out and staying out is very difficult, be that in terms of a job, somewhere to live or staying alive.

We know that two-thirds of prisoners lose their jobs simply by coming into prison. Many also lose their homes and some 30 per cent leave prison with nowhere to live. In London, that equates to 7,500 individuals from across the country released into the capital with nowhere to live. Countless others leave prison with perhaps an address on paper but in reality this is based on a tenuous relationship with anyone from a partner to a drug dealer. In the current economic climate things will undoubtedly get worse.

For those not involved in the criminal justice system, there is considerable misunderstanding about the process of release from prison. Whilst the norm is for release to occur at a prescribed time in a sentence, often with licence conditions, for many release can be as chaotic as the lifestyles that got them into custody in the first place. Many are released from court. Only half of all remand prisoners go on to receive a prison sentence and, therefore, are released – unplanned – into the community. This lack of structure is often compounded by the common problems for those involved in the criminal justice system of drugs, alcohol and mental health issues: the consequences for some can be dire. Even those who are aware of a release date may not receive support at release. Those on short sentences (less than twelve months) will be released without statutory supervision. In addition, fewer offenders are receiving flexible early release via Home Detention Curfew, parole and release on temporary licence, all of which may offer support with housing and employment.

The consequences of lack of support at release for the health of offenders can be as grave as are the consequences on their reoffending. In the first week of release men are twenty-nine times more likely to die than others in the community and women sixty-nine times more likely. One in three of the deaths involve a single drug, and 87 per cent involve drugs such as heroin. If you have been injecting drugs in prison, are still dependent on drugs like heroin, or combinations of heroin and other illegal drugs you are at even higher risk. In addition, recently released prisoners are at greater risk of suicide than the general population – at a rate equivalent to that of discharged psychiatric patients.

At the RSA the baton has been picked up. The RSA, founded in the eighteenth century, is the Royal Society for the Encouragement of Arts, Manufactures and Commerce. With its headquarters on John Adam Street just off the Strand in central London, it has adopted the strapline, 'twenty-first-century enlightenment' – exactly what the prison system in England and Wales needs. At the heart of the RSA's philosophy is 'Can we go on like this and do we need new ways of thinking?' Again, applied to prisons, the answers are no and yes.

One of the RSA's current key projects, on which I and other Fellows are collaborating, is RSA Transitions. The overall concept is not new. It was what Charles Clarke recognised on his visit to Brixton in 2005 but which his successor, John Reid, eschewed alongside other positive changes. Charities have embraced the principle and even the Ministry of Justice still flirts with it, but little has changed and the RSA project is the first to come up with well-planned and well-costed proposals.

RSA Transitions aims to provide a physical space where people can properly prepare themselves for life outside prison. Its overall aim is not to prevent escapes, it is for people whom the law has decreed must leave prison and whom society hopes will not come back. It embraces all the economic essentials of cost, value for money and payment by results. It has hardnosed financial thinking behind it but with new and important values.

The new model of prison proposed would be built and managed around a culture of learning and social enterprise and target rehabilitation through increasing people's capacity to work. Prisoners would be paid to work in social enterprises whilst in custody and be helped to develop skills and opportunities for securing employment in the community. Prisoners' salaries would make a contribution towards reparation to victims, individual savings towards setting themselves up on the outside, preferably without state benefits, and, potentially, running costs.

Transitions would be run as a social business under the RSA 'brand' with a central holding company, working with different social enterprises on a proper contractual basis (not unlike John Lewis principles). There would be rigorous evaluation linked to payment by results, designed to identify what works to reduce reoffending. To work properly it would focus on its local community for design, business, education and social integration. It must be embraced by the community or it will fail. Environmental and economic sustainability will also be integral to the ethos. There is much work still to do, not least in securing the funding, determining its size and whether it is to be on a greenfield or brownfield site. It is a bold venture but it is twenty-first-century enlightenment for a nineteenth-century prison system. If there is a 'Big Society' then this is it.

On a small scale and at a local level RSA Transitions may point out a third way and be an inspiration for imaginative thinking which has been lost in the chaos of administrative reorganisation, political disingenuousness and media misrepresentation. To cut through it all, to establish properly what we want from a prison system requires something all-embracing and truly independent.

Prisons were once designated as part of an independent agency. In reality they have become tools of Whitehall with civil servants incapable of running large people-orientated organisations running around like headless chickens, perpetually reorganising and running scared of ministers who change in a perpetual round of musical chairs. Outsiders only get the opportunity to have a say after disasters. I have documented in this book the influences of Mountbatten, Woodcock and Learmont.

There have been others, not least Lord Woolf after the Strangeways riot in 1990. We have not been short of internal inquiries that have recommended the continuance of a status quo that is patently not working. Lord Carter of Coles produced no less than two Carter Reports that led to the creation of the disastrous and dysfunctional National Offender Management Service, which the Tory party in opposition described as a 'Leviathan' and promised to scrap but which they have embraced in government. They also opposed Carter's proposals for building so-called 'Titan' prisons, those holding upwards of 2,000 prisoners, but are about to open one in the midlands in Featherstone.

Lord Ramsbotham in 2008, rattling ministerial cages and promoting rational thinking, as is his forte, said in a *Guardian* article:

> All is clearly not well, and, in my opinion, will not become better until some light and air is let into the closed shop of the Ministry of Justice and the Prison Service. Royal commissions are a well tried, but less frequently used way of doing this. They are made up of experts who take evidence in public and publish reports. I believe that such an exercise can only help both the ministry and the service resolve the problems that they appear to be unable to do, because they are too close to daily events to be able to take a dispassionate and informed look. Therefore the purpose of my exercise [on 26 June 2008 Lord Ramsbotham held a debate in the House of Lords, calling for a royal commission on the state of prisons] is constructive and not destructive. All that it requires is an acceptance of facts and a willingness to listen. I suspect that the public would not have them do otherwise.

Since then things have only worsened for prisoners, for staff and for the communities sending people to and receiving them back from prison. Outwardly there are no high-profile escapes, major riots or anything else to embarrass ministers or cause an inquiry. But behind the walls that there is much that is wrong and that needs to be changed. It remains however, out of sight and out of mind.

REFERENCES

p. 12   Michael Zander, *Cases and Materials on the English Legal System* (10th ed.), Cambridge University Press, 2007.

p. 13   Charles F. Campbell, *The Intolerable Hulks: British Shipboard Confinement 1776–1857* (3rd ed.), Fenestra Books, 2001.

p. 24   Earl Mountbatten, 'The Mountbatten Report: Inquiry into Prison Escapes and Security', Home Office, 1966.

p. 57   Coogan, Tim P., *On the Blanket: The Inside Story of the IRA Prisoners' 'Dirty' Protest*, Palgrave Macmillan, 2002.

p. 62   House of Commons, 'Prison Population Statistics', www.parliament.uk/briefing-papers/SN04334, 7 November 2011.

p. 65   Howard Marks, www.howardmarks.name, 8 December 2011.

p. 84   Archbishop of Canterbury, 'The Archbishop's address to the APPG (All-Party Parliamentary Group) on Penal Affairs', http://www.archbishopofcanterbury.org/articles.php/563/archbishops-address-to-the-appg-on-penal-affairs, 18 January 2011.

p. 99   Michael Steinberg and Larry Rothe, *For the Love of Music: Invitations to Listening*, Oxford University Press, 2006.

p. 103   David Ramsbotham, 'Arts behind bars', *The Guardian*, http://www.guardian.co.uk/commentisfree/2008/nov/05/prisonsandprobation, 5 November 2008.

p. 104   Hanna Johnson, Sarah Keen and David Pritchard, 'Only Connect', New Philanthropy Capital, www.philanthropycapital.org/publications/community/unlocking_value.aspx, October 2011.

p. 128   Ibid.

p. 138   *Porridge*, http://www.porridge.org.uk/about.html, 8 December 2011.

p. 143   Judge Michael Addison, Sentencing of Russell Throne at Guildford Crown Court, www.dailymail.co.uk/.../Sid-James-prison-governor-Russell-Thorne, 18 July 2011.

p. 153   Serious Organised Crime Agency, 'The United Kingdom Threat Assessment of Organised Crime', www.soca.gov.uk/... soca/.../54-the-united-kingdom-threat-assessment, 2009/10.

p. 156   Balios Report, 'Executive summary from strategic intelligence analysis Operation Balios', Metropolitan Police Directorate of Professional Standards, 2005, disclosed under Freedom of Information Act, 2006.

p. 161   Hansard, written answer on 'Prisons: Drugs', http://www.publications.parliament.uk/pa/cm200910/cmhansrd/cm100323/text/100323w0006.htm#10032375000088, 23 March 2010.

p. 161   Hansard, written answer on 'Prisons: Drugs', http://www.publications.parliament.uk/pa/cm200910/cmhansrd/cm100225/text/100225w0002.htm, 25 February 2010.

p. 162   Hansard, written answer on 'Prisons: Drugs', http://www.publications.parliament.uk/pa/cm200910/cmhansrd/cm100128/text/100128w0010.htm, 28 January 2010.

p.187   Ministry of Justice, 'National Offender Management Service Annual Report 2008/09', www.justice.gov.uk/publications/docs/noms-annual-report-0809-stats-addendum.pdf, March 2010.

p. 191   UNICEF statement, www.unicef.org.uk, 8 December 2010.

p. 198   HM Chief Inspector of Prisons, 'Report on an Announced Inspection of HMP Kirkham', Ministry of Justice, www.justice.gov.uk/downloads/publications/inspectorate-reports/hmipris/Kirkham_2009_rps.pdf, November/December 2009.

p.199   M. D. Barnes, letter to the *Daily Telegraph*: 'Prisoners at Work', http://www.telegraph.co.uk/comment/letters/8671717/

We-need-high-speed-rail-because-more-people-use-trains-than-ever.html, 30 July 2011.

p. 209   Law Commission, 'Murder, Manslaughter and Infanticide', Ministry of Justice, http://www.justice.gov.uk/lawcommission/docs/lc304_Murder_Manslaughter_and_Infanticide_Report.pdf, 28 November 2006.

p. 209   Committee on the Penalty for Homicide Report, 2007.

p. 216   HM Chief Inspector of Prisons, 'The Indeterminate Sentence for Public Protection', www.ohrn.nhs.uk/resource/policy/IPP.pdf, September 2008.

p. 225   Ken Clarke, Speech at Conservative party Conference, Manchester, 2010.

p. 227   Ministry of Justice, 'What are offending behaviour programmes?', http://www.justice.gov.uk/guidance/prison-probation-and-rehabilitation/before-after-release/obp.htm, 8 December 2011.

p. 237   PricewaterhouseCoopers, 'Economic Framework: outline of key issues', Ministry of Justice, www.justice.gov.uk/news/docs/prison-drug-treatment-funding-appendix-5.pdf, 8 December 2011.

p. 249   Ken Clarke, 'Punish the feral rioters, but address our social deficit too', The Guardian, www.guardian.co.uk/uk/2011/sep/05/kenneth-clarke-riots-penal-system, 5 September 2011.

p. 254   Amber Marks, 'Drug detection dogs and the growth of olfactory surveillance: Beyond the rule of law?', Surveillance and Society, 4, 257–271, 2008.

p. 273   Juliet Lyon, 'England rioters "poorer, younger, less educated"', www.bbc.co.uk/news/uk-15426720, 24 October 2011.

p. 273   HM Inspectorate of Prisons Youth Justice Board, 'Children and Young People in Custody', www.justice.gov.uk/downloads/publications/inspectorate-reports/hmipris/children-young%20people-2010-11.pdf, 2011.

p. 275   Prisons Research Centre, 'Annual Report', www.crim.cam.ac.uk/research/prc/prcrep11.pdf, June 2011.

p. 277   Royal Society for the Encouragement of Arts, Manufactures and Commerce, 'RSA Transitions: The 21st Century Prison', www.thersa.org/fellowship/journal/archive/summer-2011/features/rsa-transitions-the-21st-century-prison, 2010.

p. 279   David Ramsbotham, 'Breaking into prison', *The Guardian*, www.guardian.co.uk/profile/davidramsbotham, 26 June 2008.

INDEX